PINEAPPLE GOLD

A COLLECTION OF RECIPES

BY
JOANN HULETT DOBBINS
Meridian, Mississippi

To order copies of PINEAPPLE GOLD, send check for $10.95 plus $1.50 mailing cost (Mississippi residents add $.55 tax) to:

PINEAPPLE GOLD
419 Windover Circle
Meridian, Mississippi 39301

First Printing April, 1983
Second Printing May, 1984

International Standard Book Number 0-9610540-0-X
Library of Congress Catalog Card Number: 83-90001

Printed in the United States of America
Wimmer Brothers Books
P.O. Box 18408
Memphis, Tennessee 38181-0408
"Cookbooks of Distinction"™

TABLE OF CONTENTS

ACKNOWLEDGEMENTS

Special thank yous go to:

My Husband, Thomas Kimbell Dobbins, who has tasted, and tasted, and tasted, and who even seemed to enjoy the flops.

And to my Mother, Leta Hulett, a really fantastic teacher.

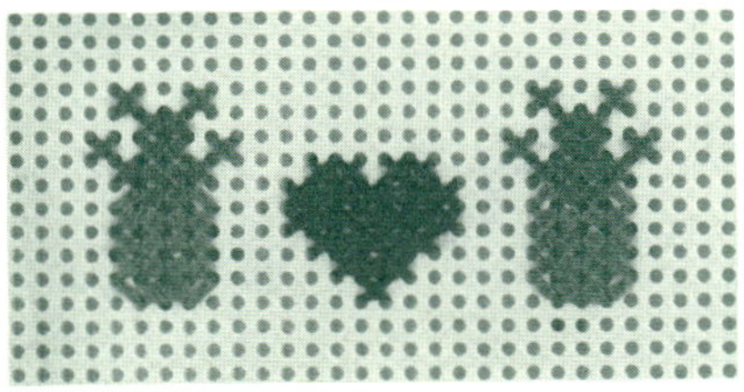

Cover Design, borders and other art work are adapted from cross stitch needlework stitched on perforated paper, sewn by the Author. This form of stitchery was popular during the Victorian Era in the 1800's. The background of the design was always left unworked.

The pineapple is, by definition, a tropical plant known for its juicy fragrant fruit. It received its name probably because the fruit looks like a large pinecone.

The beautiful pineapple has long been considered the classic symbol of hospitality in all Southern homes.

It has been said by many that hospitality is high tide in the loving and giving heart. It is a personal attribute. To be a memorable hostess one needs the background of a welcoming house in order to realize the full potential of her talent. A hostess is, among many things, a planner of delicious meals and an assembler of compatible people. These ingredients add up to the ability of creating a very special climate that makes her guests feel as if suddenly the sun were shining. It's pure gold. PINEAPPLE GOLD.

Not every recipe in this cookbook is my very own. This is really a collection of recipes that have been enjoyed by my family and our friends for a long time. Cooking good food and entertaining are a delightful hobby...even an adventure. I feel that to succeed in this endeavor is the happy hallmark of the hospitable woman. It is a legacy. It is the merrymaker of the moment.

Joann Hulett Dobbins
October 1982

Compiled for

MARILETA, TOMMY, AND ALEXA

with much love

And with the hope of preventing
instant starvation upon leaving "the nest".

Appetizers

ARTICHOKE HEARTS WITH CAVIAR

Serves 10

1 (8 ounce) package cream cheese, softened
2 tablespoons commercial sour cream
2 teaspoons mayonnaise
1 teaspoon lemon juice
1 (8½ ounce) can artichoke hearts drained and chopped
2 teaspoons grated onion
Dash of garlic salt
Caviar

Combine cream cheese, sour cream, mayonnaise, and lemon juice; mix well. Add artichoke, onion, and garlic salt. Mix well.

Shape mixture into a 5 inch mound; flatten slightly, and spread caviar on top. Serve with assorted crackers.

AVOCADO TOAST FINGERS

Mash pulp of one ripe avocado. Season with 1 tablespoon lemon juice and a little onion juice. Add 1 teaspoon salt and 1 teaspoon paprika.

Spread on 1 inch x 3 inch toast strips. Place narrow strips of bacon on top of each and broil until bacon is crisp. Delicious!

MARINATED ARTICHOKE HEARTS

Serves 8

2 teaspoons dill weed
¾ cup dressing
2 (8½ ounce) cans artichoke hearts, drained
Pimento strips

DRESSING:
1 tablespoon grated onion
2 tablespoons white wine vinegar
2 teaspoons Dijon mustard
⅛ teaspoon pepper, freshly ground
1½ teaspoons salt
½ cup olive oil
4½ teaspoons fresh lemon juice

Combine ingredients and shake until well blended. Combine dill weed and dressing. Pour over artichoke hearts and marinate for several hours. Garnish with strips of pimento.

ARTICHOKE BITES

Yield: about 30 squares

2 (6 ounce) jars marinated artichokes
1 medium onion, chopped
1 clove garlic, minced
4 eggs
¼ cup bread crumbs
Dash of hot pepper sauce
½ teaspoon oregano
Salt and pepper to taste
2 cups shredded Cheddar cheese

Drain the juice from 1 jar of artichokes into a skillet. Sauté the onion and garlic in the juice. Drain the other jar and chop all artichokes.

In a bowl, beat the eggs, then add the bread crumbs, hot pepper sauce, oregano, salt and pepper. Stir in the onion, garlic, cheese, and artichokes. Mix well.

Bake in a 9 x 13 inch pan for 30 minutes in a 325 degree oven. Cut into small squares and serve hot. Can be made ahead and rewarmed on a cookie sheet.

VARIATION: Can substitute ⅔ cup each of shredded Swiss Cheese, Parmesan, and Cheddar.

ASPARAGUS FOLD OVERS

Trim crusts from bread and roll each slice flat. Spread with Hollandaise sauce (can use a mix). Sprinkle with Parmesan cheese. Fold each side diagonally over canned asparagus spear. Insert a toothpick. Brush on melted butter. Shake on a little more Parmesan cheese. Bake at 400 degrees for 12 minutes.

These are good served with a salad in the summer.

AVOCADO DIP

Yield: 2 cups

1 carton sour cream
1 package onion soup mix
2 cans frozen avocado dip
Dill weed to taste

Mix all ingredients and chill. Serve with corn chips.

BEEF TENDERLOIN

Serves 12 to 16

1 (5 to 7 Lb.) whole beef tenderloin, trimmed
Seasoned salt
Pepper

Sprinkle beef with seasoned salt and pepper. Bake at 425 degrees until meat registers 140 degrees for rare or 160 degrees for medium rare. DO NOT OVERCOOK.

Cool, refrigerate overnight. Slice. May be served cold or warm. Serve on party rye or tiny buns with a real good spread.

Good for a cocktail buffet.

HOT CHIPPED BEEF DIP

½ cup or more coarsely chopped pecans
2 tablespoons butter
½ teaspoon salt
11 ounces cream cheese, softened
2 tablespoons milk
1 (2½ ounce) jar dried chipped beef, cut in small pieces
¼ cup chopped bell pepper
1 small onion, grated
Pepper, to taste
1 cup sour cream

Toast pecans in butter and salt in oven. Watch carefully and do not let them burn. Mix cream cheese, milk, beef, bell pepper, onion and pepper. Fold in sour cream and half the nuts. Place in baking dish and sprinkle remaining nuts on top. Bake at 350 degrees for 20 minutes. Serve in a chafing dish with Melba rounds.

Men especially like this fantastic dip.

BROCCOLI DIP FOR 100

Serves 100

6 packages frozen chopped broccoli, cooked according to package directions, and drained
4 cans cream of mushroom soup
2 medium onions, chopped and sautéed in ¼ pound butter
3 packages garlic cheese in rolled packages
2 teaspoons MSG seasoning

Mix all ingredients and heat on low so that the cheese melts. Serve in chafing dish with big corn chips.

If you halve this recipe, be sure to use 2 full packages of garlic cheese.

CHEESE AND HAM PINWHEELS

Yield: 30

2 (3 ounce) packages cream cheese
1 (5 ounce) jar bleu cheese spread
½ teaspoon onion juice
5 slices boiled ham

Soften cream cheese and bleu cheese spread to room temperature. Beat cream cheese until soft and fluffy. Gradually add bleu cheese. Stir in onion juice. Spread on ham slices and roll each slice in jelly roll fashion. Wrap each roll in aluminum foil and freeze.

To serve: Slice frozen pinwheels ¾ inches thick and place on serving tray. Excellent with a drink.

NOTE: These may be prepared up to 6 weeks ahead.

CHEESE BOXES

½ pound sharp cheese, grated
½ pint mayonnaise
1 tablespoon Durkees dressing
1 teaspoon prepared mustard
1 tablespoon Worcestershire sauce
Onion or garlic juice to taste
Salt and pepper to taste
Regular thin sliced bread

Blend cheese and mayonnaise. Add remaining sauces and seasonings.

Trim crust from bread. Spread 2 slices with cheese mixture, placing one on top of the other. Then cut into 4 squares. Repeat until desired number of two-story boxes are formed. Frost sides of boxes lightly with cheese mixture.

Toast at 400 degrees immediately before serving. Yields 1 pint of cheese spread which is enough for 2 loaves of bread.

These may be frozen until ready to bake.

CHEESE RINGS

1 pound very sharp Cheddar cheese, grated
¼ pound butter
1 tablespoon cold water
1½ cups sifted flour
1 dash salt
Cayenne pepper

Mix, creaming butter and cheese. Add flour and seasonings. Work together. Roll out very thin on waxed paper. (AND BE PATIENT).

Bake for 10 minutes at 300 degrees.

CHEESE MOLD

Soften the following cheeses and blend together.

8 ounces pasteurized process cheese
14 ounces cream cheese
6 ounces Smokey
5 ounce jar Old English
6 ounce roll Jalapeña
6 ounces grated Cheddar

Add the following:

Juice of ½ lemon
6 tablespoons Worcestershire sauce
1 scant tablespoon minced green onion
Salt and pepper to taste
Paprika

Mix well. Place in mold. Chill well or freeze. This mixture does well in any kind of metal mold. I use a double love bird mold and I have frozen it for several months successfully. When taken from the mold, I decorate birds to give them a little personality (olive slices for eyes, a red bow of pimento strips around neck, etc.) Let your imagination go wild. Place mold on tray, on top of a bed of lettuce or parsley, and serve with assorted crackers.

CHEESE-CHILI ROLL

¾ pound pasteurized processed cheese
1 (3 ounce) package soft cream cheese
2 cloves garlic, minced
¼ teaspoon salt
¼ teaspoon onion juice
¼ teaspoon Worcestershire sauce
⅛ teaspoon cayenne pepper
¾ cup finely chopped pecans
About 1½ jar chili powder

Have cheeses at room temperature. Mash processed cheese (like Velveeta) and add cream cheese, blending together. Add all other ingredients except chili powder and nuts. Mix well and stir in pecans. Roll mixture into 4 inch rolls, approximately 1½ inches in diameter to fit round crackers. Roll each roll in chili powder. Wrap in waxed paper. Place in refrigerator or freezer. When using from the freezer, allow 1½ hours for thawing. Slice and serve on round crackers.

One of these rolls makes a nice little gift.

CHEESE STRAWS

1 stick butter
2 cups sharp Cheddar cheese, grated
1½ cups flour
1 teaspoon salt
1 good dash hot pepper seasoning or use cayenne pepper to taste

Cream all together and push through a cookie press.

Bake at 325 degrees for about 10 minutes. Watch carefully and do not permit them to brown.

CHEESE WAFERS

1 pound Cheddar cheese, grated
1½ cups flour
¼ pound margarine
1 teaspoon salt
1 teaspoon red pepper

Mix together well. Make into long rolls about the circumference of a 50 cent piece. Wrap rolls in waxed paper and chill. Then slice and bake at 425 degrees for 7 or 8 minutes.

CRAB DIP OR SPREAD

8 ounces cream cheese, softened
1 tablespoon milk
1 cup crabmeat
1½ teaspoons horseradish
1 teaspoon lemon juice
Paprika

Mix ingredients together. Put in casserole and bake at 350 degrees for 15 minutes. Serve with Melba toast rounds.

RICH CRAB DIP

4 (8 ounce) packages cream cheese
2½ pounds fresh crab lumps
1½ sticks margarine, melted
3 tablespoons horseradish
½ carton chives (frozen food section of grocery)

Melt margarine and mix with softened cream cheese. Add the following seasonings to taste: Worcestershire sauce, salt, white pepper, and a few drops of hot pepper sauce.

Mix well. Fold in the crabmeat gently. Heat in oven until hot and then keep hot in chafing dish.

Serve with homemade toast rounds or Melba rounds.

CHAFING DISH CHICKEN LIVERS

Marinate livers in the following sauce for 4 to 6 hours.

SAUCE:

½ cup soy sauce
½ cup honey
½ teaspoon monosodium glutomate
1 clove garlic, crushed
½ teaspoon ginger

Other ingredients needed:

1 can sliced water chestnuts
1 pound sliced bacon
Dark brown sugar
Toothpicks

Wrap chicken liver piece, water chestnut slice, with ½ slice of bacon and secure with a toothpick. Then roll in brown sugar. Repeat this process until you have used all the livers. Grill in a 400 degree oven or over coals until bacon and livers are tender, about 15 to 25 minutes. Turn often and watch them closely.

These take a fairly long time to prepare but are well worth the effort. Just before your guests arrive, place livers in chafing dish and warm thoroughly.

NOTE: THESE DO NOT FREEZE.

ESCARGOTS BOURGUIGNON

(Snails in garlic butter)

1 can escargots
⅓ pound butter
2 garlic cloves, crushed
1½ teaspoons parsley, chopped
1 teaspoon shallots, chopped
Salt and pepper, to taste

In a bowl cream ⅓ pound butter and blend in thoroughly 2 garlic cloves, crushed, 1½ teaspoons finely chopped parsley, a teaspoon finely chopped shallots, and salt and pepper to taste.

Put a little of the butter mixture into each of 24 shells. Put a snail in each shell, and cover the snails with the remaining butter mixture. Bake the snails in the shells in a very hot oven (450 degrees) until the butter begins to bubble and turn brown. Serve at once, with French bread.

NOTE: Escargots may be purchased in cans at gourmet shops. Snail shells may also be purchased at the same place.

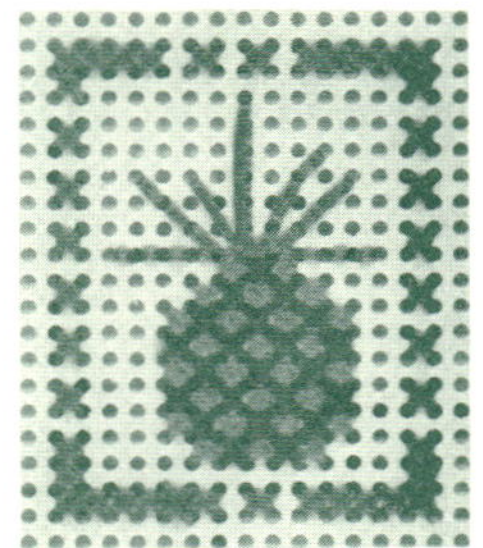

COCKTAIL CREAM PUFFS AND THEIR FILLINGS

1 cup water
½ cup butter
1 cup sifted all-purpose flour
Dash salt
4 eggs

Bring water to a boil. Add butter, stirring until melted. Add flour and salt all at once. Stir well until mixture is smooth and forms a soft ball. Cool mixture slightly. Add eggs, one at a time, beating well after each addition. After last addition continue beating until mixture is shiny. Drop batter by teaspoonfuls on to lightly greased baking sheet to make 36 small puffs. Bake at 375 degrees for 50 minutes. Allow to cool in a warm place, away from drafts. When cool, fill with your favorite filling. Delicious for teas, cocktail parties, etc.

FILLINGS:

Shrimp Salad

1½ cups chopped cooked shrimp
½ cup finely chopped celery
1 teaspoon caraway seed
2 teaspoons lemon juice
¾ cup mayonnaise

Combine ingredients and mix well. Adjust seasoning to taste. Refrigerate for at least an hour. This is enough filling for 36 cream puffs.

Salmon Salad:

1½ cups flaked salmon (1 pound can)
½ cup chopped nuts
½ cup finely chopped green pepper
½ cup mayonnaise
Dash hot pepper sauce

Combine ingredients and mix well. Refrigerate for at least an hour.

Other: Chicken salad and Ham salad are other good fillings for these puffs.

CORNELIA'S HAM TURNOVERS

Yield: 20 turnovers

PASTRY:

¼ pound butter
½ pound cream cheese
1 cup plain flour

Mix together, form ball, and chill.

FILLING:

¾ cup ground, boiled or baked ham
1½ teaspoons prepared mustard
2 tablespoons catsup
½ teaspoon Worcestershire
Dash hot pepper seasoning

Mix well and set aside.

Roll out pastry on a lightly floured surface. Cut in 1½ inch circles.

Place a teaspoon of filling in center of each circle. Fold over making a half circle. Prick edges with a fork to seal.

Bake on cookie sheet at 400 degrees for about 10 minutes.

This recipe may be doubled easily.

Mrs. Earl Laird

CHUTNEY SPREAD

Yield: 1 cup

1 (9½ ounce) jar chutney
1 (8 ounce) package cream cheese, cut into 6 pieces
1 tablespoon fresh lemon juice

Combine all ingredients in work bowl of food processor until blended (about 5 seconds), stopping once to scrape down sides of bowl. Transfer to small serving bowl. Cover and refrigerate until ready for use.

Delicious with thinly sliced onion bread.

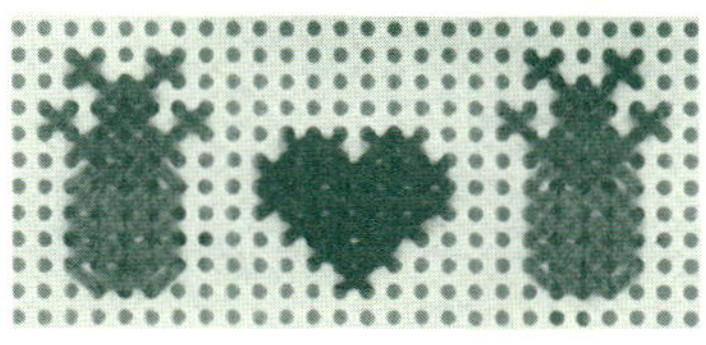

BOURBON HOT DOGS

2 pounds wieners
1½ cups catsup
½ cup brown sugar
½ cup good bourbon

Cut wieners into bite sized pieces. Simmer uncovered in a saucepan in the sauce made of catsup and brown sugar. Add bourbon and cook in covered saucepan 30 more minutes. Refrigerate overnight. Serve hot in chafing dish.

Very Tasty.

POLYNESIAN GINGER DIP

1 cup mayonnaise
1 cup sour cream
¼ cup finely chopped onion
¼ cup minced parsley
¼ cup chopped water chestnuts
2 tablespoons crystalized ginger, chopped fine
1 clove minced garlic
1 tablespoon soy sauce
Pinch salt

Combine mayonnaise and sour cream. Add remaining ingredients and mix well.

Superb as a dip for raw vegetables. Also delicious dip using sesame seed crackers.

MUSHROOM CAPS STUFFED WITH CRAB

1 cup crab lumps
1 tablespoon bread crumbs
1 tablespoon each, chopped fine: onion, parsley, chives
1 teaspoon salt
1 egg
1½ pounds large mushrooms
Parmesan cheese

Combine 1 cup lump crabmeat with 1 tablespoon dry bread crumbs. Add 1 tablespoon each of onion, parsley, and chives, all finely chopped and 1 teaspoon salt. Stir in 1 egg, lightly beaten.

Trim the stems of 1½ pounds large mushrooms and reserve them for another use. Fill the caps with the crabmeat mixture. Sprinkle mushrooms with buttered breadcrumbs and freshly grated parmesan cheese.

Bake in a moderate oven (350 degrees) for about 20 minutes.

These are Heavenly...

TINY MEATBALLS, A LA MARILYN

1½ pounds ground chuck (as lean as possible)
5 slices bread soaked in milk. Squeeze dry and then discard milk
2½ teaspoons salt
2 teaspoons mace
2 teaspoons paprika
1 teaspoon bouquet garni seasoning
1 teaspoon dry mustard
½ teaspoon pepper

Mix well the above ingredients and form into tiny bite-sized meatballs. Brown well in skillet, drain, and set aside. Be sure they are DONE. Meanwhile make the following sauce:

1 cup catsup
1 cup good red wine (Never use cheap wine)
½ teaspoon oregano
1 tablespoon Worcestershire sauce
Salt and pepper to taste

Pour sauce over meatballs and keep hot in chafing dish. This recipe, when doubled, makes enough to fill a large chafing dish.

NOTE: I always double the sauce recipe for use with 1 recipe of meatballs. You may make the meatballs way ahead and freeze for later use. Make sauce when ready to use.

Mrs. Jerry Greene

HOT OLIVES

Yield: about 50

1 jar Old English cheese spread or 1 cup grated sharp Cheddar cheese
1 stick margarine
1 cup flour, sifted
2 dashes red pepper

Mix well. Then wrap each stuffed green olive in about 1 teaspoon of cheese dough and roll in palm of hand. Wrap and freeze, or chill 4 hours before baking.

To serve: Bake in 400 degree oven for 15 minutes on ungreased pan.

NOTE: You can do this same thing with cocktail onions and bits of vienna sausage, too.

(To store in freezer, freeze first on a cookie sheet and then put in plastic bags).

RIPE OLIVE SPREAD

1 (8 ounce) package cream cheese
1 can ripe olives, chopped
3 tablespoons mayonnaise
Dash Worcestershire
Juice of ½ lemon
½ cup chopped nuts

Mix well in blender or mixer. Chill. Serve with crackers.

PEANUT DIP FOR VEGETABLES

Yield: 3 cups

1 tablespoon butter
1 large onion, sliced
3 garlic cloves, minced
1¾ to 2 cups chicken consommé
¾ cup peanut butter
1 tablespoon whipping cream
1 tablespoon fresh lime juice
1 small green chili pepper, finely chopped or 1 tablespoon each minced bell pepper and chili powder

Melt butter in large skillet over medium high heat. Add onion and garlic and sauté until browned, about 10 or 15 minutes. Lower heat and stir in 1¾ cups consommé with peanut butter, whipping cream, lime juice and pepper. Simmer about 10 minutes. Transfer to food processor or blender and puree until smooth, adding remaining consommé if the mixture seems too thick. Pour into a serving bowl, cover and chill.

To serve, arrange dipping sauce in center of large platter and surround with raw or blanched vegetables. (green beans, fresh asparagus, cucumber, carrots, cherry tomatoes, etc.)

PICKLED BLACK-EYED PEAS

2 (No. 2) cans black-eyed peas, drained
1 cup salad oil
¼ cup wine vinegar
1 clove garlic or garlic seasoning
¼ cup thinly sliced onion
½ teaspoon salt
Cracked or freshly ground pepper to taste

Drain peas. Place in bowl and add other ingredients. Mix thoroughly. Store tightly covered in refrigerator at least two days before serving. Can store up to two weeks. Serve in a bowl with a slotted spoon for dipping. Serve with saltine crackers.

GREAT AND UNUSUAL FOR A COCKTAIL PARTY.

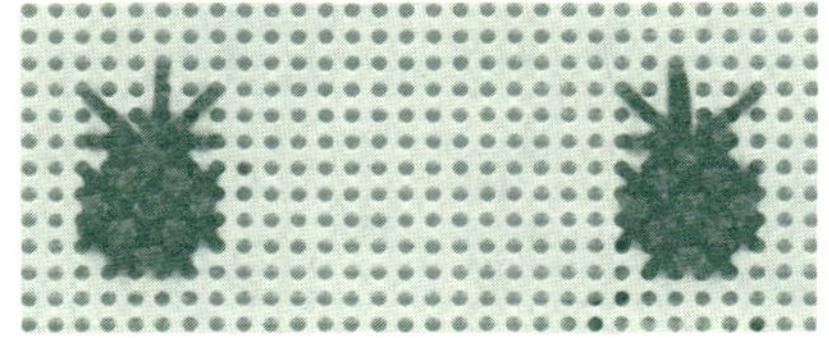

LITTLE PIZZA APPETIZERS

Yield: 80

PIZZA SAUCE:

1 large onion, chopped
1 large bell pepper, chopped
1 stalk celery chopped fine
1 can tomato sauce (15 ounce)
1 teaspoon chili powder
½ teaspoon oregano
½ teaspoon thyme
½ teaspoon salt
½ teaspoon pepper
1 tablespoon Worcestershire sauce
1 clove garlic, minced
1 pound hot pork sausage

Cook the above all together until onion, bell pepper, and celery are well cooked and tender. (about 30 to 45 minutes) Drain. Fry sausage. Drain well. Mix sausage into sauce. Refrigerate overnight. Next morning, lift hardened grease off top, discard, and proceed.

PASTRY:

1 (13¾ ounce) package hot roll mix prepared according to the directions on package. Be sure to let dough rise twice (2 hours each time). After first time, punch dough down and let rise second time.

TOPPING:

1 package mozzarella cheese, grated
1 can grated Parmesan cheese
Paprika
Olive oil

FOR FINISHED PIZZAS: Roll dough out as thin as possible and cut with a 2 inch round cutter. Place on cookie sheet. Brush each round with olive oil. Sprinkle mozzarella cheese on each round. Spread sauce mixture on rounds. Sprinkle with paprika and then Parmesan cheese.

Bake in 350 degree oven for 25 minutes. Serve hot.

These may be made ahead and frozen and then reheated.

TOASTED PECANS

12 cups pecan halves
1 stick butter (¼ pound)
Salt

Place nuts in a 17 x 12 inch pan in a 300 degree oven. Toast for 30 minutes. Then add a stick of butter sliced in pieces.

Let pecans get completely buttered all over. Stir several times. Sprinkle generously with salt. Toast for about 2 hours or more, until butter has been absorbed. Store in a tin.

VARIATION: Can add Worcestershire sauce and a dash of hot pepper sauce.

COCKTAIL REUBENS

Serves 4 to 6

1 (8 ounce) package refrigerated crescent rolls
Mustard
Sauerkraut, rinsed and drained
1 package cocktail franks
1 egg yolk, lightly beaten
Caraway seeds

Preheat oven to 375 degrees. Separate dough into triangles. Spread with mustard. Top with very thin layer of sauerkraut and 1 cocktail frank. Roll to enclose. Brush with egg yolk and dip into caraway seeds.

Place on ungreased baking sheet and bake until golden brown, about 10 to 13 minutes. Serve immediately.

COCKTAIL SAUSAGE BALLS

Yield: about 200

3½ cups biscuit baking mix
1 pound hot sausage
1 (10 ounce) package sharp Cracker Barrel cheese

Put biscuit mix in mixer on low speed. Add uncooked sausage to flour mix and slowly flake. Melt cheese and add to flour-sausage mix. Mix well, using your hands. Form into marble size balls.

Place on cookie sheets and freeze. Then you may store in freezer bags.

Thaw and bake in 350 degree oven for 25 to 30 minutes, until brown. Serve hot.

ROTEL DIP

1 (10 ounce) can tomatoes and green chilies
2 (1 pound) packages pasteurized process cheese

Melt cheese in a double boiler. Add tomatoes. Blend well. Serve hot in chafing dish with big corn chips.

VARIATION: Add a can of chili without beans to the above. Great for a crowd. Teenagers love it.

SALMON MOUSSE

Great for a cocktail party...

2 envelopes unflavored gelatin
½ cup water
1 (15½ ounce) can red salmon
1 cup mayonnaise
2 tablespoons vinegar
2 tablespoons catsup
Dash of cayenne pepper
Dash of pepper
15 pimento stuffed olives, sliced
2 hard cooked eggs, chopped
2 tablespoons India Relish
1 cup whipping cream, whipped
Lettuce, lemon halves, paprika and parsley

Combine gelatin and water in a small saucepan; and place over medium heat until gelatin is dissolved, stirring constantly. Remove from heat and set aside.

Drain salmon, remove skin and bones, and flake it with a fork. Add mayonnaise, vinegar, catsup, cayenne, and pepper. Mix well. Stir in olives, eggs, relish, and dissolved gelatin.

Fold in whipped cream. Spoon mixture into a well-greased 5½ to 6 cup mold. Chill overnight. Unmold on lettuce or other greens. Garnish with lemon halves dipped in paprika and topped with parsley.

SHRIMP BALL

2 cans (7 ounce each) small shrimp (or use fresh)
1 package (8 ounce) cream cheese
1 tablespoon lemon juice
2 teaspoons grated onion
1 teaspoon prepared horseradish
¼ teaspoon liquid smoke
¼ teaspoon salt

Wash, strain, and flake shrimp. Combine with cheese, lemon juice, horseradish, onion, smoke, and salt. Mix thoroughly and chill until firm. Shape mixture into ball, roll in chopped pecans and garnish with parsley. Serve with assorted crackers.

SHRIMP DIP

1 can (10½ ounce) cream of tomato soup
3 packages (3 ounce each) cream cheese
1 envelope gelatin
¼ cup water
1 cup chopped celery
Dash hot pepper seasoning
1 tablespoon chopped bell pepper
1 tablespoon chopped onion
2 cups shrimp, cut fine or mashed
1 cup mayonnaise
1 cup sour cream

Bring to a boil the tomato soup. Remove from heat. Add cream cheese and the gelatin that has been dissolved in water. Add celery, pepper, onions, shrimp, mayonnaise, and sour cream. Chill. Serve with thin wheat crackers.

PICKLED SHRIMP

Cover 2½ pounds shrimp with boiling water. Add ½ cup celery tops, 3½ teaspoons salt, ¼ cup mixed pickling spices or cook shrimp in packaged "crab boil" for 10 to 12 minutes. Drain. Cool. Peel under cold running water and clean.

Alternate shrimp and sliced onions (about a pint) in a shallow glass dish. Add 7 or 8 bay leaves.

DRESSING: Combine the following:

1¼ cups salad oil
¾ cup white vinegar
1½ teaspoons salt
2½ teaspoons celery seed
2½ tablespoons capers and juice
Dash hot pepper seasoning

Mix dressing and pour over shrimp and onions. Cover and store in refrigerator at least 24 hours for best flavor. These will keep at least a week in the refrigerator.

These are grand served with crackers at a cocktail party. Also good as a first course served in small shells.

SWISS SANDWICH PUFFS

Combine ½ cup mayonnaise, ¼ cup chopped onion, and 2 tablespoons finely snipped parsley.

Spread on 32 toasted little rye bread slices (Party Rye). Top each slice with ¼ slice Swiss cheese. Broil 2 or 3 minutes. Serve hot.

This is really easy and tastes great.

INDIVIDUAL SPINACH QUICHES

Serves 12

1 (10 ounce) package frozen chopped spinach
2 tablespoons chopped onion
3 tablespoons melted butter
1 teaspoon salt
1 teaspoon pepper
½ teaspoon ground nutmeg
3 eggs, beaten
1½ cups half and half cream
¼ cup shredded Swiss or Gruyere cheese
12 or 13 (2¾ inch) individual tart shells, unbaked

Cook spinach according to package directions. Drain well and set aside. Sauté onion in butter until soft. Add spinach. Cook and stir over medium heat about 3 minutes. Blend in salt, ½ teaspoon pepper, nutmeg, and set aside.

Combine eggs, cream, and remaining pepper in bowl. Blend well. Stir in spinach and cheese. Spoon into tart shells. Bake at 375 degrees about 20 minutes.

Arrange on serving tray. Garnish with egg slices and parsley.

NOTE: You may also use tiny pastry shells for bite sized quiches.

TOMATO LOBSTER CUPS

Yield: 5 or 6 dozen

1 can (6 ounce) lobster meat, drained, boned, chopped fine
1 cup finely diced celery
½ cup finely chopped walnuts
1 teaspoon grated onion
¼ teaspoon salt
2 tablespoons thin French dressing
½ cup mayonnaise
2 pints cherry tomatoes (60 to 70)
10 pitted ripe olives cut in strips or sliced

Combine all ingredients except tomatoes and olives in a medium bowl. Toss lightly to mix and set aside.

Wash and stem tomatoes. Cut a thin slice off the bottom. Scoop out pulp with the quarter teaspoon of a measuring spoon set or a demitasse spoon. (Tomatoes will sit flat on stem end)

Stuff each tomato with lobster salad; garnish with a piece of ripe olive. Cover and chill.

For variety, you can stuff with ham, chicken, or other seafood salad.

To serve 100 people, triple the recipe.

CHEESE STUFFED SNOW PEAS

A most interesting and delicious hors d'oeuvre.

Yield: 100 Stuffed Peas

FILLING:

1 pound cream cheese, softened
¼ cup freshly grated Parmesan cheese
3 tablespoons catsup
2 teaspoons dillweed
1 teaspoon dry mustard
1 teaspoon Worcestershire sauce
½ to 1 teaspoon salt
½ teaspoon freshly ground white pepper

Combine all ingredients in a large mixing bowl and blend well. Using pastry tube fitted with ¼ to ⅛ inch tip, pipe filling into cut end of each pea pod. Chill until ready to serve.

PEAS: Arrange snow peas in a large bowl and cover with boiling water. Let stand about 1 minute. Drain peas well and immediately plunge into ice water. Drain again. Trim ¼ inch from stem end of each pod, using sharp knife and discard. Set peas aside until ready to stuff.

TO SERVE: Using a round silver (or other) tray, layer snow peas between leaves of a head of curly cabbage. This makes a lovely color contrast with the shiny green pea pods and the pale ruffles of cabbage. Place core of cabbage on top of the spiral with cabbage leaves arranged to resemble a rose.

TURKEY CHEESE BALL

Yield: 2½ cups

1 package (8 ounce) cream cheese
1 cup finely chopped cooked turkey
¾ cup finely chopped toasted almonds
⅓ cup mayonnaise
2 tablespoons chutney, chopped
1 tablespoon curry powder
¼ teaspoon salt
Chopped parsley
Assorted crackers

Mix together the first 7 ingredients. Chill for several hours. Shape into a ball. Roll ball in chopped parsley. Serve with crackers.

IDEAS FOR QUICK APPETIZERS

1. Wrap ½ strip of bacon around a piece of watermelon rind pickle. Place on cookie sheet and bake in oven at 400 degrees until bacon is crisp.
2. Wrap bacon pieces around Waverly Wafer Crackers. Put on cookie sheet and bake at 350 degrees until crisp. May be frozen and reheated. Shake on Parmesan cheese before baking.
3. Artichoke leaves (fresh, of course) and cooked. Dab end with mayonnaise and top with 1/8 hard boiled egg. Arrange on a plate in a sunburst fashion.
4. A big block of cream cheese is so versatile:
   a. Frost an 8 ounce bar with liverwurst sausage. Serve with crackers
   b. Pour Pic-a-Pepper sauce over bar of cream cheese. Serve with crackers.
   c. Cover with green pepper jelly. Serve with crackers
   d. Cover block of cheese with caviar garnished with sliced lemons. Serve with crackers.
   e. Pour a can of smoked oysters over cheese. Serve with crackers.
5. Good Dip: Sour cream mixed with a can of French fried onions.
6. Good Dip: Spaghetti-sour cream. Combine 1 (1½ ounce) envelope spaghetti sauce mix with 2 cups commercial sour cream and ½ cup finely chopped bell pepper. Blend well and chill a couple of hours. Serve with chips.

TOAST ROUNDS

Pepperidge Farm French rolls (they come in a package of four to the package).

Slice to make rounds. Toast in a 225 degree oven for 1½ to 2 hours until dry and crisp. They may be frozen or they keep a long time in tightly covered tins.

Use as you would Melba toast rounds.

Beverages

AMARETTO FREEZE

Delicious as an after dinner drink or as a frozen dessert.

Serves 6 as an after dinner drink. Double recipe to serve 6 for a parfait.

1/3 cup Amaretto liqueur
1 tablespoon dark brown sugar
1 quart vanilla ice cream
Whipped cream
Maraschino cherries

Mix Amaretto and brown sugar together and stir until the sugar is dissolved.

Combine the Amaretto mixture and the ice cream in container of blender and process until smooth.

You may serve immediately in brandy snifters or pour mixture into parfait glasses. Fill 3/4 full and freeze. When ready to serve, top with a spoon of whipped cream and a cherry.

This is a grand dessert after a heavy meal.

BLOODY MARYS

Yield: 4 quarts

3 quarts tomato juice
3 cups vodka
1/3 cup steak sauce
1/4 cup Worcestershire sauce
2 1/2 tablespoons salt
3 teaspoons sugar
1/4 teaspoon hot sauce
Juice of 12 limes
Lime slices
Celery sticks

Combine first 8 ingredients, stirring well. Pour into punch bowl. Float lime slices on top.

BLOODY MARYS FOR TWELVE

1 (46 ounce) can tomato juice
23 ounces vodka (Really half of the juice can)
1 ounce lemon juice
1 ounce Worcestershire sauce
Hot pepper seasoning to taste (try 12 to 15 drops)
1 1/2 teaspoons celery salt
1 1/2 teaspoons salt
6 pinches garlic powder
Black pepper to taste

Mix all ingredients well and pour into pitchers and refrigerate until ready to serve.

NOTE: I sometimes use bloody Mary mix for the tomato juice.

BRANDY ALEXANDERS A LA GLORIA

May be served as an after dinner drink or a divine dessert

½ gallon vanilla ice cream
½ cup cream de cacao
1 cup brandy
1 tablespoon instant coffee powder
Nutmeg

Whip in blender or food processor. Serve in brandy snifters or some other beautiful glass.

Mrs. Lowry Moore

COFFEE BRULOT

This is a grand way to prepare coffee for a very special dinner party.

In a large chafing dish marinate the following:

¼ cup brandy
40 whole cloves
45 lumps sugar
2 or 3 sticks whole cinnamon broken in several pieces
½ lemon sliced very thin
½ orange sliced very thin
1 lemon rind and 1 orange rind, spiraled and studded with some of the cloves.

Cover and let set for a while...the longer the better.

Make 1 quart of strong fresh coffee.

Just before serving, heat 1 cup brandy over low heat in a small saucepan.

At the table, in the presence of your guests and having only candle light...Pour the warmed brandy into chafing dish with marinated spices. Flame. Allow to flame a few seconds as you lift the ladle high. Then slowly pour in the hot coffee. Serve in demitasse cups. Serve Brulot after dessert. A magnificent way to end a fabulous meal.

SPECIAL COMPANY COFFEE

Have ready on a silver tray:

Bowl of semi-sweet chocolate chips
Small pitcher fine brandy
Bowl of fresh whipped cream
Pot of freshly made hot coffee

Each guest prepares his own coffee, according to taste. It is recommended that a little of each of the above ingredients be used. This is wonderful after a good dinner. It is also a fun thing to do at a morning meeting.

HOT SHERRIED CONSOMMÉ

Delicious for a winter time ladies lunch

In a sauce pan heat:

2 cans condensed consommé
$1\frac{1}{3}$ cups water
6 tablespoons dry sherry

Serve warm in wine glasses as an appetizer before lunch, with a tray of cheese straws.

CHAMPAGNE COCKTAIL

Into a champagne glass, put 1 lump of sugar and a curled twist of lemon. Pour chilled champagne into glass and serve. A most elegant cocktail before dinner.

FROZEN DAIQUIRI

1 can frozen lemonade or limeade
1 or 2 cans light rum
3 cans water

Mix and freeze in a plastic container. When ready to serve, spoon frozen mix into blender. Fluff and serve. Garnish with a cherry.

GUS' MINT JULEPS

Fill a gallon container full of washed, drained, fresh mint. Pour in almost a gallon of bourbon whiskey. Add 3 or 4 tablespoons sugar. Close container and leave for 48 hours. Strain liquid into another glass container. Keeps indefinitely in refrigerator.

TO SERVE: Pack glass with crushed ice. Pour julep mix over ice. Garnish with a sprig of mint that has been dipped into powdered sugar.

Sip slowly and enjoy.

George Hintgen

EASY MOCK CHAMPAGNE PUNCH

Make as You Need...

1 bottle sparkling Catawpa grape juice
2 quarts ginger ale

Pour over ginger ale ice ring in punch bowl. This is delicious and almost tastes like the real thing. A good punch for a teenage gathering.

CHAMPAGNE PUNCH

Serves 100

12 bottles sauterne wine
3 cups cognac
12 lemons
6 oranges
12 bottles dry champagne

To prepare punch base: Use ½ gallon containers. Into each container pour 2 bottles sauterne, ½ cup cognac, the juice of two lemons, the juice of 1 orange. Chill.

When ready to serve, pour the punch base over ice and add 2 bottles of champagne for each portion of base.

EPISCOPAL PUNCH

Yield: 8 quarts

1 cup water and 2 cups sugar boiled until it spins a thread (about 16 minutes)
3 cups pineapple juice
3 cups orange juice
¾ cup lemon juice
4 quarts ginger ale

Before adding ginger ale, add enough water to make 4 quarts of liquid. Serve over ice.

GRADUATION PUNCH

Yield: Approximately 2 gallons

1 large can pineapple juice
3 small cans frozen orange juice concentrate
2 small cans frozen lemonade concentrate and 3 or 4 cans water
5 quarts Ginger ale
2 (10 ounce) packages frozen strawberries

Mix pineapple juice, orange juice, lemonade, and water together and let chill a while. Just before serving add thawed strawberries and chilled ginger ale.

Looks beautiful in punch bowl. Make ice ring using ginger ale instead of water so punch will not be diluted.

MILK PUNCH

Serves one

1¼ ounces bourbon or brandy
3 ounces light cream or milk
1 teaspoon superfine sugar
1 dash vanilla extract

Stir in blender and pour into an 8 ounce highball glass. Add a couple of ice cubes. Can also add 1 dip vanilla ice cream. Top with nutmeg.

MILK PUNCH FOR A CROWD

Yield: about 1 gallon

1 quart vanilla ice cream
½ gallon milk
3 cups bourbon

In mixer, blend together softened ice cream and milk. Add bourbon and mix well. Mixture fits into 2 gallon milk cartons. Put in cartons and then in freezer until ready to use. Take from freezer and place in refrigerator 3 or 4 hours before serving. Do not thaw completely, leave icy. Serve from a silver pitcher. Really good. You will need grated nutmeg. (For garnish)

MARTHA ANN'S PUNCH

35 to 40 servings.

BASE:
1 can frozen lemonade
3 cans water
1 (46 ounce) can grapefruit-pineapple drink
1 (46 ounce) can pineapple juice
Sugar to taste (Try about 2 tablespoons)

Make base ahead and refrigerate. Just before serving add 2 large bottles of ginger ale.

FOR PINK PUNCH: Use pink lemonade and pink grapefruit drink.

FOR ORANGE PUNCH: Use regular lemonade and regular grapefruit-pineapple drink and substitute 1 (46 ounce) can orange juice for the pineapple juice.

This punch is delicious for a morning meeting especially in the spring or Summer.

Mrs. Ronnie Hampton

STRAWBERRY PUNCH

Yield: 1 gallon

1 (6 ounce) can frozen lemonade concentrate
1 (8 ounce) can crushed pineapple
1 (10 ounce) package frozen strawberries, thawed
2 quarts cold ginger ale

Put lemonade, pineapple, and strawberries in blender or food processor. Blend. Add ginger ale just before serving.

Looks delicious in punch bowl.

WHISKEY PUNCH

1 or 2 fifths whiskey (use good bourbon)
9 small bottles Sprite, 7-Up, or Upper Ten
2 small cans frozen lemon juice
1 large bottle club soda

Mix just before serving. Serve in punch bowl with a pretty ice ring. (Have all ingredients cold before mixing together) Makes about 2 gallons and you can stretch it by adding a little more club soda.

WHISKEY SOUR PUNCH

For 50

1 quart lemon juice
1 quart orange juice
1 quart whiskey
3 quarts sparkling water (club soda)
Sugar to taste

Pour juices and whiskey over block of ice in punch bowl. Add club soda just before serving. So good.

SIMPLE SYRUP

1 cup sugar and 1 cup water

Combine in saucepan. Simmer about 3 minutes after sugar is dissolved. Stores indefinitely in refrigerator in covered jar.

24 HOUR COCKTAIL

1 pint whiskey
6 lemons (juice and rind)
Simple syrup

Mix water and sugar. Boil. Add whiskey and lemons. Let stand 24 hours. Serve over ice. Makes a good potent punch for a party.

SCREWDRIVERS

Yield: 4 quarts

3 quarts orange juice
3 cups vodka
¼ cup lime juice
Lime slices

Combine orange juice, vodka, and lime juice. Mix well and pour into punch bowl. Float lime slices on top. To serve, pour into ice filled glasses.

ROSEMARY'S NECTAR SODA

BASE:
3 cups sugar
1 cup water

Boil sugar and water in saucepan until it spins a thread.

ADD:
1 teaspoon vanilla extract
1 teaspoon almond extract
Pink coloring
1 large can evaporated milk

Stir.

TO SERVE: Put 2 scoops vanilla ice cream in a tall glass. Add about ¼ cup pink syrup. Add cold club soda. Can put a couple of small ice cubes in bottom of glass.

Serve with a straw, iced tea spoon and a good cookie.

HOT BUTTERED RUM BATTER

¼ pound butter
1 pound dark brown sugar
¼ teaspoon cinnamon
¼ teaspoon nutmeg
¼ teaspoon ground cloves

Cream butter and sugar. Sprinkle in spices and mix thoroughly. Store in refrigerator in a covered container.

TO MAKE THE DRINK:
Place 1 heaping tablespoon of batter in a mug.
Add 1½ ounces DARK RUM.
Fill mug with boiling water.
Stir well and serve hot.

A WONDERFUL DRINK ON A COLD WINTER NIGHT and even better when it snows.

STRAWBERRY FRAPPÉ

Serves 6

2 (10 ounce) packages frozen strawberries, unthawed
2 cups vodka
3 cups finely crushed ice

Combine 1 package strawberries, 1 cup vodka, and 1½ cups ice in container of electric blender. Blend until no ice chunks remain. Repeat process with remaining ingredients. Serve the frappé immediately in stemmed glasses.

MINT TEA

Yield: 1 Gallon

7 or 8 teabags
12 sprigs mint
Rind of 3 lemons (in halves)
Juice of 7 lemons
2 cups sugar
8 cups boiling water
8 cups water

Steep tea, mint, and lemon rinds in boiling water for 15 minutes. Remove teabags, rinds and mint from liquid and discard. Add juice and sugar. Strain. Add water. Makes 1 gallon.

Serve over ice in tall glasses with a sprig of mint. Delicious.

FROZEN WHISKEY SOUR

1 (6 ounce) can frozen lemonade
3 cans water
1 tablespoon frozen orange juice concentrate
2 (6 ounce) cans bourbon whiskey

Mix and freeze in a plastic container. When ready to serve, whip in blender. Serve with a cherry and a slice of orange.

Salads and Salad Dressings

APRICOT CONGEALED SALAD

Serves 8

1 (16 ounce) can apricot halves
1 (8¾ ounce) can pineapple chunks in syrup
2 tablespoons vinegar
1 teaspoon whole cloves
2 or 3 sticks cinnamon
2 (3 ounce) packages orange gelatin
¾ cup apricot nectar
½ cup dairy sour cream

Drain apricots and pineapple, reserving syrups. Combine syrups with vinegar, cloves, and cinnamon sticks. Bring to a boil and simmer for 10 minutes. Strain and add enough hot water to make 2 cups. Pour over 1 package orange gelatin. Stir until dissolved and chill until partially set. Fold in well-drained apricot halves, cut in half and pineapple. Pour into a 6 cup ring mold. Chill until almost firm.

Dissolve the other package orange gelatin in ¾ cup boiling water; stir in ¾ cup apricot nectar. Chill until partially set, then whip until fluffy. Stir in the sour cream and swirl it around. Pour over first layer. Chill for at least 8 hours.

Very spicy and refreshing.

LETA'S TOMATO ASPIC

Serves 8

3 cans (16 ounce) tomato juice
2 tablespoons sugar
Salt, cayenne pepper, bay leaves, cloves
½ garlic clove
3 stalks outside celery
2 small onions, chopped fine

Simmer until vegetables are tender. Then strain.

Add the following ingredients:

2 tablespoons lemon juice
1 tablespoon vinegar
1 tablespoon Worcestershire sauce
3 envelopes unflavored gelatin

Mix well and pour into molds.

NOTE: You may add boiled shrimp and chopped celery for another delicious salad.

ARTICHOKE SALAD

Serves 4 to 6

1 can (10½ ounce) consommé
1 envelope unflavored gelatin
Salt, pepper, garlic, salt, and onion salt, to taste
1 cup celery, cut fine
1 can artichoke hearts

Heat consommé and add gelatin. Add seasonings. Set aside.

Oil well individual salad molds or custard cups. Divide the celery and artichoke hearts into each mold. Pour in the liquid to cover. Refrigerate until set. Serve unmolded on lettuce leaf. Top each serving with a dab of mayonnaise. Shake on a little paprika for color.

NOTE: Shrimp are good added to this salad.

BROCCOLI SALAD

Serves 6 to 8

1 can consommé
1 envelope gelatin
2 boxes frozen broccoli, chopped
Large dash of Worcestershire
Large dash of hot pepper seasoning
Lemon juice to taste
¾ cup mayonnaise
3 eggs, hard boiled
¾ cup cottage cheese

Soak gelatin in 2 tablespoons cold water until soft. Heat consommé and dissolve gelatin in it. Cook broccoli according to directions on box. Let consommé partially congeal and then add broccoli, mayonnaise, and finely chopped eggs. Put in ring mold. To serve: Turn out on a bed of lettuce.

CALIFORNIA SALAD

1 cup pineapple chunks, drained
1 cup Mandarin orange slices, drained
1 cup spiced grapes, drained (or use fresh green grapes)
1 can flaked coconut
1 cup tiny marshmallows

Blend fruits gently. Add 1 cup sour cream and blend. Garnish with fresh mint leaves and fresh strawberries.

Cool and refreshing.

AVOCADO SALAD

Serves 8

1 package lime gelatin dissolved in 2 cups hot water
1 avocado, mashed
1 package cream cheese, mashed
½ bell pepper, chopped
A few drops onion juice
½ cup mayonnaise
¼ cup celery, cut extra fine
½ teaspoon salt

When gelatin is nearly set, add all other ingredients. Mix well and place in mold.

BASIC CHICKEN SALAD

Yield: about 1 quart

2 cups diced chicken or turkey
1 cup finely diced celery
2 hard-boiled eggs, chopped
1 cup mayonnaise
Salt and pepper to taste

This salad is heavenly when stuffed in a ripe tomato.

CHICKEN SALAD ROLLS: Hollow out bought dinner rolls and fill with chicken salad. Years ago this was a specialty at a restaurant across from Randolph Macon Women's College in Lynchburg, Virginia.

VARIATION: Can add to the salad: toasted almonds, seedless grapes, pineapple chunks, and fresh strawberries.

CRAB SALAD, WEST INDIES STYLE

1 medium onion, chopped (or less)
1 pound fresh lump crabmeat
4 ounces vegetable oil
3 ounces cider vinegar
Salt and pepper to taste

Spread half of onion over bottom of large bowl. Cover with separated crab lumps, add the remaining onion. Add salt and pepper. Pour oil and vinegar over all. Cover and marinate for 2 to 12 hours. Toss lightly before serving.

This is one of Norma's good recipes.

NOTE: A variation to this is to mix it all with fresh spinach. Makes a fabulous lunch.

CRAB MOUSSE

1 tablespoon gelatin
¼ cup mayonnaise
2 tablespoons lime juice
2 tablespoons lemon juice
1 tablespoon parsley, chopped
1 tablespoon chives, chopped
1 tablespoon prepared mustard
Salt and pepper to taste
2 cups flaked crabmeat
¾ cup heavy cream, whipped

Soften 1 tablespoon gelatin in 3 tablespoons cold water and dissolve it over hot water. Mix gelatin with ¼ cup mayonnaise, 2 tablespoons each of lime and lemon juice, 1 tablespoon each of parsley and chives, 1 tablespoon prepared mustard, and salt and pepper to taste. Fold in 2 cups flaked, fresh crabmeat. (The lump crabmeat is not as delicate as the other) Fold in the ¾ cup heavy cream, whipped.

Pour the mixture into a buttered ring mold and chill until set. Unmold the mousse on a chilled platter and garnish with thin slices of lime.

Fill the center with avocado mashed with lemon juice, a little mayonnaise, and a dash of Worcestershire. Sprinkle top with chopped chives.

This can also be made into individual salads and is delicious for a luncheon. It is pretty in a fish mold without the avocado.

SOUR CREAM CUCUMBERS

Cucumbers
½ teaspoon seasoned salt
1 scant teaspoon sugar
2 tablespoons chopped chives
1 teaspoon celery seed
Chopped parsley
Pinch of dill weed
2 tablespoons tarragon vinegar
1 cup sour cream

Dissolve salt and sugar in vinegar. Add sour cream and stir until smooth.

Peel cucumbers or not. If you do not peel, score all over lengthwise with a fork to make ridges. Slice them paper thin. Mix with dressing and chill.

Serve as a "side dish" vegetable or these are delicious at a cocktail party served with crackers.

NOTE: Can also mix in thin slices of small onions, red or white.

CUCUMBER MOUSSE

Fills a 6 cup mold

3 to 4 cucumbers, peeled, seeded, and finely chopped
1 tablespoon vinegar
½ teaspoon sugar
½ tablespoon unflavored gelatin
½ cup cold water
1 (3 ounce) package lime flavored gelatin
1 cup boiling water
1 (8 ounce) package cream cheese, softened
½ cup mayonnaise
Juice of 1 lemon
3 dashes of hot sauce
½ teaspoon Worcestershire sauce
½ teaspoon salt
½ teaspoon seasoned pepper
3 to 5 green onions, minced
Salad greens
Mayonnaise, optional

Sprinkle cucumber with vinegar and sugar; cover with ice water and soak for 30 minutes. Drain well.

Soften unflavored gelatin in ½ cup cold water. Dissolve lime flavored gelatin in boiling water. Add enough water to unflavored gelatin to make 2 cups liquid. Stir in lime-flavored gelatin mixture. Chill until slightly thickened.

Combine cream cheese and ½ cup mayonnaise, beating until smooth. Stir in lemon juice, hot sauce, Worcestershire sauce, salt, pepper, and thickened gelatin mixture. Fold in cucumber and green onion. Pour into a lightly oiled 6-cup mold. You may also use individual molds. Chill until firm. Unmold on salad greens. Put a little dab of mayonnaise on top and shake with paprika for color.

CUCUMBER SALAD

Serves 4 to 6

1 (3 ounce) package lime gelatin
¾ cup hot water
¼ cup lemon juice
1 teaspoon onion juice
1 cup sour cream
1 cup chopped cucumber

Dissolve gelatin in hot water. Add lemon juice and onion juice. Chill until partially set. Fold in sour cream and cucumber. Pour in oiled mold and chill until firm. Garnish with tomato wedges. Serve on lettuce.

GOLDEN GLOW SALAD

Serves 8

1 package lemon gelatin
1 cup boiling water
1 cup crushed pineapple
1 cup pineapple juice
½ cup chopped celery
1 cup raw grated carrot
1 tablespoon vinegar
¼ teaspoon salt
½ cup chopped pecans

Dissolve gelatin in water. Cool. Add juice and other ingredients. Pour into molds and chill until firm.

LUNCHEON SALAD

Serve with potato chips and toasted cheese sandwiches

1 package lemon gelatin dissolved in 1 cup hot water
Add ¼ envelope plain gelatin
1 cup peach pickle juice
2 cups diced peach pickle

Fill molds ½ full and let congeal (I use custard cups).

2 cups diced chicken breast (cooked)
2 tablespoons gelatin
½ cup cold water
1 pint mayonnaise
½ cup chopped celery
1 cup tiny canned English peas and juice
1 cup chopped almonds or pecans
Cayenne pepper and salt to taste

Mix the above ingredients with salad dressing. Fold in chicken, etc. Add this chicken salad on top of molds and let congeal again. Unmold on lettuce.

Makes for a delightful ladies luncheon.

SPICED GRAPE SALAD

Serves 8

1 can spiced grapes (drain and save juice)
1 package lemon gelatin
1 cup sliced stuffed green olives, drained
1 cup chopped pecans

Heat grape juice, adding enough water to make 1 cup. Dissolve gelatin and add 1 cup cold water.

Put other ingredients into 8 molds that have been greased with mayonnaise or cooking oil. Pour in gelatin. Chill until firm.

Serve on lettuce with a spoon of mayonnaise on top. Sprinkle mayonnaise with paprika for color.

LAYERED GOURMET SALAD

Serves 12 to 15

8 cups chopped lettuce
12 hard boiled eggs, chopped
½ pound Gruyere cheese, chopped or grated
1½ cups diced celery
1 cup green onions, sliced thin with tops
½ pound fresh raw mushrooms, sliced
16 ounces bacon fried crisp, drained and crumbled
1 (10 ounce) package frozen tiny English peas (uncooked)

Layer into deep large bowl. Start with lettuce, then half of the other ingredients. Then repeat. Spread the following dressing over the top, sealing to edge of bowl. Cover tightly and chill at least 24 hours.

DRESSING:
2 cups mayonnaise
3 tablespoons Dijon mustard
5 tablespoons lemon juice
Salt and pepper to taste
2 teaspoons Worcestershire sauce

Mix ingredients well.

Use your imagination in creating this fabulous, refreshing salad. Can add cucumbers, tomatoes, garbanzo beans, or anything. Toss well before serving.

VARIATION TO LAYERED GOURMET SALAD

DRESSING:

1 carton (8 ounce) sour cream
1½ cups mayonnaise
⅓ cup minced fresh parsley
2½ teaspoons dill weed, dried
1½ teaspoons Beau Monde seasoning
¼ teaspoon garlic powder

Mix well. If seems not smooth enough, add a little canned chicken broth.

LAYER THE SALAD AS FOLLOWS:

Lettuce
1 package frozen, thawed, uncooked tiny English peas
½ of the dressing
1½ cups shredded carrots
Chicken (canned, boned, baked, boiled) cut into small pieces
4 hard cooked eggs, sliced
1½ cups celery, chopped
1 small red onion, sliced and separated into rings
Remaining half of dressing

Sprinkle with Parmesan cheese, cover with plastic wrap and chill overnight. Before serving, sprinkle 8 slices bacon, cooked and crumbled on top of salad.

COLD MARINATED SALAD

DRESSING:

½ cup oil
¼ cup tarragon vinegar
1 tablespoon fines herbes
¼ teaspoon hot pepper sauce
½ teaspoon MSG
1 teaspoon salt
1 teaspoon sugar

Mix well and set aside.

SALAD:

1 can cut green beans, drained
1 can red kidney beans or tiny English peas, drained
1 (7 ounce) can pitted ripe olives
1 (6 or 8 ounce) can sliced mushrooms or use fresh
1 (4 ounce) jar pimento, diced
1 (15 ounce) can artichoke hearts, quartered and drained
½ cup celery, diagonally sliced
1 medium onion, sliced thin
Can add bell pepper, cucumbers, tomatoes

Marinate salad ingredients in dressing overnight. Drain well before serving. Looks beautiful on a buffet in a crystal bowl.

This is a good salad for a tailgate picnic.

MARINATED VEGETABLES

Artichoke hearts
Carrots, peeled and cooked until almost tender
Broccoli, cook fresh broccoli about 10 minutes
Asparagus
Cherry tomatoes
Green beans, cook, in salted water 20 minutes
Cauliflower florets, cook 10 minutes

MARINADE:
1 cup white vinegar
1 tablepoon salt
1 tablespon granulated sugar
1 teaspoon cracked pepper
3 cups vegetable oil

Pour over warm vegetables in a shallow dish. Cover and refrigerate overnight.

Serve by arranging beautifully on a large platter. Can serve with it a side dish of green mayonnaise.

GREEN MAYONNAISE:
3 cups mayonnaise
6 tablespoons lemon juice
6 tablespoons parsley
3 tablespoons chives

Mix together well and pass to your guests.

HEARTS OF PALM SALAD

Serves 6

1 can hearts of palm
2 ripe tomatoes
2 medium onions
3 hard boiled eggs
8 anchovie fillets (optional)
1 clove garlic, crushed
½ cup vinegar
1 cup oil
Salt, pepper, dash of tarragon flakes, 1 heaping teaspoon sugar, dash parsley flakes

Chop all ingredients into bite size pieces. Season with salt and pepper, sugar and crushed garlic. Mix with vinegar and oil and add rest of seasonings. Marinate at least several hours before serving. Can marinate over night.

Sometimes I add 1 can artichoke hearts and 2 or 3 stalks celery, chopped fine.

PICNIC SALAD

1 can shoe peg corn
1 can tiny English peas
1 can French style green beans
1 jar pimento, cut up
4 stalks celery, chopped fine
1 large bell pepper, chopped fine
1 purple onion, thinly sliced, to make rings

Combine the following ingredients:

½ cup vegetable oil
1 cup sugar
¾ cup white vinegar
1 teaspoon salt
1 teaspoon pepper

Boil and then cool the above. Pour slowly over vegetables. Let marinate at least 24 hours covered in refrigerator. Drain and serve cold.

NOTE: A great dish to take on a tailgate picnic.

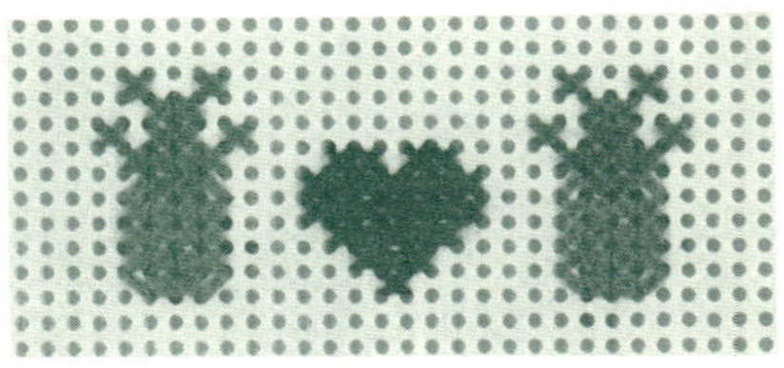

POTATO SALAD

Serves 6 to 8

6 to 8 large red potatoes
3 eggs, hard boiled
1 cup celery, chopped
2 or 3 tablespoons India relish
Seasonings: salt, pepper, celery salt, dill weed, parsley, and dry mustard
½ to 1 cup mayonnaise (amount depends on your own desire for moistness)

Either pare potatoes and cut in bite size pieces and boil in salted water until just tender enough to prick with a fork, or boil whole in the skins, cool, and then peel and cut up. Mix all ingredients gently and refrigerate until ready to serve.

IMPORTANT NOTE: Throw away left over potato salad after the third day.

Some people like a little grated onion in potato salad. I think onion is too strong for this delicious dish.

BOBBI'S SALMON MOUSSE

Serves 12

2 tablespoons gelatin
½ cup cold water
1 pound can red sockeye salmon
2 tablespoons grated onion
1 cup finely diced cucumber
½ cup diced celery
¾ cup diced green pepper
1 tablespoon Worcestershire
Dash hot pepper seasoning
Salt to taste
½ teaspoon pepper
1 tablespoon vinegar
3 tablespoons lemon juice
1 cup thick mayonnaise
½ pint whipping cream

Pour water over gelatin; then melt over hot water. Discard bones and skin from salmon. Mix salmon and its oil with vegetables. Add seasonings and set aside. Whip cream and mix with mayonnaise. Fold gelatin mixture into cream mixture. Pour all over salmon, blending well. Pour into oiled fish shaped mold and refrigerate overnight. Turn into tray lined with lettuce and surrounded by sliced cucumbers, parsley and cherry tomatoes.

Mrs. Everett Crudup

ALICE'S SPAGHETTI SALAD

Serves 12 generously

1 (8 ounce) package spaghetti
½ pound sharp cheese, cut in small cubes
1 medium onion, chopped fine
1 medium bell pepper, chopped fine
1 cup chopped celery
½ cup chopped dill pickle
1 small jar chopped pimento
1 small jar stuffed green olives, sliced
4 hardboiled eggs, cut up
3 medium firm ripe tomatoes cubed (drain and fold in last)
1 teaspoon celery seed
Salt and pepper to taste
½ teaspoon dry mustard
Mayonnaise to moisten

Cook spaghetti in salted water. Drain. Then pour 2 tablespoons vinegar over spaghetti. Dry pickle, celery, olives, and pimento on a paper towel. Add mayonnaise to spaghetti, then add other ingredients. Fold in the tomatoes last.

Make this salad the day before you plan to use it. This gives a better flavor. Delicious with turkey, ham, or fish.

Mrs. Sam Bailey

SENSATION SALAD

DRESSING:

1 clove garlic or garlic powder
½ teaspoon salt
¼ teaspoon pepper
2 tablespoons Parmesan cheese
1 tablespoon lemon juice
¼ cup salad oil
Dash dry mustard

Mix ingredients well and put in bottom of wooden salad bowl.

Break lettuce on top and add all other salad ingredients. Cover and refrigerate as long as 2 hours. Toss just before serving.

This is a wonderful time saver when you are rushed and are having guests for dinner.

All the salad ingredients stay very crisp.

SHRIMP RICE SALAD

Serves 4

¼ cup raw rice. Cook and store in refrigerator so it will be cold when salad is mixed.
¾ pound shrimp, cooked, peeled, cleaned and left whole
¾ teaspoon salt
1 teaspoon lemon juice
1 teaspoon minced onion
2 tablespoons 1890 French dressing
1 tablespoon slivered green pepper
¾ cup diced raw cauliflower or celery or both
Pinch of pepper
⅓ cup of mayonnaise

Mix all ingredients and serve cold on lettuce.

SPINACH SALAD

Serves 10

1 pound fresh spinach
1 large cucumber or several small ones
2 cups coarsely chopped celery
2 large ripe avocados, peeled and cubed
Bleu cheese dressing **(See Index)**

Remove stems from spinach, wash thoroughly and pat dry on a paper towel. Tear into bite size pieces.

Wash cucumber well. With the tines of a fork, forcefully pull down the cucumber, all around. Makes the cucumber look striped. Slice. Add cucumber and remaining vegetables to spinach. Add dressing and toss gently until well coated.

SLAW

This can really be a creative dish

1 head of cabbage, washed in cold water, drained and shredded
3 or 4 stalks celery, chopped
2 carrots, coarsely grated
1 or 2 tablespoons pickle relish
1 teaspoon celery seed
Salt and pepper, to taste
1 teaspoon white vinegar
¼ to ½ teaspoon dill weed
½ to 1 cup mayonnaise

Mix above ingredients well and refrigerate. Sometimes I add thinly sliced cucumber and tomato wedges just before serving. Makes it look pretty.

DEANNA'S STRAWBERRY SALAD

2 packages strawberry gelatin (3 ounces each)
1 cup hot water
1 cup cold water
3 mashed bananas
1 carton frozen strawberries with juice
1 small can crushed pineapple, drained
Sour cream

Mix all. Pour half in mold and let congeal. Spread congealed surface with layer of sour cream. Then pour other half of mix in mold to congeal. Delicious for a ladies luncheon. Children like it better if sour cream is omitted.

Mrs. Richard Wilbourn

TABOOLEY

This is a Syrian wheat garden salad

Serves 6

1 cup cracked wheat, fine
1 bunch green onions
2 large bunches parsley
½ bunch mint
4 large tomatoes
Juice of 4 lemons
½ cup olive oil
Salt and pepper, to taste

Soak wheat in water a few minutes. Squeeze dry by pressing between palms.

Chop onions, parsley, mint leaves, and tomatoes very fine. Add wheat, lemon juice, olive oil, salt and pepper. Mix well. Serve with fresh, crisp lettuce leaves.

KAY'S SAUERKRAUT SALAD

1 can (1 pound 11 ounce) sauerkraut

Drain for at least 20 minutes.

Prepare 1 cup each of diced celery, diced onion and diced bell pepper
¾ cup sugar
3 tablespoons vinegar
½ teaspoon salt
1 teaspoon pepper
1 teaspoon celery seed
1 small jar pimento, chopped

Chop sauerkraut up with scissors. Stir in other vegetables. Mix sugar, vinegar, salt, pepper, and celery seed together well and pour over vegetables. Add pimento.

Make this salad at least 24 hours before you wish to serve it. Keeps indefinitely and tastes better with age.

Mrs. Kay Pearce Dickson

TACO SALAD

A delicious Sunday Night Supper

Serves 6 to 8

In a big salad bowl place:

1 head chopped lettuce and 4 chopped tomatoes

SKILLET:

2 pounds ground chuck, very lean
1 big onion, chopped
1 bell pepper, chopped
1 cup celery, finely chopped
1 tablespoon cumin
¼ teaspoon chili powder

DOUBLE BOILER:

1 pound pasteurized process cheese
½ can or more tomatoes and green chilies

Corn Chips

Brown meat with onion, bell pepper, and celery. Add remaining skillet ingredients. Pour meat mixture over salad mixture. Pour cheese mixture over all and crunch corn chips over top.

Avocado is great in this salad, too.

CURRIED TURKEY SALAD IN CANTALOUPE HALVES

Serves 6

Diced turkey (from a 3½ to 4 pound turkey breast)
1½ cups thinly sliced celery
1 cup curry mayonnaise (use 2 teaspoons curry powder)
Salt, pepper, and chopped chutney to taste

Mix well and chill.

Meanwhile, prepare cantaloupes. Halve them lengthwise and seed them. Wrap in plastic wrap and put back in refrigerator.

Prepare the following condiments:

½ pound toasted cashews
½ pound lean bacon, cooked and crumbled
¼ pound golden raisins
½ cup minced scallions
¼ cup each chopped green and red bell pepper

Serve the curried turkey in the cantaloupe halves and top with the condiments.

Great for a ladies lunch. Serve with assorted small sandwiches.

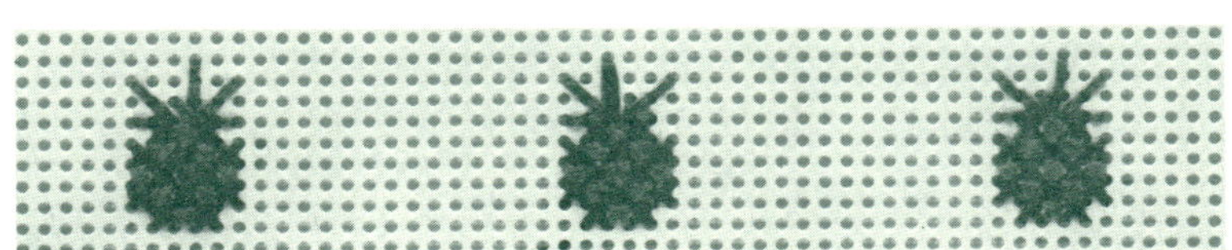

WALDORF SALAD

Serves 6

2 apples, peeled and chopped in small pieces
1 cup celery, chopped
1 can (15 ounce) pineapple chunks in natural juice, drained
¼ cup or more raisins
¼ cup or more chopped pecans
Juice of ¼ lemon
Enough mayonnaise to hold together (I use about 1 heaping tablespoon)

This is easy, quick, and delicious for supper with almost anything.

WATERMELON FILLED WITH FRESH FRUIT

A Spectacular Fruit Salad for a Party

Buy a large, beautiful watermelon. Slice off the top fourth. With a melon baller, make as many watermelon balls as you can (no seeds please). Put these balls in a plastic bag and in the refrigerator. Then with your hands, scoop out the rest of the melon. With a sharp knife, cut a zig zag edge around top edge of melon. Invert on paper towels for a while to drain. I always freeze the melon shell so that it can keep the fruit cold during a party.

Prepare other fresh fruits and refrigerate. (Cantaloupe, honeydew, strawberries). Chill in refrigerator cans of pitted bing cherries, pineapple chunks, mandarin orange sections, and spiced grapes. All this can be done a day ahead. (NO BANANAS). Be sure to drain fruit.

About 2 hours before serving time, combine the fruits and place in frozen melon shell. Garnish top with fresh mint. Refrigerate again until ready to serve.

Serves from 10 to 24 depending upon how much fruit you use. Allow at least 1 cup per person. Make the following dressing and serve it in a large bowl beside the watermelon.

CUSTARD SAUCE:

Beat slightly, 3 or 4 egg yolks.
Add: 1/4 cup sugar and
1/8 teaspoon salt.
Scald and stir in slowly, 2 cups milk.

Place the custard over very low heat and stir it constantly. Take care that it DOES NOT BOIL. OR stir over simmering water until it begins to thicken. Strain and cool the custard. Add to it: 1 teaspoon vanilla and 1/2 teaspoon almond extracts. Chill it thoroughly. Add one package of tiny marshmallows melted. The marshmallows may be added after the sauce begins to thicken and before chilling. Remember that this sauce is not a firm custard, but a sauce. Near serving time, fold in 2 half pints of whipped cream.

Poppy seed dressing is also good with a fruit salad.

SALADS AND SALAD DRESSINGS

MISCELLANEOUS SALADS

1. Pink grapefruit sections and avocado slices on lettuce. Serve with a good French dressing or poppy seed dressing.
2. A ring of cantaloupe on lettuce filled with other fresh fruit is a pretty salad. Poppy seed dressing is good on this.

HELPFUL HINTS:
1. When you make a big molded salad, use ¼ cup less liquid than the recipe calls for to guarantee that it congeals. Minimum time for gelatin to set well is usually 6 hours.
2. For crisp salad greens, wash well in cool water. Drain well, and wrap in a cloth dish towel. Put towel wrapped greens in refrigerator for several hours.

APRICOT DRESSING

½ cup apricots put through a sieve
Juice of a fresh lime
1 tablespoon mayonnaise
1 cup heavy cream, whipped

Mix apricots and lime juice and add to mayonnaise. Fold into whipped cream. Spoon on fruit salad and dust with finely ground nuts.

BLEU CHEESE DRESSING

Yield: 1¼ cups

2 ounces bleu cheese, crumbled
2 tablespoons half and half cream
¼ cup mayonnaise
3 tablespoons vegetable oil
2 tablespoons vinegar
½ teaspoon prepared mustard
Dash of salt
Dash of pepper
1 (0.4 ounce) package buttermilk salad dressing mix

Combine cheese and half and half in a small mixing bowl and beat with electric mixer until creamy. Add remaining ingredients except buttermilk salad dressing mix and mix until smooth.

Prepare buttermilk salad dressing according to package directions. Add ½ cup buttermilk dressing to the bleu cheese mixture, mixing well. Reserve remaining buttermilk dressing for another use.

Delicious on spinach salad.

ELLA'S CELERY SEED SALAD DRESSING

¼ cup sugar (scant)
1 teaspoon each of celery seed, paprika, salt, dry mustard, and grated onion
4 tablespoons vinegar
1 cup salad oil

Mix dry ingredients with 1 tablespoon vinegar. Alternate oil and remaining vinegar, beating well. (Can use blender).

Delicious with fresh fruit.

COLLENE'S FRENCH DRESSING

1 can tomato soup
½ cup salad oil
½ cup vinegar
1 teaspoon salt
2 teaspoons Worcestershire sauce
½ cup sugar
3 cloves garlic (let stand in dressing overnight and remove)
Chopped bell pepper
Minced onion

Put all ingredients in jar and shake well. Leave overnight. Makes extra large quantity but keeps well for a long time. Delicious on fresh spring vegetables.

FLUFFY PINEAPPLE PECAN DRESSING

Yield: 4½ cups

1 (15¼ ounce) can pineapple tidbits in their own juice
Cold milk
1 (3¾ ounce) package instant vanilla pudding and pie filling
½ cup finely chopped pecans
1 teaspoon ground cardamon
½ teaspoon ground ginger
1 cup heavy cream, whipped

Drain pineapple and reserve juice. Add enough milk to the pineapple juice to make 1 cup liquid. Combine the juice mixture and the pudding mix and beat with electric mixer until thick. Stir in pineapple, pecans, cardamon, and ginger. Fold in whipped cream. Delicious served over fresh fruit.

POPPY SEED DRESSING

½ cup sugar
1 teaspoon finely grated onion
3 tablespoons lemon juice
1 teaspoon dry mustard
¼ teaspoon salt
⅓ cup honey
6 tablespoons tarragon vinegar
1 cup salad oil
1 teaspoon paprika
2 teaspoons poppy seeds

Put all ingredients in a jar and shake thoroughly until well blended. OR: Put all ingredients except poppy seeds into blender container and blend at high speed about ten seconds. Add poppy seeds and turn blender on and off very quickly. Store in a covered container in refrigerator. Will keep at least two weeks. Delicious over fruit, especially a salad of grapefruit and avocado.

SWEET FRENCH DRESSING

Yield: about 1½ cups

⅓ cup sugar
1 teaspoon celery seed
1 teaspoon salt
1 teaspoon dry mustard
4 tablespoons vinegar
1 cup salad oil
1 teaspoon paprika
1 scant teaspoon grated onion

Mix all ingredients in blender. Put in covered jar in refrigerator. Keeps well. Delicious on fruit.

DIANNE'S DIP FOR FRUIT

1 (8 ounce) tub whipped cream cheese
1 (7 ounce) jar marshmallow cream

Mix until well blended.

Serve in a bowl in the center of a large tray of assorted fresh fruit. Can include strawberries, apple slices, pear slices, pineapple, banana, and green grapes.

MILDRED'S THOUSAND ISLAND SALAD DRESSING

1 cup mayonnaise
½ cup Chili sauce
⅓ cup India relish
Salt to taste
2 hard boiled eggs, chopped fine
½ teaspoon grated onion

Mix well. Keep refrigerated.

Mrs. Mildred Noblin

Soups, Eggs, and Cheese

CHICKEN SOUP

8 cups chicken stock
4 cups or more diced chicken
2 or 3 stalks celery, chopped
2 or 3 carrots, peeled and sliced thin
2 Irish potatoes, diced
3 small onions, chopped
1 (8 ounce) can stewed tomatoes
2 beef bouillon cubes
6 drops hot pepper seasoning
Seasonings: salt, pepper, celery salt, parsley flakes
You may also add: green beans, rice, etc.

Make stock by simmering chicken pieces (I use 2 or 3 whole chicken breasts) in water seasoned with 1 onion, halved, 2 (2 inch) pieces celery, 1 tablespoon parsley, 3 bay leaves, and 1 teaspoon tarragon flakes in 8 cups water until tender. Remove chicken to another container to cool. Strain broth.

Place into soup pot the strained broth and add enough water to have 8 cups. Add all other ingredients and simmer for several hours. Taste and correct seasonings.

NOTE: You may use left over diced turkey. You may wish to have a thinner soup. (Add canned chicken broth or bouillon cubes and water).

LINDA'S CRAB BISQUE

Serves 8 to 10 generously

1 can cream of mushroom soup
1 can cream of celery soup
1 can cream of chicken soup
3 soup cans milk
¾ to 1 pound fresh crabmeat, picked over well for shells
Salt and pepper to taste

Heat soups and milk together on low heat. Stir until well blended. Add crabmeat. Season to taste with salt and pepper.

NOTE: As a variation, you may pass a small pitcher of sherry. Just a little adds a very interesting taste.

Mrs. William Billups

CREAM OF MUSHROOM SOUP

Serves 6 to 8

¼ cup minced onions | **3 tablespoons butter**

Cook the onions slowly in butter for 8 to 10 minutes until tender but not brown. (Use a 2½ quart heavy stainless steel or enamel saucepan).

ADD: 3 tablespoons flour and stir over moderate heat for 3 minutes but do not brown. Remove from heat.

ADD: 6 cups boiling chicken broth, either homemade or canned. Blend it in thoroughly with the flour. Season to taste, with salt and pepper.

ADD: 2 parsley sprigs, ⅓ bay leaf and ⅛ teaspoon thyme and the chopped stems from 1 pound fresh mushrooms. Simmer partially covered for 20 minutes or more. Strain, pressing the juices from the mushroom stems. Return the soup to the pan.

IN A SEPARATE SAUCEPAN:
2 tablespoons butter
1 pound thinly sliced mushroom caps
¼ teaspoon salt
1 teaspoon lemon juice

Melt the butter. When it is foaming, toss in the mushrooms, salt, and lemon juice. Cover and cook slowly for 5 minutes.

Pour the mushrooms and their cooking juices into the strained soup base. Simmer for 10 minutes.

If not serving immediately, set aside uncovered. Reheat to simmer just before proceeding to the next step.

2 egg yolks
½ to ¾ cup whipping cream
1 to 3 tablespoons softened butter

Beat the egg yolks with a wire whip and cream in a 3 quart mixing bowl with a wooden spoon. Then beat in hot soup by spoonfuls until a cup has been added. Gradually stir in the rest. Correct seasoning. Return the soup to the pan and stir over moderate heat for a minute or two to poach the yolks, but DO NOT LET THE SOUP COME NEAR THE SIMMER. Remove from heat and stir in butter by tablespoons. Pour into a tureen or soup cups. Decorate with fluted mushrooms caps and a parsley sprig.

Even people who say they don't like mushroom soup like this. Delicious.

ROSEMARY'S GUMBO BASE

4 quarts water in pot with 4 bouillon cubes (beef and chicken) or part chicken broth. Simmer.

ADD: 1 cup minced ham with most of the fat removed.

ALSO ADD: 2 pounds fresh okra that has been washed, dried, and sliced, then browned on both sides in a skillet in 2 tablespoons bacon fat. Be careful not to burn. Drain on paper towels.

THEN: MAKE ROUX. Take 3 tablespoons bacon fat and 3 tablespoons flour. Brown in iron skillet REAL SLOW to make the roux. If this scorches, start over. It is not hard, just a slow process.

Add the following ingredients to the beautiful brown roux:

6 green onions, chopped fine in food processor
2 red onions, chopped fine in food processor
1 green pepper, chopped
1 cup celery, finely chopped
4 large pods garlic, minced
2 tablespoons parsley, chopped

Simmer all until the onions are gold in color and sort of transparent looking.

ADD: 2 big (#2) cans tomatoes which have been chopped in blender. Simmer all for 10 minutes and then put in soup pot (what you started with). Add salt, pepper, red pepper, Tabasco, 4 bay leaves, and simmer slowly for 1 hour.

Pour into containers. Refrigerate overnight. Then skim off the fat and throw away. At this point, the gumbo mix may be frozen for later use.

When ready to use, add the seafood.

3 pounds raw, peeled, cleaned shrimp

(Let cook 7 minutes in the base).

ADD:

2 jars oysters
1 can fresh lump crabmeat (be sure to pick over well)
1 pound crab fingers

Just let the gumbo get piping hot.

Serve in gumbo bowls with a great big spoon of steaming hot rice.

Rosemary Frugé Robinson

COLD CUCUMBER SOUP

Serves about 6

3 tablespoons butter
2 leeks, cubed
1 small onion, chopped
2½ cups cucumber, diced and unpeeled
1 cup watercress leaves (optional)
1 cup raw potatoes, finely diced
2 tablespoons parsley, coarsely chopped
3 cups chicken broth
½ teaspoon dry mustard
1 cup heavy cream
Chopped dillweed and cucumber slices for garnish

Melt butter and cook leeks and onion in butter until transparent. Add all ingredients except cream and the garnish. Boil, then simmer for 30 minutes, or until potatoes are tender. Puree in food processor or blender or a food mill. Season to taste. Chill. Before serving, stir in the cream. Garnish by sprinkling dill weed over top. Serve cold.

Very refreshing.

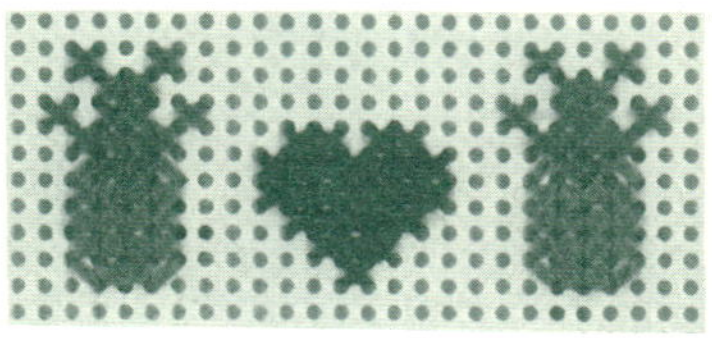

OYSTER STEW

Serves 6

1 pint oysters
1 stalk celery
½ bunch parsley
1 bunch green onions
1 cup butter
Salt and pepper
1 pint coffee cream
1 pint milk

Put parsley, celery, onions, in food processor and chop fine.

Melt butter in saucepan. When melted, add chopped vegetables and sauté until tender but not brown. Add oysters and cook until ends curl. Bring milk and cream almost to the boiling point but do not boil. Add the oysters and vegetables to the milk mix and serve hot.

FRENCH ONION SOUP

(This recipe takes about 2½ to 3 hours to prepare).

Serves 6 to 8

5 cups thinly sliced yellow onions (about 1½ pounds)
3 tablespoons butter
1 tablespoon oil
1 teaspoon salt
¼ teaspoon sugar (this helps the onions brown)
3 tablespoons flour
2 quarts boiling brown stock, canned beef bouillon or use half stock and half water.
½ cup dry white wine or dry white vermouth
Salt and pepper to taste
3 tablespoons cognac
Rounds of hard toasted French bread
1 to 2 cups grated Swiss or Parmesan cheese

Cook the onions slowly with the butter and oil in a heavy bottomed 4 quart saucepan, covered, for 15 minutes. Uncover, raise heat to moderate, and stir in the salt and sugar. Cook for 30 to 40 minutes, stirring frequently, until the onions have turned an even, deep golden brown.

Sprinkle in the flour and stir for about 3 minutes. Remove from heat. Blend in the boiling liquid. Add the wine, and season to taste. Simmer partially covered for 30 to 40 minutes or more, skimming occasionally. Taste and correct the seasoning. Set aside uncovered until ready to serve, then reheat to the simmer.

Just before serving, stir in the cognac. Pour into a tureen or soup cups over the rounds of bread and pass the cheese separately.

continued on next page

VARIATION:

ONION SOUP GRATINÉED WITH CHEESE
(You will need individual onion soup pots for this).

2 ounces Swiss cheese cut into very thin slivers
1½ cups grated Swiss or Swiss and Parmesan cheese combined
1 tablespoon grated raw onion
1 tablespoon melted butter or olive oil
12 to 16 rounds of hard toasted French bread

Preheat oven to 325 degrees. Bring soup to the boil and pour into soup pots. Stir in the slivered cheese and grated onion. Float the rounds of toast on top of the soup, and spread the grated cheese over it. Sprinkle with melted butter or oil. Bake for 20 minutes in the oven, then turn on broiler for a minute or two to brown the top lightly. Serve immediately.

WILLIAMSBURG CREAM OF PEANUT SOUP

Serves 10 to 12

1 medium onion, chopped
2 ribs of celery, chopped
¼ cup butter
1 tablespoon all purpose flour
2 quarts chicken broth
1 cup smooth peanut butter
2 cups light cream
Chopped peanuts

Sauté onion and celery in butter until soft, but not brown. Stir in flour until well blended. Add chicken broth, stirring constantly, and bring to a boil. Remove from heat and rub through a sieve. Add peanut butter and cream, stirring to blend thoroughly. Return to low heat, but do not boil, and serve, garnished with peanuts.

Serve the soup hot or cold. Delicious.

BEST OF ALL VEGETABLE SOUP

Serves 6 to 8

IN A LARGE POT:

3 pounds lean stew meat cut in small pieces, seasoned with seasoning salt and pepper, dusted with flour and browned in bacon fat.

Just a little ham, chopped fine, for flavor

ADD:

1 quart water

1 quart chicken stock or broth

1 can tomato-flavored vegetable juice (8 ounce)

2 (#2) cans tomatoes or fresh tomatoes, chopped

Simmer the above on low heat.

MEANWHILE, Prepare vegetables:

Potatoes, peeled and cut small

Onions, peeled and chopped

Carrots, peeled and sliced

Cabbage, shredded

1 small can green beans, cut and drained

1 small can corn kernels, drained

Add vegetables to soup and simmer for a long time. Maybe 2 or more hours. Serve hot with wedges of buttered corn bread. Freezes well.

May also add other vegetables such as butterbeans, peas, a little bit of raw spaghetti or macaroni, or noodles, broken up, celery, chopped. You can really be creative.

BREAKFAST ROLL WITH SHRIMP

(Like a jelly roll, only a breakfast dish).

4 tablespoons butter
½ teaspoon salt
5 eggs, separated
½ cup flour
1/8 teaspoon white pepper
2 cups milk

Preheat oven to 400 degrees. Grease, line with wax paper, grease again, a jelly roll pan. Dust it with flour.

Melt butter in sauce pan, blend in flour, salt, pepper, stirring in milk gradually.

Bring to a boil, stirring and cooking for exactly one minute. Beat yolks, adding a little of the hot sauce while beating. Then mix all together and cook over medium heat one more minute, stirring constantly. DO NOT BOIL. Cool to room temperature. (CAN DO THIS MUCH THE DAY BEFORE SERVING).

Beat egg whites until stiff and fold into cooled sauce. Pour into jelly roll pan and bake 25 to 30 minutes until puffed and brown.

Turn onto a clean towel immediately. Carefully pull off wax paper. Spread with filling and roll from long side with the aid of the towel, putting on a serving platter with seam side down.

FILLING:

1 package frozen chopped spinach, cooked and drained
3 cans (4½ ounce) shrimp (or use fresh, boiled, peeled and cleaned)
1 scant teaspoon dill weed
4 green onions, chopped
1 can (3 ounce) mushrooms, drained
2 packages (3 ounce) cream cheese
Salt and pepper to taste

Melt butter in skillet and sauté onions until tender. Add mushrooms, shrimp, spinach, dill weed, and cream cheese.

Season to taste with salt and pepper. Spread on roll evenly before rolling it up.

Filling can be made as much as 2 days ahead and refrigerated. (To use, bring to room temperature before spreading on roll).

Serve with fruit and cheese grits casserole for a very special breakfast or brunch.

CANADIAN BACON BRUNCH CASSEROLE

Serves 4

Canadian bacon
Swiss Cheese
Eggs
Light cream
Parmesan cheese

Line an oven-proof casserole with slices of Canadian bacon. Place a layer of Swiss cheese over each slice of bacon. Break an egg over each slice, then drizzle cream over the eggs until the yolks peek through. Put in a 450 degree oven for 10 minutes. Take out and sprinkle with Parmesan cheese. Return to oven for 5 more minutes. Cut in squares and serve immediately. If you like your eggs more done, cook a little longer the first time.

CHEESE SOUFFLÉ

This is a never fail recipe

Serves 4

1 cup grated sharp cheese (more if you like)
1 cup thick cream sauce (See section on Sauces)
3 egg yolks, well beaten
¼ teaspoon cream of tartar
3 egg whites

Heat oven to 350 degrees. Blend cheese into cream sauce; add egg yolks. Add cream of tartar to egg whites and beat until stiff (use electric mixer). Fold in cheese mixture. Pour into ungreased 1½ quart soufflé dish. Make a groove with the back of a spoon 1 inch from the edge. Bake in a pan of hot water (1 inch deep) for 50 to 60 minutes, until puffed and golden brown.

You may double this recipe successfully.

REMEMBER that the soufflé does not wait for the guests, but the guests must wait for the soufflé.

NOTE: Try serving a Seafood Newberg over servings of the soufflé for a most elegant entreé.

EGGS BENEDICT

Top crisp Rusks (English Muffin Halves) with slices of grilled Canadian bacon and soft poached eggs.

Ladle Hollandaise sauce over eggs and sprinkle with paprika. Garnish with a little parsley, or if you feel real fancy, a slice of truffle.

Serve immediately.

EGGS HUSSARDE

Lay slices of grilled Canadian bacon on crisp rusks and cover with Marchand de vin sauce. Top with tomato slices (can grill first if desired). Then put on soft poached eggs. Ladle Hollandaise sauce over top and sprinkle with paprika.

Recipes for the sauces will be found in the sauce section of this book.

SOFT POACHED EGGS

In a large saucepan, heat water to boiling. Add a little vinegar and salt. Break each egg into a saucer, then slide egg into the water, tipping dish toward edge of pan. Keep heat low. Do not let boil. When soft cooked, (3 to 5 minutes), remove eggs with a slotted spoon.

To keep hot until ready to serve, transfer eggs to warm water, 3 inches deep.

DEVILED EGGS (OR STUFFED EGGS)

Hard boiled eggs

Shell eggs. Cut in half lengthwise. Remove yolks to a bowl and reserve shells.

Crush yolks with a fork. Add India relish or a sweet pickle relish, salt and pepper to taste, and mayonnaise. Mix into a heavy like paste.

Fill whites with mixture. Shake paprika over tops for color. Cover and refrigerate until ready to serve.

Great for a picnic.

MOT'S BRUNCH SOUFFLÉ

Serves 6 to 8

Everyone will want seconds of this delicious dish.

8 slices white bread cut in fourths
⅓ cup margarine, spread on bread
2 cups grated sharp cheese
3 cups milk
4 eggs
1⅓ teaspoons salt
½ teaspoon dry mustard

Alternate layers of bread pieces and cheese, ending with cheese on top. Mix milk, eggs, etc. Pour over bread and cheese. Refrigerate for *24 hours.*

Bake at 325 degrees for 40 minutes. Sprinkle paprika on top before cooking...looks pretty.

Mrs. Fred Hulett

GRITS AND CHEESE CASSEROLE

1 cup grits cooked in boiling salted water for 20 minutes
Add 2 or 3 beaten eggs
½ stick butter (4 tablespoons)
½ pound or more grated Cheddar cheese

Put all in casserole and bake in a slow oven at 350 degrees for 35 to 40 minutes. Sprinkle paprika on top.

ARRINGTON'S SPANISH FRIED BANANAS

Melt 2 tablespoons butter in frying pan. Add four sliced bananas. Top with cinnamon sugar and the juice of one lemon. Cook over low heat for 10 minutes. This is good plain, when camping. It is also delicious over vanilla ice cream.

Mrs. George Arrington

QUICHE LORRAINE

2 frozen unbaked pie shells or your own homemade ones
20 slices bacon, fried crisp, drained and crumbled
10 slices Swiss cheese
2 large onions, chopped fine

Pre-heat oven to 375 degrees. Fry bacon until crisp and crumble. Chop onions and sauté in bacon drippings until light brown. Remove to drain on paper towels. Beat together: 4 eggs, 1 tablespoon flour, dash of nutmeg, ½ teaspoon salt, dash of cayenne pepper. Add 2 cups light cream. Beat and then stir in 1½ tablespoons melted butter.

Take bacon and crumble into bottom of pie shells. Tear 4 or 5 slices of Swiss cheese into bits on top of the bacon. Over this spread the sautéed onion. Pour custard over this. Bake at 375 degrees for 40 minutes. Bake ahead of time so it can cool to warm. Do not serve hot. Delicious for a bridge luncheon.

Serve with a green salad and a good white wine.

Seafood

CRAB CASSEROLE

Serves 6

1 pound fresh crabmeat (pick over well for shells)
1 grated onion
1 tablespoon Worcestershire sauce
1 tablespoon lemon juice
¾ cup buttered bread crumbs
1¼ cup medium cream sauce seasoned with salt, pepper, and nutmeg (see Sauce section).

Mix all, top with crumbs, and cook in a casserole for 30 minutes at 350 degrees.

PENNY'S CRABMEAT MORNAY

Serves 12

2 sticks butter (1 cup)
2 small bunches green onions, chopped small
1 cup finely chopped parsley
4 tablespoons flour
2 pints cream (half and half)
1 pound grated Swiss cheese
2 tablespoons sherry
Red pepper to taste
Salt to taste
2 pounds fresh crabmeat (be sure to pick out shell)

Melt butter in heavy pot and sauté onions and parsley. Blend in flour, cream and cheese until cheese is melted. Add other ingredients and gently fold in crabmeat.

This may be served in chafing dish with Melba toast or served as a luncheon dish in patty shells.

Mrs. Jimmy Purnell

PHYLLIS'S FISH FRY BATTER

2 cups self-rising flour
1 tablespoon sugar
Dash of salt and pepper
2 eggs
3 tablespoons salad oil
Iced water

Mix all ingredients. Add enough of the cold water to make a waffle-like batter. Cut fish into fingers. Dip in batter and fry.

Mrs. W.G. Campbell, Jr.

QUENELLES OF FISH

Yield: about 3 dozen

2 tablespoons butter
½ cup sifted all purpose flour
1 pound boned, skinned fish fillets
6 tablespoons butter
1 egg
2 egg whites
¾ cup whipping cream
1½ teaspoons salt
¼ teaspoon ground nutmeg
⅛ teaspoon white pepper
1 recipe Mornay Sauce (see Sauce section of this book)

In small saucepan, bring ½ cup water and 2 tablespoons butter to boiling, stirring until the butter melts. Remove from heat and add the flour and a dash of salt; beat until smooth. Cook over low heat, beating constantly until mixture forms a ball that does not separate. Remove from heat and cool, cover and chill thoroughly.

Cut the fish in small pieces and grind, using the finest blade on food grinder or processor. Place in small mixer bowl; add the 6 tablespoons butter and beat with electric mixer on high speed until very smooth and fluffy. Chill for 30 minutes.

Transfer the chilled flour mixture to a large mixer bowl. Beat in the egg and egg whites, one at a time, until very smooth. Gradually beat in the chilled fish mixture. Add the cream gradually, beating until very light and fluffy. Beat in the salt, nutmeg, and pepper. Chill thoroughly, at least 2 to 3 hours. Heavily butter two medium skillets. Using 2 soup spoons, mold each quenelle into an oval shape and gently place in skillet. Repeat until all fish mixture is used.

Heat 6 cups water to boiling. Gently pour three cups water over spoon and down side of each skillet around the quenelles. Add 1 teaspoon salt to each skillet. Cover and simmer very gently for 12 to 15 minutes or until quenelles are set. Remove from skillet with slotted spoon; drain on paper towels and serve immediately with Mornay Sauce.

Makes about 3 dozen. This recipe may be prepared a day ahead up to the last step of poaching the quenelles. This is an elegant first course.

LEMON BAKED FISH

Serves 4 to 6

Fish fillets (may use trout, sole, red fish)
1 onion, chopped
2 tablespoons butter
1 tablespoon flour
1 teaspoon salt
1 teaspoon grated lemon rind (coarsely grated)
¼ teaspoon nutmeg
⅛ teaspoon pepper (or just a pinch)
1 cup light cream

Place fillets in buttered oven dish. Sauté onion in butter. Blend in the remaining ingredients and cook them until thick. Pour over fillets. Cook covered at 300 degrees for about 20 minutes.

LOBSTER NEWBERG

Serves 8

½ cup butter
3 tablespoons flour
1 quart milk
Chopped bell pepper to taste
2 cans mushrooms, drained
¼ cup dry Sherry, or more, if desired
1 cup or more grated sharp Cheddar cheese
Salt and pepper to taste
2 teaspoons Worcestershire sauce
3 drops hot pepper seasoning
Paprika and cayenne pepper, if desired
Lobster tails (these come frozen 3 to a box, use 3 boxes).

Cook the 3 boxes lobster tails for 10 minutes in boiling water, timing exactly by the clock. Break tails open and tear meat apart.

Butter casserole dish. Put in lobster chunks. In a saucepan, melt butter. Blend in flour. Add the quart of milk and stir until thick. Add remaining ingredients. Save a little cheese to sprinkle on top of casserole. Pour cream sauce over lobster. Sprinkle with cheese, paprika and dot with butter. Serve hot in patty shells or in noodle nests, or over rice.

HOW TO COOK A WHOLE LOBSTER

1. Buy live lobsters on the day they will be served. Keep chilled until cooking time in a large bowl. Bring 12 cups water and 1 tablespoon salt to boiling in a large kettle. Hold lobster just behind the eyes. Rinse under cold running water. Drop it head first into the boiling water. Add the second lobster.
2. Return water to boiling. Reduce heat and simmer, uncovered, for 20 minutes. Remove lobster with tongs.
3. Place lobster on its back on a cutting board. Halve lengthwise with poultry shears, leaving back intact.
4. With a knife cut away membrane on the tail to expose the meat.
5. Remove the black vein that runs the length of the body and all organs in body cavity near head except the red coral roe (only in females) and liver which are delicacies.
6. Crack open large claws with a nutcracker. Remove from body.
7. Use a seafood fork to remove the meat. Dip in melted butter into which you have squeezed lemon juice. Be sure to eat the meat from the smaller claws.

FABULOUS

NEWBERG SAUCE FOR SEAFOOD

Yield: about 2½ cups, for 6 to 8 servings

2 tablespoons butter
2 tablespoons flour
¾ teaspoon salt
Dash cayenne pepper
2 cups cream (half and half)
4 egg yolks, beaten
¼ cup dry sherry

Melt butter, and stir in flour, salt, and cayenne. Blend well. Then add cream. Cook over low heat until smooth and the mixture comes to a boil. Stir some of the hot sauce into the egg yolks and then add to the sauce mixture.

At this point you may add the seafood. This can be shrimp, lobster, crab, or a combination, which has been sautéed in a little butter. Then add the sherry and keep warm until ready to serve.

Divine served hot over cheese soufflé.

Also good in patty shells or over steaming hot rice.

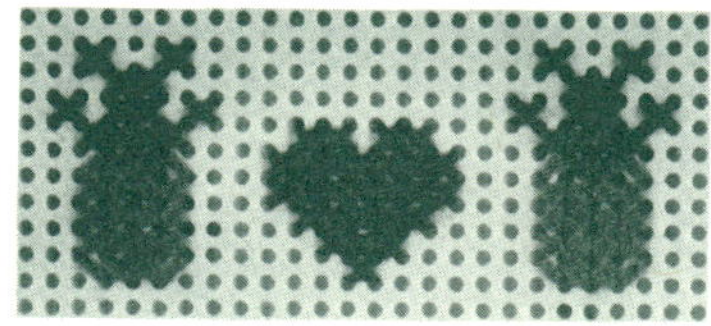

WILD RICE AND SEAFOOD CASSEROLE

Serves 6

2 pints oysters or 1 pound cooked shrimp
6 cups beef broth (or half water)
1½ cups raw wild rice
1 stick butter (¼ pound) at room temperature
3 cups mushroom oyster sauce

Drain oysters, reserve liquid and set aside. Bring beef broth to a boil in a large saucepan. Add rice and cook until tender (about an hour). All liquid will have gone away.

Place oysters in skillet over medium heat, just until the edges of the oysters curl. Drain well.

TO MAKE THE CASSEROLE: Combine hot rice with stick of butter. Mix well. Spoon ½ the rice over bottom of a 2 quart casserole. Arrange oysters on top. Cover with remaining rice. Spoon mushroom sauce over all. Bake at 325 degrees for 30 minutes.

MUSHROOM SAUCE:
2½ tablespoons butter
1½ tablespoons flour
1 cup oyster liquor
Salt, pepper, to taste
4 shallots, crushed, peeled, and minced
¼ pound button mushrooms, chopped fine
1 small onion, chopped fine
¾ cup heavy cream
1 teaspoon curry powder (optional)

Heat 1½ tablespoons butter. Stir in flour and cook until frothy. Add oyster liquor and cook while beating with wire whisk until sauce is thickened. Add salt and pepper and set aside.

Place onion and shallots in food processor until fine. Melt remaining butter and add onions, etc. Add chopped mushrooms. Cook until most liquid has gone. Add curry, oyster sauce, and cream. Cook while stirring about 5 minutes.

NOTE: If you use shrimp, substitute milk and cream for the oyster liquor.

SEAFOOD THERMIDOR

A great dish for a crowd.

Yield: 3 quarts

3 (6½ ounce) cans crabmeat or use fresh
5 (1½ to 2 ounce) lobster tails, cooked (comes frozen)
2 pounds shrimp, cooked, peeled, cleaned
¾ cup butter
1½ cups sliced mushrooms
1 big onion, chopped and sautéed
¾ cup flour
3 cups chicken broth
1 cup heavy cream
2 cups light cream
1 tablespoon salt
2 tablespoons prepared mustard
Few drops hot pepper seasoning
1 tablepoon lemon juice
¼ cup sherry to each quart
1 cup Parmesan cheese

Pick over crab carefully. Cut lobster into bite size pieces. Cook and prepare shrimp.

Melt butter, add onions and mushrooms; sauté. Stir in flour. Blend well. Add broth and seasonings. Add seafood. Mix well and cool.

Pack into 3 refrigerator cartons (quart size) and freeze. Thaw in refrigerator for several hours. Transfer to casserole and bake at 350 degrees for 30 minutes. Remove from oven and stir in sherry. Sprinkle with cheese. Bake until bubbly.

(Of course, you do not have to freeze).

CREOLE SAUCE

(For Shrimp Creole)

Yield: about 3 cups sauce

½ cup onion, chopped
1 clove garlic, crushed
½ cup celery, finely cut
¼ cup bell pepper, finely cut
2 tablespoons olive oil
2½ cups tomatoes
1 bay leaf
2 teaspoons salt
2 teaspoons sugar
2 teaspoons parsley, chopped
4 cloves
1 teaspoon flour

Sauté onion, garlic, celery, and bell pepper until soft. DO NOT BROWN. Add remaining ingredients except the flour. Cook on low heat until thick. Remove garlic and cloves. Add the flour dissolved in a little water. Add shrimp for shrimp creole and serve over rice. Also a delicious sauce for veal cutlets.

DEVILED SHRIMP

Serves 12

4 teaspoons minced onion
3 pounds shrimp
1 can sliced mushrooms
6 tablespoons flour
6 hardcooked eggs, diced
1 cup butter
2 cups buttered breadcrumbs
1 teaspoon mustard
3 cups milk
2 teaspoons paprika
1 teaspoon salt
Dash cayenne pepper

Sauté onions in butter. Add cooked shrimp which have been peeled and cleaned, paprika, mustard, salt, cayenne, and flour. Mix well. Add milk and cook slowly until thickened, stirring constantly. Add eggs.

Place in ramekins or scallop shells. Sprinkle with bread crumbs. Bake in hot oven (425 degrees) for 15 minutes or until brown and bubbly.

SHRIMP AND CRABMEAT CASSEROLE

Serves 16

4 pounds shrimp, cooked and peeled
1 (1 pound) can fresh crab lumps
5 hard-boiled eggs, chopped or grated
Juice of 1 lemon (add last)
1 can mushrooms, sliced
½ cup chopped parsley

Sauté 2 extra large onions in 4 tablespoons margarine.

Mix seafood and eggs with cream sauce. Add onion, parsley, and lemon juice. Put in buttered casserole. Sprinkle buttered bread crumbs over top. Bake 20 minutes at 350 to 375 degrees.

CREAM SAUCE:
3 cups milk (heat in double boiler)
6 tablespoons flour dissolved in a little of the milk
1 teaspoon salt
½ teaspoon dill weed
½ teaspoon pepper
½ teaspoon dry mustard
2 teaspoons Worcestershire sauce
Pinch of thyme
2 teaspoons paprika
1 dash cayenne pepper
2 teaspoons Durkee's Dressing (heaping)
Seasoned salt
Few drops hot pepper seasoning

Stir until medium thick and smooth over medium heat.

SHRIMP ROCKEFELLER

Serves 8 to10

2 packages frozen, chopped spinach, defrosted
1 clove garlic, crushed
6 green onions, chopped
2 tablespoons parsley
½ head lettuce, chopped
3 stalks celery, chopped
½ cup butter
1 tablespoon Worcestershire sauce
2 tablespoons anchovy paste
1½ teaspoons salt
3 pounds shrimp, peeled and cleaned

Heat together butter and seasonings. Add chopped lettuce and spinach and simmer 10 minutes. Add ½ cup soft bread crumbs. Spread over shells or in bottom of casserole and cover with cooked shrimp. Just before heating, cover greens and shrimp with cream sauce.

SAUCE:
3 tablespoons butter
3 tablespoons flour
2 cups milk
Dash of Worcestershire sauce
1 package Swiss Gruyere cheese

Cut up cheese, and cook with other ingredients until melted and season to taste. Pour cream sauce over casserole of shrimp and bake at 350 degrees for 20 minutes.

BAKED RED SNAPPER IN CREAM SAUCE

Serves 6

3 pounds red snapper
2 chopped hard boiled eggs
1 pint hot cream sauce (see Sauce section)
½ teaspoon chopped parsley
½ cup Hollandaise sauce (see Sauce section).

Add eggs and parsley to cream sauce; fold in the hollandaise. Pour over broiled red snapper. Divine.

TOMMY'S RED SNAPPER

1 whole large red snapper (5 or 6 pounds)

OR a small to medium whole snapper per person

Score whole fish by cutting deep gashes in both sides crosswise of the fish.

Season fish inside and out with salt and pepper. Place a slice of lemon in each fish or several slices in the large fish. Also place lemon slices on top.

Place fish in broiler pan without rack. Bake at 325 degrees for about 20 minutes. Then pour the lemon juice over the fish. Spoon the mushroom and artichoke sauce over the fish. Continue baking fish until it is tender and flaky (15 minutes or more).

MUSHROOM-ARTICHOKE SAUCE:

1 stick butter (¼ pound)
2 little green onions, chopped
1½ cups fresh mushrooms, sliced
1 can artichoke bottoms, cut in bite size pieces, if you are feeling extravagant
OR you may use 1 can artichoke hearts, quartered
¼ cup chopped fresh parsley
½ to 1 cup dry white wine
3 tablespoons lemon juice, freshly squeezed

Melt butter and sauté onions. Add sliced mushrooms and artichoke bottoms and sauté gently. Add parsley and wine and toss lightly. Set aside until ready to use.

FRIED OYSTERS

Select large oysters. Rinse and lay on colander to drain. Dry gently with a piece of paper towel. Handle oysters as little as possible.

Take a long fork and catch it in the eye of the oyster, dip in egg and then in just enough fine cracker dust. Use 2 eggs for a dozen and a half oysters. Beat them, add a pinch of salt and 1 tablespoon of boiling water. Have ready a frying pan, not too deep, with plenty of smoking-hot oil to which add a little butter to aid in making oysters crisp and brown. Put in only enough oysters to cover bottom without crowding. When brown on one side, turn over. Serve hot.

SOUTHERN FRIED OYSTERS

1 quart large oysters, drained
Cracker meal
3 eggs mixed with ½ cup water
1 teaspoon salt
2 tablespoons baking powder

Drain oysters; coat them with cracker meal. Dip each oyster in egg and water mixture. Have another dish of cracker meal mixed with the salt and baking powder. Dip oysters in this and fry in deep fat about 5 minutes.

OLD SOUTHERN BAKED OYSTERS

12 to 15 servings

2 quarts oysters, drained
½ cup chopped parsley
½ cup chopped shallots or onions
Salt, pepper, hot pepper seasoning, to taste
1 tablespoon Worcestershire
2 tablespoons lemon juice
½ cup melted butter
2 cups finely ground cracker crumbs
Paprika
¾ cup half and half cream (use ½ cup if using 1 quart oysters)

Place layer of oysters in bottom of greased, shallow, 2 quart baking dish. Sprinkle with half the parsley, shallots, seasonings, lemon juice, butter and crumbs. Then make another layer of same. Sprinkle with paprika. Just before baking, pour in cream, being careful not to moisten topping.

Bake at 375 degrees for 30 minutes.

OYSTER DRESSING

2 cups cooked rice
½ stick margarine (4 tablespoons)
Sauté 1 cup chopped celery and 1 cup chopped parsley
Salt, pepper
3 big onions, chopped
1 or more pints oysters

Melt margarine in skillet. Add oysters and juice. Let cook until edges of the oysters curl. Add sautéed celery, parsley, and onions. Add to rice. Blend gently.

Serve hot from a chafing dish. Delicious.

A good dish for a buffet supper.

OYSTERS BIENVILLE

Serves 4 to 6

48 or more oysters
1½ pounds cooked shrimp, diced fine
2 cans (No. 1) mushrooms, diced
1 clove garlic
1 large onion, finely chopped
1½ cups milk
1½ cups chicken broth
¼ cup or more butter
3 tablespoons flour
1 teaspoon onion juice
2 tablespoons Worcestershire sauce
¼ teaspoon celery seed
1 cup white wine
Parmesan cheese, or grated Cheddar cheese, or both

Dice the shrimp and mushrooms fine. Make a sauce of the butter, flour, garlic, onion juice, Worcestershire sauce, celery seed. Add liquids except wine. Blend well. Should look like a cream sauce. Add mushrooms and shrimp. Stir gently. Add wine. Simmer slowly for about 15 minutes.

Put oysters in shells on rock salt. Run under hot broiler for about 2 minutes, until the edges curl. Drain off liquid accumulated in oysters.

Sprinkle each oyster with Parmesan cheese, then cover with sauce. Shake on bread crumbs and a little more cheese and paprika on top. Put back under broiler for about 5 minutes, until bubbly. Serve hot.

It is most interesting to serve these along with oysters Rockefeller as a first course with a glass of wonderful white wine. We usually serve these for Christmas dinner. We like a Vouray wine.

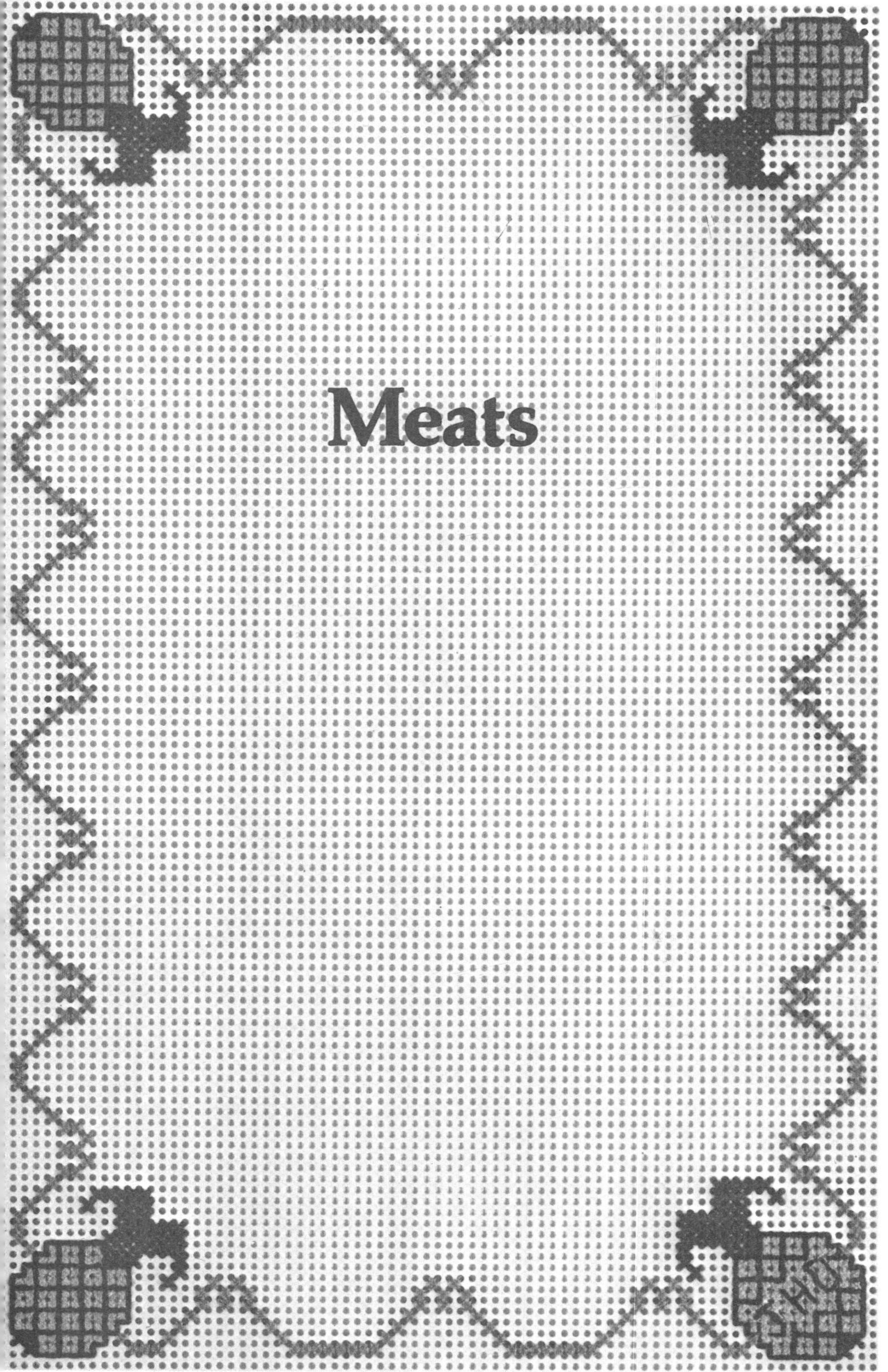

Meats

PEG'S BEACH BURGERS

Delicious for a crowd

Serve on hamburger buns.

4 onions, chopped fine
2 cups celery, finely chopped
¼ cup butter

Sauté the above until browned.

ADD:
4 pounds lean ground chuck and brown.

ADD:
1 teaspoon garlic powder
2 teaspoons seasoned salt
½ teaspoon pepper
3 tablespoons Worcestershire sauce
2 (12 ounce) bottles catsup

Simmer all at least an hour.
Freezes well.

BEEF CASSEROLE

Serves 4 to 6

2 pounds beef cubes, browned
1 can French onion soup
1 can cream of mushroom soup
Noodles (5 oz. package) cooked according to package directions

Mix together in casserole and bake at 350 degrees for 2 hours or more. Serve over noodles.

Can add: Burgundy wine for flavor, fresh or canned mushrooms during the last 15 minutes of cooking time.

NOTE: A teaspoon of poppy seeds added to cooked noodles makes for a delicious feast.

Freezes well.

SWEDISH MEAT BALLS OVER RICE

Serves 4 to 6

1 pound ground beef
1 cup soft bread crumbs
1 cup milk
1 egg, well beaten
2 medium onions, chopped
2 teaspoons salt
¼ teaspoon nutmeg
2 tablespoons cooking oil
1 cup boiling water
1 tablespoon flour
2 tablespoons cold water
Hot cooked rice

Put meat and the next 7 ingredients in a mixing bowl and mix well. Form into 1 inch balls. Set dial on electric skillet to 350 degrees and preheat. Heat a little fat and brown meat balls well on all sides, using more fat as necessary. Remove from pan as they brown and drain. Set dial at 210 degrees. Add boiling water to meat drippings. Blend flour and cold water. Stir into hot mixture. Cook until thickened, stirring constantly. Return meat balls to pan. Cover and cook for 30 minutes, adding more water if necessary.

Serve hot over hot rice.

BRISKET

1 (4 to 5 pound) brisket with fat trimmed
½ teaspoon seasoned salt
½ teaspoon cayenne pepper
½ teaspoon garlic powder
Paprika

Season brisket. Coat with paprika. Wrap meat in aluminum foil. Bake fat side up for 4 hours in a 300 degree oven.

Serve with the following sauce:

1 carton sour cream
1 tablespoon horseradish
1 teaspoon lemon juice

Mix well and refrigerate.

BEEF BOURGUIGNON

Serves 12

Butter or margarine
5 pounds boneless beef chuck, cut into 1½ inch cubes
6 tablespoons brandy
1 pound small white onions, peeled (about 24)
1 pound small fresh mushrooms
½ cup potato flour (can use plain flour)
5 teaspoons meat extract paste
¼ cup tomato paste
3 cups Burgundy wine
1½ cups dry sherry
1½ cups ruby port
1 can (10½ ounce) condensed beef broth, undiluted
¼ teaspoon pepper
2 bay leaves
24 small new potatoes
Chopped parsley

On the day before: Slowly heat an 8 quart Dutch oven with a tight fitting lid. Add 4 tablespoons butter. Heat but do not burn. In the hot butter, over high heat, brown the beef cubes well all over. Brown about one fourth of them at a time. Lift out beef as it browns. Continue until all beef is browned, adding more butter as needed. Then return beef to Dutch oven.

In a small saucepan, heat 4 tablespoons brandy just until the vapor rises. Ignite and pour over beef. As flame dies, remove beef cubes and set aside.

Add 2 tablespoons butter to Dutch oven and heat slightly. Add onions and cook over low heat, covered, until onions brown slightly. Then add mushrooms and cook, stirring for 3 minutes. Remove from heat.

Stir in flour, meat-extract paste and tomato paste until well blended. Stir in Burgundy, sherry, port and beef broth.

Preheat oven to 350 degrees.

Bring wine mixture just to boiling, stirring. Remove from heat. Add beef, pepper, and bay leaves, mixing well.

Bake, covered and stirring occasionally, 45 minutes, adding remaining brandy little by little. Bake with a sheet of waxed paper placed over Dutch oven and lid placed on top. Discard any liquid collecting on top of paper.

Meanwhile, scrub potatoes, leaving skins on. Cook, covered, in small amount of lightly salted, boiling water for 10 minutes. Drain. Add potatoes to beef mixture, spooning liquid over potatoes.

Let cool; refrigerate, covered, overnight.

TO SERVE: Heat gently, covered for about 1 hour, stirring in a little more wine, if necessary, to thin sauce.

NOTE: For 24 servings, you will need to make recipe twice.

TOMMY'S BEEF JERKY

Perfect for Boy Scout trips as well as divine with a drink

Round steak or flank steak (7 pounds will net about 3 pounds of jerky)
Lemon pepper
Seasoned salt
Garlic salt
Soy sauce
Juice of 2 lemons
Worcstershire sauce

Have butcher slice meat thin with the grain into strips. If you choose to slice it yourself, it is easier to do if meat is slightly frozen. Be sure to trim off all fat.

Season both sides of meat and marinate in soy sauce, Worcestershire sauce and lemon juice for about 6 hours or overnight in the refrigerator. When ready to bake, place strips on a rack with a drip pan underneath. Cook at 200 degrees for about 6 hours. The meat will be dark and very dry in appearance.

This meat will keep safely for a long time, however, it is so good you'll have trouble keeping it at all.

GRILLED BEEF TENDERLOIN

Serves 8 to 10

Buy a whole tenderloin of beef at your grocery. To serve 8 to 10 people the tenderloin should weigh about 6 pounds.

PREPARATION FOR COOKING: Strip off the dark thick fat, the gristle-like yellow substance that resembles cord and the thin sinewy sheath between the fat cover and the meat. Don't destroy the round shape of the meat. Use a small, sharp paring knife to help you.

Season meat all over with seasoned salt, and lemon pepper. Let stand about an hour. Make a basting sauce of the following:

½ cup melted butter
Juice of 1 lemon
2 tablespoons Worcestershire sauce

Sear meat on all sides over hot fire on grill. Baste with sauce. Then cover and cook from 20 to 40 minutes to desired doneness. (Medium rare is divine).

Baste several times during the cooking and do not let meat burn.

MEAT LOAF

1½ to 2 pounds ground lean chuck. Season well with seasoned salt and pepper.

ADD:
1 teaspoon dried onion flakes
1 teaspoon prepared mustard
A big pinch of bouquet garni
Bread crumbs (made in food processor from 2 slices stale bread)
¼ cup milk
1 egg, beaten

Mix meat with seasonings and crumbs gently with your hands. Add egg and milk. Mix and shape into a loaf. Place in a glass baking dish. Bake at 350 degrees for 1 hour.

When meat loaf is halfway done, mix together ½ cup chili sauce and ½ cup water and pour over meat loaf. Serve hot.

SIRLOIN TIP ROAST WITH VEGETABLES

3 to 4 pound sirloin tip roast (buy U.S. choice, heavy beef without the proten additive)
Flour, salt, pepper
1 medium onion, thinly sliced
2 bay leaves
1 clove minced garlic
½ cup hot water
8 small onions, peeled
8 medium carrots, peeled
8 small potatoes, peeled and halved

Sprinkle meat with salt, pepper, and flour. Brown slowly on all sides in a little hot fat in a Dutch oven. Add sliced onion, bay leaves, garlic and water.

Cover and cook in moderate oven at 350 degrees for about 1½ hours or until almost tender. This roast may be cooked in an electric skillet instead of oven cooking.

Add vegetables. Sprinkle with 1½ teaspoons salt. Cover and continue to cook 1 hour or until done. Remove to a platter. Thicken juices for pot roast gravy.

ANOTHER METHOD FOR COOKING ROAST: If roast is from top grade beef, cook uncovered and without water. Roast at 325 degrees with meat thermometer inserted in roast to desired doneness. Usually 30 minutes per pound for medium doneness. Cook vegetables separately on top of stove.

EYE OF THE ROUND ROAST

Red wine
Olive oil
Freshly ground pepper
Salt, either plain or seasoned
Mashed garlic clove

Marinate roast overnight in refrigerator in a mixture of 3 parts wine to 1 part olive oil, adding a great deal of freshly ground pepper, seasoned salt, and a mashed garlic bud. Turn occcasionally. Bake in a 400 degree oven for about 20 minutes for rare. Cook longer for more well done meat. (A meat thermometer is the best gauge).

ALTERNATE COOKING METHOD: Cook out on the grill, using charcoal and hickory chips. Takes longer but tastes divine.

TO SERVE: Serve with hot artichoke bottoms and pass Bearnaise sauce.

NOTE: Remember that Bearnaise sauce is not served hot. It will curdle if you heat it.

PHYLLIS'S SPAGHETTI MEAT SAUCE

Serves 5

1 pound ground round steak
½ cup vegetable oil
1 onion, chopped
¼ bunch parsley, chopped
5 small cans tomato sauce
5 cans water
1½ tablespoons sweet basil
1 teaspoon anise seed
4 bay leaves
1 teaspoon rosemary
½ teaspoon ground cinnamon
½ teaspoon ground nutmeg
1 tablespoon sugar
Salt, pepper, and garlic salt to taste

Mix salt, pepper, garlic salt, onion, and meat. Brown for about 15 minutes. Add other ingredients. Simmer approximately 12 hours. Divine.

NOTE: I always at least double the recipe and sometimes more. The sauce freezes well and always tastes richer and better the second day.

Mrs. W.G. Campbell

SPANISH NOODLES

Serves 10

1 onion, large, chopped
2 pounds ground chuck
1 can mushrooms, sliced
Bacon fat
½ pound grated sharp cheese
1 large package medium egg noodles or 2 (5 ounce) packages
1 (No. 2) can cream style corn
1 (3 ounce) can sliced ripe olives
1 clove garlic, minced (optional)
2 small cans tomato sauce

Brown chopped onion in bacon fat. Remove to another dish. Then brown meat, seasoned with salt and pepper. Return onion to skillet with meat. Stir in tomato sauce, creamed corn, olives with the juice, minced garlic, mushrooms with the juice. Let all this simmer for several hours.

Boil noodles and rinse well in colander. Put noodles in pyrex dish, pour sauce and cheese over them, mixing well. More cheese may be added on top.

Bake in a 350 degree oven for 30 minutes.

This recipe may be doubled and it also freezes well.

Great for a crowd. Serve with a green salad.

BEEF STROGANOFF I

Serves 6

4 cups meat (either a fresh round steak or left-over roast. Trim all fat from meat and cut in strips about 1 inch long and ¼ inch wide)
2 tablespoons olive oil
2 tablespoons butter
1 cup thinly sliced or chopped onion
1½ cups sliced mushrooms (fresh or canned)
1 cup beef stock or consommé
1½ tablespoons flour
1 teaspoon seasoned salt
Dash of pepper and nutmeg
1 teaspoon Worcestershire sauce
½ to 1 cup sour cream

Heat oil and butter in skillet. Sauté onions and mushrooms on low heat until soft. Add meat and continue cooking for about 10 minutes. (If fresh meat, shake a little flour on it and brown it). Add consommé and cook about 30 minutes. (Dissolve flour in a little of the consommé until dissolved and smooth, then add to skillet).

Just before serving, add sour cream. Stir and smooth. DO NOT LET IT BOIL. Can serve over rice or noodles.

BEEF STROGANOFF II

2 pounds round steak, sliced in thin strips
2 large onions, sliced
2 medium cans sliced mushrooms
¾ cup sherry
1 can mushroom soup
½ cup sour cream

Slice steak into strips, dredge in seasoned flour. Brown in bacon drippings. Remove and set aside.

Slice onions thin and sauté.

Drain mushrooms, reserving liquor. Brown lightly. Add meat to onions and mushrooms.

Add mushroom soup, juice from mushrooms, and ½ soup can of water. Cover and stew slowly about an hour. (You may have to add more water). Add sherry. Stir often.

Just before serving add sour cream and blend well. Serve over rice.

Baked or broiled whole tomatoes are good with this.

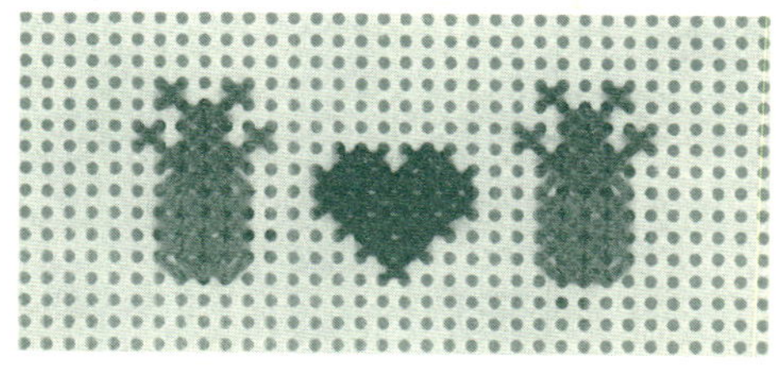

VEAL CUTLETS WITH TOMATO SAUCE

Dip seasoned veal cutlets in flour, then in beaten egg, then in bread crumbs. Cook in skillet until well browned, using butter or some other fat to brown.

SAUCE:

3 tablespoons chopped onion
1 tablespoon chopped bell pepper
Garlic
1 tablespoon butter
1 can tomato paste
3 cans water
¼ teaspoon thyme
¼ teaspoon sweet basil
½ teaspoon sugar
1 bay leaf, crushed
Salt and pepper, to taste

Sauté onion and bell pepper. Add everything else. Bring to a boil. Lower heat and simmer for 15 to 20 minutes. Pour over browned meat and simmer until meat is done. Delicious.

LEG OF LAMB (BONED)

Have butcher bone leg of lamb and secure together well. Marinate lamb for 24 hours, refrigerated, in the following sauce:

⅓ cup vegetable oil
1 bay leaf
Oregano
½ cup scallions
2 or 3 cloves garlic
Pinch of rosemary
Italian seasonings

If the above ingredients don't seem to be enough marinade, just add a little Italian salad dressing to it.

When ready to cook the meat, drain for a few minutes and then rub meat with curry powder, ginger, and seasoned salt. Pour in 1 cup Port or Madiera wine, after roast has cooked for about 30 minutes. Bake uncovered on a rack in a 300 degree oven until done. A 5 pound roast should cook 3 hours.

Serve with Cumberland sauce. Add ½ cup of good Brandy and 1 lump of sugar and ignite. (You will find the sauce recipe in the Sauce section).

Looks beautiful and tastes divine.

LAMB SHISH KABOBS

10 servings

1 (3½ pound) boned leg of lamb
1 large onion, finely chopped
½ cup salad oil
½ cup dry sherry
1 to 1½ tablespoons cumin seed
1 tablespoon salt
1½ teaspoons rosemary
1 teaspoon coarsely ground black pepper
1 teaspoon garlic salt
1 (1 pint) box cherry tomatoes
3 bell peppers, cut into 1 inch squares
2 (16 ounce) jars onions, drained

Remove fell from lamb. This is the tissuelike covering. Cut lamb into 1½ inch cubes and set aside.

Combine chopped onion, oil, sherry, and seasonings. Add lamb. Cover and marinate at least 24 hours in the refrigerator.

Remove meat from marinade. Alternate meat and vegetables on skewers. Broil 5 minutes; turn and broil an additional 5 minutes or to desired degree of doneness. (You may also use large mushrooms on the skewers).

BUTTERFLIED LEG OF LAMB

Serves 25

2 eight pound legs of lamb, trimmed and butterflied

MARINADE FOR LAMB:
4 large onions, cut into chunks
4 garlic cloves
2 cups pomegranate juice
1 cup dry red wine
1 lemon, unpeeled and cut into chunks
4 teaspoons basil leaves
1 tablespoon salt
1 teaspoon freshly ground pepper

Combine all ingredients in processor or blender and puree.

Arrange lamb in 2 (10 x 14 inch) roasting pans. Pour half of marinade over top of each leg of lamb, turning lamb to cover completely. Marinate 8 to 10 hours at room temperature or chill 1 or 2 days.

Preheat broiler. Wipe excess marinade from lamb. Arrange in pan and broil 5 to 6 inches from heat source, turning frequently to brown evenly (inside should be pink), about 30 to 35 minutes. Slice thinly to serve.

Lamb can also be barbecued.

NOTE: Pomegranate juice can be found in specialty food shops. If you cannot obtain it, just substitute the same amount of red wine.

BAKED CANADIAN BACON

2 pounds Canadian bacon
½ cup beer
¾ cup sugar
½ teaspoon dry mustard
Beer to make paste

Place bacon, fat side up, in a roasting pan. Pour ½ cup beer over it and bake 45 minutes at 350 degrees. Baste with beer in pan.

Make a paste with the sugar, mustard and a little beer. Remove bacon from oven and spread paste over it. Return to oven and bake 1 hour longer, basting frequently.

Serve warm.

CASSEROLE OF PORK CHOPS ON RICE

4 servings

4 lean center cut pork chops
Seasoned salt and pepper
2 cups cooked rice
1 small onion, chopped
¼ cup chopped celery
1 can (10¾ ounce) mushroom soup
1 cup milk

Grease skillet and brown seasoned chops on both sides. Combine other ingredients. Put rice in buttered casserole. Lay chops on top. Add fat from skillet. Cover. Bake in hot oven (400 degrees) for 30 minutes or longer.

ROLLED PORK LOIN ROAST

Have your butcher prepare a rolled loin of pork weighing at least 3 to 4 pounds. Rub it with seasoned salt, pepper, garlic salt, and a little ground nutmeg. Brown on top of stove.

Place in roasting pan and add the following:

¼ cup chopped onion
A big pinch chopped parsley
1 bay leaf
1 can (10½ ounce) beef consommé

Bake at 350 degrees about 2 hours until done.

NOTE: A divine variation is to add 1 can sauerkraut on top of roast during the last half of the cooking time. (This little trick came from my friend, Joy Mitchell).

Can also add a little red wine in the beginning.

GOLDEN SUGARED HAM

1 precooked ham
1 (16 ounce) jar apricot-pineapple preserves
½ cup brown sugar (dark)
Pecan halves and maraschino cherries for garnish

Combine preserves and brown sugar and heat in saucepan, stirring well. Spread mixture over a precooked ham for the last half hour of baking.

TO GARNISH: Alternate diagonal rows of pecan halves and cherry halves.

CROWN ROAST OF PORK

1 roast weighing 6 pounds should serve 10 people

Make friends with your butcher and then ask him to prepare a crown roast for you.

Sprinkle roast with salt and pepper. Place on a rack in a shallow roasting pan rib ends up. Fill center cavity with crumpled aluminum foil to help retain crown shape. Cover rib ends with foil to keep them from looking burned. Roast in a 350 degree oven for 35 minutes per pound or until meat thermometer reaches 185 degrees.

TO SERVE: Fill cavity with some kind of rice dish, as sausage-rice stuffing or wild rice and mushrooms. Garnish platter with crab apple rounds and curly parsley.

SAUSAGE-RICE STUFFING:

1 pound bulk pork sausage
1 cup package pre-cooked rice
1 tablespoon parsley flakes
4 oranges, sectioned
¾ cup chopped pecans
Salt and pepper
1½ cups chopped onion
½ cup orange juice
½ teaspoon poultry seasoning
¾ cup raisins

Break up sausage in large skillet and cook with onion until meat is done and onion is golden. Add rice, orange juice, parsley. Cover and simmer 5 minutes. Add orange sections, raisins, and pecans. Mix lightly.

One hour before end of roasting time, remove roast from oven. Remove foil. Fill cavity with stuffing mixture, piling high in the center. Return to oven and cook one hour longer. To Serve: place on platter and garnish with parsley and orange roses. Serve with orange sauce.

ORANGE ROSES: Cut peel in long strips spiral fashion. Roll strip of peel to look like a rose and fashion with a toothpick which you will remove at serving time.

ORANGE SAUCE:

3 tablespoons pork drippings from pan or use butter
2 cups orange juice
¼ teaspoon poultry seasoning
3 tablespoons flour
¾ teaspoon salt
1 orange, sectioned

Blend drippings and flour. Gradually stir in orange juice and add seasonings. Stir constantly over medium heat until mixture thickens and comes to a boil. Stir in brown particles from bottom of pan. Add orange sections. Heat. Serve with roast. Yield: 2 cups sauce.

BAKED HAM

Place a "cook before eating" ham or half a ham fat side up on a rack in a shallow roasting pan. Insert meat thermometer. Bake at 325 degrees until thermometer reads 160 degrees. For a 12 pound ham, baking time should be about 4 hours. Half an hour before end of cooking time, remove from the oven. Pour fat drippings from pan, reserving 2 or 3 tablespoons.

Score ham fat in diamond shapes. Insert 1 whole clove in center of each diamond. Combine 1 cup brown sugar, 1 teaspoon dry mustard, and reserved drippings. Spread over ham.

Continue baking about 30 minutes, spooning glaze over ham two or three times.

You may also decorate ham with pineapple slices and cherries.

BAKED HAM WITH BLACK CHERRY SAUCE

Serves 6

1 sliced ready to eat ham (2 or 3 pounds)
1 (1 pound) can pitted dark Bing cherries (2 cups)
2 teaspoons cornstarch
Dash salt
1 tablespoon finely chopped candied ginger
2 teaspoons lemon juice

Slash fat edge of ham. Place in shallow baking dish. Bake at 350 degrees for 45 minutes. Serve with warm cherry sauce.

SAUCE: Drain cherries, and reserve syrup. Add water to syrup to make 1 cup. Gradually stir reserved syrup into cornstarch. Add cherries, salt, and ginger. Cook and stir until mixture thickens and boils. Cook 2 minutes. Stir in lemon juice.

BAKED HAM WITH PINEAPPLE WHEELS

Good supper dish.

1½ pounds ham cut in thick slices
1 can sliced pineapple
1 tablespoon brown sugar
1 teaspoon pepper
1 tablespoon prepared mustard

Sprinkle ham with pepper and spread with mustard. Then put brown sugar all over top. Put ham in hot iron frying pan and pour pineapple juice all around. Cover pan and place in oven. Cook slowly for 1 hour (about 300 degrees). When ham is tender, remove cover and brown. Top with slices of pineapple centered with a cherry for garnish.

HAM DIVAN

Serves 4 to 6

2 packages frozen broccoli
8 or 10 slices baked ham (this can be left over)
2 cups medium cream sauce (see Index)
3 tablespoons Parmesan cheese
4 tablespoons dry sherry

Cook broccoli according to package directions. (Undercook a little so vegetable will be crisp). In a glass baking dish arrange a layer of broccoli, then a layer of ham. Pour the sherry evenly over the above. Top this with the cream sauce to which Parmesan cheese has been added. Sprinkle the top with a little more Parmesan cheese. Brown under the oven broiler until hot, just before serving.

This is a quick substitute for Chicken Divan. It can be prepared ahead and heated at serving time.

A fruit salad is nice with this.

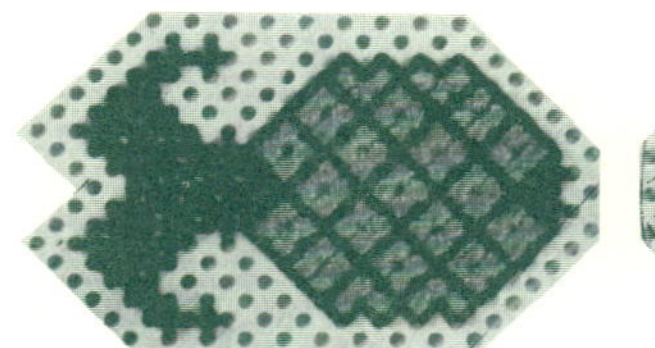

FRUITED HAM KABOBS

Serves 6

3 pounds boneless fully cooked ham, cut into 1½ inch cubes
24 large pitted prunes
3 (¾ inch thick) slices fresh pineapple, cut into 6 wedges
1 (12 ounce) can apricot nectar
½ cup honey
¼ teaspoon ground ginger
1 lime, cut into 6 wedges

Place ham, prunes, and pineapple in a bowl. Combine apricot nectar, honey, and ginger in a saucepan; simmer for 5 minutes, stirring occasionally. Cool and pour over ham and fruit. Marinate in refrigerator 4 to 6 hours. Drain well, reserving marinade.

Alternate meat and fruit on 6 (12 inch) skewers; thread a lime wedge on end of each skewer. Grill kabobs 5 to 6 inches from low heat for 20 to 25 minutes, turning and brushing with marinade occasionally.

HAM MOUSSE

¼ pound butter
1 can consommé
1 tablespoon gelatin
2 cups ground ham
1 tablespoon mustard
2 eggs
½ cup chopped bell pepper
½ cup chopped celery

Separate eggs. Beat yolks well. Mix with mustard, consommé, and butter in double boiler. Cook slowly until it is like custard. Stir in ham, celery, pepper, and gelatin which has been softened in ¼ cup cold water. Let cool and fold in stiffly beaten egg whites. Put in a WET loaf mold (oven-proof glass). Serve garnished as you like.

Delicious served with a green salad on a hot summer day.

VENISON, COUNTRY-FRIED

Serves 6

1½ pounds (¾ thick) venison
1 cup flour
Salt and pepper
¼ teaspoon seasoned salt
4 tablespoons bacon drippings
2 cloves garlic, minced
1 quart water
⅓ cup all purpose flour
1½ teaspoons bottled brown bouquet sauce
1 medium onion, sliced thin
½ pound fresh mushrooms, sliced
Hot cooked rice

Prepare venison by trimming off all fat and removing connective tissues. Cut meat into serving-size pieces, like little steaks. Pound each piece to ¼ to ½ thickness.

Combine flour, salt, pepper, seasoned salt, and dredge the venison in the flour mixture.

Heat 1 tablespoon bacon drippings in a large heavy skillet. Add garlic and sauté until golden. Remove garlic and set aside. Add remaining bacon drippings to skillet. Cook venison until it is browned on both sides. Remove from skillet and set aside.

Gradually stir about ½ cup water into ⅓ cup flour. Mix until smooth and add the remaining water. Stir flour mixture into pan drippings and cook over medium heat, stirring constantly, until thickened. Stir in bottled bouquet, ½ teaspoon salt and ⅛ teaspoon pepper. Return venison and garlic to skillet, reduce heat. Cover and simmer for 30 minutes. Add onion. Cover and simmer 15 minutes. Add mushrooms, cover, and simmer for 15 more minutes.

Poultry

BREAST OF CHICKEN IN FOIL

Delicious for a super easy supper

Place 1 piece chicken breast on a large square of aluminum foil. Add 2 small peeled carrots, 1 small peeled potato, salt, pepper, ¼ teaspoon grated onion, parsley, a little piece of celery or celery salt, 2 tablespoons heavy cream, 2 tablespoons butter, and 1 teaspoon dry sherry.

Fold up sealing edges well. Place in shallow pan and cook in 350 degree oven for 45 minutes.

Serve with a salad.

ROLLED CHICKEN BREASTS I

Serves 6

½ cup chopped mushrooms, drained (more if you wish)
2 tablespoons butter
2 tablespoons flour
½ cup light cream
¼ teaspoon salt
Dash cayenne pepper
1¼ cups shredded sharp Cheddar cheese
6 or 7 boned whole chicken breasts (have butcher do this for you)
All purpose flour
2 slightly beaten eggs
¾ cup dry fine bread crumbs

FOR CHEESE FILLING: Cook mushrooms in butter about 5 minutes. Blend in flour. Stir in cream. Add salt and cayenne. Cook and stir until very thick. Add cheese and cook over low heat, stirring constantly until cheese is melted. Turn mix into pie plate. Cover and chill thoroughly about 1 hour. Cut into equal portions and shape into short sticks.

CHICKEN: Skin chicken breasts. Pound to ¼ inch thickness. Sprinkle with salt. Place a cheese stick on each breast, roll chicken like a jelly roll, tucking in the sides. Press together to seal well. You will need toothpicks. Dust rolls with flour. Dip in beaten egg, then roll in bread crumbs. Cover and chill about an hour.

BEFORE SERVING TIME: Fry in deep hot fat for 5 minutes until crisp. Drain. Then place in a shallow baking dish and bake in a 325 degree oven for about 45 minutes to 1 hour.

Serve on a platter garnished with grapes.

ROLLED CHICKEN BREASTS II

6 Servings

3 large chicken breasts, boned skinned, and halved
6 thin slices boiled ham
6 ounces Swiss cheese, cut in 6 sticks
¼ cup all purpose flour
2 tablespoons butter
½ cup water
1 teaspoon chicken flavored gravy base
1 (3 ounce) can broiled sliced mushrooms, drained
⅓ cup sauterne wine
2 tablespoons all purpose flour
½ cup cold water
Toasted sliced almonds

Place chicken pieces, boned side up, on cutting board. Working from the center out, pound chicken lightly with mallet to make cutlets about ¼ inch thick. Sprinkle with salt. Place a ham slice and a cheese stick on each cutlet. Tuck in sides of each and roll up like a jelly roll, pressing to seal well. Skewer with toothpicks. Coat rolls with the ¼ cup flour. Brown in the butter. Remove chicken to an 11 x 7 x 1½ inch baking pan.

In the same skillet, combine first ½ cup of water, the gravy base, mushrooms and wine. Heat, stirring to incorporate any crusty bits from skillet. Pour mixture over chicken in baking pan. Cover and bake in moderate oven (350 degrees) for 1 to 1¼ hours, or until tender.

Transfer chicken to warm serving platter. Blend the 2 tablespoons flour with the other ½ cup cold water. Add to gravy in baking pan. Cook and stir until thickened. Pour a little gravy over chicken. Garnish with toasted, sliced almonds. Pass the remaining gravy.

LOWELL'S FRIED CHICKEN

1 frying chicken, cut up (or more, if desired)
⅓ cup buttermilk
2 eggs
2 cups flour
1 teaspoon salt
1 teaspoon black pepper
2 teaspoons cayenne pepper
Vegetable oil for frying

Mix salt, black pepper, cayenne pepper, buttermilk and eggs in a shallow bowl. Place flour in another bowl. Dip chicken, piece by piece, in egg mixture and then roll in flour mixture. Deep fry at 350 degrees until done. Crisp and delicious.

Mr. H. Lowell Bloodworth (my son-in-law)

BARBECUED CHICKEN IN A PAPER BAG

Serves 4

Use a 3 pound chicken cut for frying.

Grease the inside of a medium size heavy paper sack and place in roasting pan. Set oven to 500 degrees.

Salt and pepper the chicken, dip in barbecue sauce, and place in sack along with remaining sauce. Carefully fold sack so as not to leak. Cover. Cook 15 minutes at 500 degrees, then lower the temperature to 350 degrees and cook for 1¼ hours. Do not open the sack until the time is up.

NOTE: Barbecue sauce recipe is found in the Sauce section of this book. (Use Sauce I).

ELLEN'S CHICKEN CASSEROLE

Put small amount of oil or butter in pan. Brown chicken (use breasts, thighs, and wishbones). Use lots of salt, pepper, and garlic powder. Drain.

Sauté fresh sliced mushrooms in real butter. To this add: 1 can chicken broth, 3 tablespoons flour, and 2 cups dry sherry.

Cook frozen artichoke hearts according to package directions, using salt. Drain, then put in sauce. You may use canned, drained artichokes. Use as many as you wish.

In casserole or big broiler pan from your stove, put in chicken, mushrooms and artichokes along with sauce which is fairly thin. Add 1 small can sliced ripe olives, drained.

Bake for 1 hour at 325 degrees, uncovered. The last 10 minutes of baking, add as many cherry tomatoes (tiny ones) as desired.

Serve with rice and a tossed salad. The recipe for green rice casserole is excellent served with this.

NOTE: A very versatile dish, both for family suppers as well as a party.

Mrs. William O. Dobbins, III

CHICKEN DIVAN

Serves 8

FIRST SAUCE:

1 cup butter, softened
6 egg yolks
1 lemon, squeezed
1 teaspoon salt
Dash of red pepper

Place the above ingredients in the top of a double boiler. Stir well before putting it over hot water. Stir constantly until done. This is a Hollandaise sauce. Set aside.

SECOND SAUCE:

4 tablespoons butter
4 tablespoons flour
2 cups milk
2 teaspoons Mei Yen seasoning
1 tablespoons Worcestershire sauce

Make a cream sauce with the above ingredients. Stir constantly until smooth and thick. Add the Worcestershire sauce last and set aside.

MAIN DISH:

4 packages, broccoli spears, cooked and drained
8 large boned chicken breasts or nice slices of chicken or turkey, cooked
½ pint whipping cream, whipped
Grated Parmesan cheese

In a large pan or flat casserole dish, make individual servings by placing the broccoli. Sprinkle it with Parmesan cheese. Place the chicken on the broccoli.

Mix together the two sauces and the whipped cream. Pour over the casserole. Sprinkle the top with lots of Parmesan cheese. Heat in a 450 degree oven for 15 to 20 minutes. Broil the last few minutes to brown on top.

Makes for beautiful servings for a luncheon.

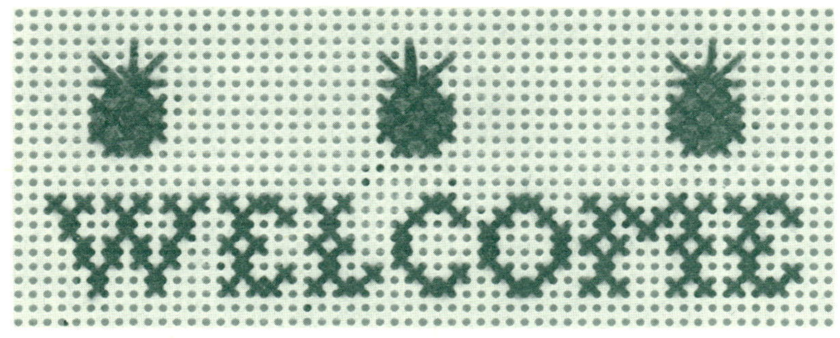

CHICKEN BREASTS WELLINGTON

12 Servings

This recipe was given me by a good friend, Faye O'Leary.

6 whole chicken breasts, boned and split
Seasoned salt and pepper
1 (6 ounce) package Uncle Ben's Long Grain & Wild Rice
¼ cup grated orange peel
2 eggs, separated
3 (8 ounce) cans refrigerator cresent dinner rolls
1 tablespoon water
2 (10 ounce) jar red currant jelly
1 tablespoon prepared mustard
3 tablespoons port wine
¼ cup lemon juice

Pound chicken breasts with mallet to flatten. Sprinkle each with seasoned salt and pepper.

Cook rice according to package directions for drier rice. Add orange peel. Cool. Beat egg whites until soft peaks form. Fold whites into the rice mixture.

On floured surface, roll 2 triangular pieces of dinner roll dough into a circle. Repeat with remaining rolls until you have 12 circles. Place a chicken breast in center of each circle. Spoon about ¼ cup rice mixture over chicken. Roll chicken jelly roll fashion. Bring dough up over stuffed breast. Moisten edges of dough with water and press together to seal.

Place seam side down on large baking sheet. Slightly beat yolks with water. Brush over dough. Bake uncovered, at 375 degrees for 45 to 50 minutes, or until breasts are tender. If dough is browning too much, cover loosely with foil.

Heat currant jelly in saucepan. Gradually stir in mustard, wine, and lemon juice. Serve warm with the chicken. DELICIOUS.

(This recipe was used as the main course for Marileta's bridesmaid's luncheon).

CURRY

Can be Chicken, Shrimp, Lamb, or Whatever

2 small onions, finely chopped
2 tablespoons celery, finely chopped
½ cup butter
½ teaspoon salt
Up to 1 tablespoon curry powder (I use 1 teaspoon)
½ cup flour
3 cups milk or half milk and half chicken broth
1 cup cream
2 tablespoons dry sherry (optional)
3 cups large diced chicken, cooked OR whole shrimp, cooked, OR lamb, cooked

Sauté onions and celery in butter. Add salt and curry powder and mix well. Add flour and cook until bubbly. Add milk and cream and stir until smooth and thick. Add sherry and then the meat. Keep hot but do not let boil.

Serve over rice with accompaniments of your choice served in individual bowls. You may pass all the accompaniments on a tray. Use at least 5 and preferably 7 (called 5 boy or 7 boy).

SUGGESTED ACCOMPANIMENTS FROM WHICH TO CHOOSE:

Diced crisp bacon
Chutney, Major Grey variety, chopped
Finely chopped salted nuts (peanuts, pecans, or almonds)
Ripe olives, chopped
Seedless raisins
Chopped pickles
Hardboiled eggs, finely chopped (sometimes whites and yolks are served separately)
Shredded coconut
Green olives, chopped
Crushed pineapple.

CHICKEN JAMBALAYA

Serves 4 to 6

1 (3 pound) fryer, cut into frying pieces
1 cup flour
1 tablespoon salt
¼ cup olive oil
⅔ cup uncooked rice
1 clove garlic, minced
1 medium onion, chopped
2 tablespoons olive oil
1 large can (No. 2½) tomatoes
2 teaspoons chili powder (optional)
1 teaspoon salt
Red and black pepper to taste

Coat chicken pieces by placing in paper bag with flour and salt. Shake well. Brown lightly in oil and place in a 3 quart casserole with a tight fitting cover.

Brown rice, garlic, and onion in the pan in which the chicken was browned, using the additional oil. Add tomatoes, additional salt, and other seasonings. Pour over chicken.

Cover and bake in a 350 degree oven for 1 hour and 15 minutes. (This may also be simmered on top of stove).

TARRAGON CHICKEN WITH PEACHES AND ALMONDS

Serves 6 to 8

¼ cup butter
4 chicken breasts, halved
½ teaspoon salt
3 green onions sliced, including tops
½ cup slivered almonds
½ teaspoon tarragon
1 tablespoon chopped parsley or more if desired
1 can (1 pound, 13 ounce) cling peach halves
½ cup grated parmesan cheese

Melt butter in skillet. Add chicken and brown lightly. Place chicken in pyrex baking dish. Add salt, onions, tarragon, almonds and parsley to melted butter in skillet. Stir mixture and pour over the chicken.

Cover and bake in a 350 degree oven for 45 minutes. Uncover, add drained peach halves around the chicken. Sprinkle both peaches and chicken with parmesan cheese and bake uncovered for 15 minutes longer.

CHICKEN PAPRIKA

Serves 4

2 chickens, halved
2 tablespoons onion, chopped
3 tablespoons butter
1 teaspoon paprika
2 tablespoons lemon juice
1 tablespoon flour
Salt and pepper, to taste
1 cup sour cream

Sauté onions in butter and remove to saucer. Brown chicken lightly. Add paprika and lemon juice and then the browned onions. Cover and simmer until tender. When done, remove chicken from skillet and keep hot.

Add flour, salt and pepper to skillet. Blend and scrape skillet. Then add sour cream, blending well and stirring constantly, until smooth and thick.

Pour sauce over hot chicken and serve with buttered noodles.

CHICKEN PARMESAN

1½ cups Italian bread crumbs or use homemade
½ cup Parmesan cheese
1 tablespoon salt
1 teaspoon pepper
6 chicken breast halves
1½ to 2 sticks butter, melted

Combine crumbs, cheese, salt, and pepper. Dip breasts in melted butter, then in the crumb mixture, being careful to coat the breasts evenly.

Place the breasts skin side up in a buttered baking dish and bake in a 350 degree oven for 35 to 40 minutes. Do not turn the chicken.

Recipe may be prepared the day before and refrigerated, then baked. Also freezes well both before and after baking. To reheat after thawed, heat in a 325 degree oven.

Mrs. W.O. Dobbins, III

CHICKEN, SAUCE PIQUANT

1½ medium onions, chopped fine
1 bell pepper, chopped fine
2 or 3 stalks celery, chopped fine
3 tablespoons oil or enough to cover bottom of saucepan

Let all this simmer until wilted looking. Add: 1 or more chickens, cut up. Brown first. Pour water to cover and add tomato sauce to taste and color. If too thin, make a roux and add to sauce, stirring well.

Serve over hot cooked rice.

Recipe from a Louisiana friend from Army days in Oklahoma.

SESAME CHICKEN

5 to 6 servings

3 pound fryer, cut up
1 cup evaporated milk (can use plain old homogenized)
1½ teaspoon salt
¼ teaspoon pepper
1 teaspoon onion salt
¼ cup butter
1 cup flour
½ cup sesame seeds

Combine milk and seasonings. Melt butter in shallow pan. Dip chicken in milk mixture, then in flour, and again in seasoned milk. Place in buttered pan, skin side up in a single layer. Sprinkle sesame seeds over each piece. Do not cover. Bake in a 350 degree oven for 1 hour.

ANN'S CHICKEN SPECTACULAR

Serves 10 or 12

3 cups cooked, boned, chicken, cut up
1 package wild rice mix cooked according to package directions
1 medium onion, chopped
1 medium jar pimento (optional)
1 (No. 2) can french style green beans, drained
1 can celery soup (10¾ ounce)
1 cup mayonnaise
1 can water chesnuts, sliced
Salt and pepper to taste

Bake at 350 degrees for 25 to 30 minutes until hot and bubbly. Makes one 3 quart casserole.

NOTE: To freeze, do not bake. When ready to bake, thaw first. Add butter and bread crumbs on top before baking.

Mrs. Tom Maynor

HOT CHICKEN SALAD

This is a great luncheon dish.

Serves 6 to 8

2 cups diced chicken
2 cups chopped celery
½ cup toasted almonds
¾ teaspoon salt
¼ teaspoon pepper
2 teaspoons grated onion
1 cup mayonnaise
2 tablespoons lemon juice
½ cup grated Cheddar cheese
Potato chips

Mix all ingredients together except potato chips. Pour into casserole dish. Crush potato chips over top. Bake at 350 degrees about 40 minutes.

TURKEY CRUNCH CASSEROLE

Serves 6

3 cups diced cooked turkey
2 hard cooked eggs, chopped
1 can (4 ounce) sliced mushrooms
¾ cup diced celery
½ cup slivered blanched almonds or pecans
1 tablespoon chopped onion
1 can (10½ ounce) condensed cream of chicken soup
¾ cup mayonnaise
Chow Mein noodles or crushed potato chips

Mix together first 6 ingredients. Stir soup into mayonnaise, then toss with turkey mixture. Put in a 2 quart casserole. Sprinkle with noodles or chips. Bake at 350 degrees for 30 minutes or until bubbly.

SMOKED TURKEY

TURKEY: Use a 12 to 16 pound whole turkey or use a turkey breast. While you are doing this, you might as well do two. They are divine.

Juice of 1 lemon
Seasoned salt
Black pepper
2 teaspoons prepared mustard
1 clove minced garlic or garlic powder
½ teaspoon sugar
2 teaspoons flour
Tarragon vinegar
1 cup butter or margarine, melted
Dash Worcestershire sauce
Dash Soy sauce

Combine dry ingredients, lemon juice, and sauces with almost a cup of the vinegar. Mix well. Add to the melted butter and cook until thickened.

Cook turkey on charcoal grill for 1 hour and then begin basting with the marinade. Be sure cavity of turkey gets some of the sauce.

Turkey should cook between 4½ to 5½ hours. You may use a meat thermometer to be sure of doneness.

Flavor is enhanced by adding water soaked hickory chips to the fire.

TURKEY TETTRAZINI

Serves 8 or 10

1 (4 pound) hen or a turkey breast. Boil in water seasoned with salt, pepper, 1 quartered onion, 1 stalk celery, ½ carrot, When done, cut up meat and save broth.
½ pound raw spaghetti, broken into short lengths
1 small bottle stuffed green olives
½ pound grated hoop cheese (more if you like)
1 cup chopped pecans
1 pint chicken stock (still save remainder)
1 can mushroom soup
2 medium onions, chopped
1 cup chopped celery
3 tablespoons butter
1 tablespoon Worcestershire sauce
Salt and pepper to taste

Boil hen or turkey breast until tender and falls from bone. Remove from stock and let cool at room temperature while preparing other ingredients.

Put spaghetti on to boil. Cook celery and onions in butter in a 3 quart saucepan on low heat. Add 1 pint chicken stock and simmer for 15 minutes. Add mushroom soup slowly while stirring until smooth. Slowly add cheese while stirring. Let stand one hour.

Meanwhile, cut up turkey and slice olives and then add to well drained spaghetti. Pour the cheese mixture and the spaghetti mixture together and mix well. Add Worcestershire sauce and other seasonings. Mix well. Put in greased casserole. Can freeze or bake at 350 degrees for 30 minutes or until bubbly.

PECANS: You can mix them with the other ingredients or they may be sprinkled on top. I like them best mixed in.

This recipe has been a wonderful crowd server for me. Can be doubled if you have a large enough container for mixing. Serve with a salad, a good white wine and a fabulous dessert.

MY MOTHER'S DRESSING FOR TURKEY

There is none better.

About 24 servings

12 slices bread, toasted and grated
2 packages cornbread mix, cooked, or 2 pans of cornbread made from scratch
2 cups seasoned croutettes
6 cups chicken broth
2 cups finely chopped celery
½ cup chopped parsley (fresh)
2 big onions and 1 bunch green onions, chopped and sautéed
1 stick margarine for sautéing (½ cup)
Season to taste with salt and pepper
3 grated hard-boiled eggs
4 raw eggs
Can put in oysters that have been sautéed in juice

Sauté onion and celery in margarine. In big bowl, combine toasted bread, cornbread (broken into small pieces) and croutettes. Moisten with some of the broth. Put in onions and celery, then hard boiled eggs and parsley. Mix well. Cover and put in refrigerator until ready to bake.

About an hour before cooking, beat the raw eggs and add to the dressing mix. The fowl can be stuffed with dressing. The dressing can be put into a greased casserole, or it can be made into patties and baked.

TO BAKE: If turkey is stuffed with dressing, bake as long as the turkey cooks.

If dressing is to be in casserole or in patties, bake at 350 degrees for 30 to 45 minutes.

If you have too much dressing mix for one use, freeze the left-over dressing *before you add the raw eggs.* To cook what is frozen, thaw and then add beaten raw egg.

This dressing is really very good and basic. Seasonings can be adjusted to individual taste.

If you are preparing for a big feast, the dressing may be made weeks ahead and frozen. Just wait until feast day to add the raw eggs.

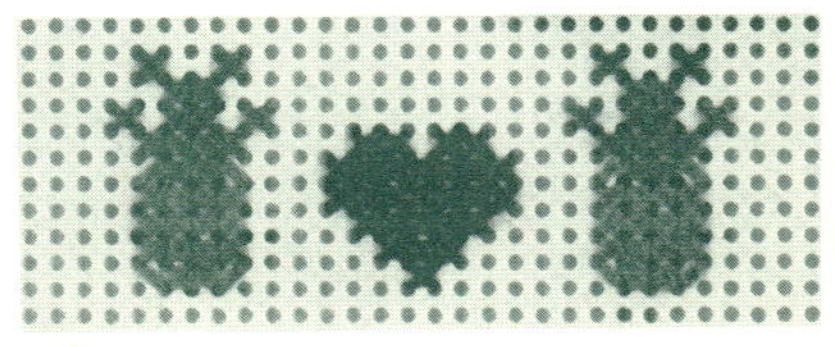

TO ROAST A TURKEY

PREPARING THE BIRD:

WAYS TO THAW:

1. Thaw in the refrigerator on a tray in its original wrap. Takes two or three days.
2. Follow directions and thaw in microwave.
3. Another quick thaw method: Fill sink or a deep pan with cold water; place the turkey in its wrapper or in a plastic bag in water for 6 to 8 hours. Be sure to change the water frequently.

TO PREPARE FOR ROASTING:

Remove the wrappings and free the legs and tail. Remove the giblets and neck from the body cavity. Rinse the bird well and pat it dry. If not already cleaned thoroughly, do so at this time. Especially the inside. Sprinkle the cavity with salt, if desired. DO NOT STUFF THE TURKEY UNTIL JUST BEFORE COOKING.

TO STUFF THE TURKEY:

Spoon some stuffing into the neck cavity; pull the neck skin over the stuffing and fasten the skin securely to the back of the bird with a short skewer. Lightly spoon more stuffing into the body cavity. Holding the turkey by its legs, gently shake the stuffing down, but do not pack it. Remember that the stuffing will swell while cooking. If the turkey has a band of skin across its tail, tuck the drumsticks under the band. Otherwise, tie the legs to the tail. Twist the wing tips under the back.

FOR UNSTUFFED TURKEY:

Place quartered onions and celery in the body cavity to obtain great flavor.

ROASTING THE BIG BIRD:

Place the prepared bird, breast side up on a rack in a shallow roasting pan. Brush the skin of the turkey with melted butter. If you are using a meat thermometer, insert it in the fleshy part of the inside thigh muscle; also make sure that the bulb does not touch the bone. Cover neck loosely with an aluminum foil cap. Place the pan in a 325 degree oven; baste the bird occasionally with pan drippings.

When turkey is ⅔ done, cut the band of skin or string between the legs. About 45 minutes before turkey is done, remove foil.

TEST FOR DONENESS:

Turkey is done when the meat thermometer registers 185 degrees or when the thickest part of the drumstick is very soft and moves up and down easily. Remove bird from oven and cover loosely. For easier carving, let turkey stand for at least 15 minutes.

COOKING GUIDE:

6 to 8 pound bird	325 degrees	3½ to 4 hours
8 to 12 pounds	325	4 to 4½ hours
12 to 16 pounds	325	4½ to 5½ hours
16 to 20 pounds	325	5½ to 6½ hours
20 to 24 pounds	325	6½ to 7½ hours

OLD TIMEY GIBLET GRAVY

Simmer, covered, turkey giblets until tender in lightly salted water to cover, along with a small cut piece of celery and the leaves, 1 small onion, quartered. Cook until they are tender when pierced with a fork. Let giblets cool in the broth. (Giblets consist of the liver, the gizzard, and the heart. The neck is usually boiled with the giblets to give more flavor, but it is thrown away).

Remove giblets and chop. Add 2 hard boiled eggs, chopped. After transferring cooked turkey to a warm platter, leave crusty bits in pan and pour the liquid from pan into a measuring cup. When fat comes to the top, skim it off. Then, for each cup of gravy, measure 2 tablespoons of fat back into roasting pan. Add 2 tablespoons flour and blend thoroughly with a wire whisk. Cook and stir over low heat until frothy. (This does not have to be made in roasting pan; a saucepan will do just as well). Remove from heat and add 1 cup lukewarm liquid (meat juices from the turkey and the giblet broth). If not brown enough, add a few drops of bottled brown bouquet sauce. Stir smooth, return to heat, and stir until it is as thick as you want it. Test seasonings and adjust. Keep warm until ready to serve.

QUAIL IN SHERRY

Sprinkle quail with seasoned salt and coarse ground pepper. Then flour each one. Allow two birds per person.

Melt ¼ pound butter and 2 or 3 tablespoons bacon fat in skillet. (I use an electric skillet). Fry quail until nice and brown on both sides.

Pour ¾ cup dry sherry over the quail. Turn heat to simmer and add 2 cups water. Simmer, covered until tender. If all the liquid evaporates, add more sherry and water. When tender, keep warm until ready to serve.

A wild rice casserole is an excellent accompaniment to quail along with a fruit dish.

BAKED QUAIL WITH MUSHROOMS

⅓ cup all purpose flour
1 teaspoon salt
½ teaspoon pepper
6 quail, dressed and cleaned
2 tablespoons butter
½ pound fresh mushrooms, sliced
½ cup butter
¼ cup plus 1 tablespoon all purpose flour
2 cups chicken broth
½ cup dry sherry
Hot cooked rice

Combine ⅓ cup flour, salt and pepper. Dredge quail in flour mixture and set aside.

Melt 2 tablespoons butter in skillet, add mushrooms and sauté. Remove and set aside.

Melt ½ cup butter in skillet and brown quail on both sides. Remove quail to a 1½ quart casserole. Add ¼ cup plus 1 tablespoon flour to drippings in skillet. Cook 1 minute, stirring constantly. Gradually add broth and sherry. Cook over medium heat, stirring constantly until gravy is thick and bubbly. Put in mushrooms.

Pour mushroom gravy over quail. Cover and bake at 350 degrees for 1 hour. Serve over hot rice.

Fruits and Vegetables

RED CINNAMON APPLES

Serves 4 unless you just love 'em

4 big apples (Rome beauty or Delicious)

Peel and core without cutting through stem end if you wish to serve them whole. OR cut in quarters OR just nice slices.

½ cup sugar
1 cup water
¼ cup red hot candies (see candy section at the grocery)

Stir and boil in saucepan until dissolved, the sugar, water, and candy. Add apples. Cook gently until tender. Pour into a bowl, juice and all. Chill before serving.

A delicious side dish to use with pork in the early fall. If you have children, be sure to double the recipe. It's a favorite.

BAKED APRICOTS

Serves 10 to 12

2 or 3 large cans apricot halves, drained
2 boxes light brown sugar (you probably won't need this much)
1 large box round buttery crackers
Butter (real creamery) and LOTS of it

(Original recipe calls for peeled apricots but I use them with the peel on and it works nicely).

In a greased baking dish put a layer of the apricot halves. It's okay to crowd them. Cover this layer with brown sugar, then add a layer of crumbled crackers (crumbling them with your hands), then dot HEAVILY with butter. Repeat this to the top of dish.

Bake slowly in about a 300 degree oven, approximately 1 hour. It should be thick and crusty on top.

If the apricots appear very ripe (soft), be sure to drain them well. If they are not sort of soft, you might need to use a little of the juice in the casserole.

You may also use dark brown sugar.

This is such a popular dish in our family that I always use more apricots than called for.

Delicious as a side dish with almost any meat, especially quail and wild game.

CURRIED FRUIT CASSEROLE

Serves 10

1 very large can peach halves
1 can apricot halves
1 very large can pear halves
3 small cans pineapple pieces
2 jars mixed fruit (fruits for salad)
10 or 12 maraschino cherries
⅓ cup melted butter
¾ cup brown sugar, packed
4 teaspoons curry powder

Drain fruit well. Mix butter, brown sugar, and curry powder. Lay fruit in shallow baking dish, hollow side up. Dot all over with butter and sugar mixture.

Bake at 325 degrees for 1 hour, basting frequently. Cool and refrigerate at least 1 day. Warm over at 350 degrees for 30 minutes.

BAKED PEACHES AND MINCEMEAT

Canned peach halves, drained
1 jar mincemeat

Fill each peach half with mincemeat. Place filled peach halves in a shallow pan with a little peach juice. Bake in a slow oven for 15 to 20 minutes.

Looks beautiful with a broiled breast of chicken or a slice of baked ham.

ARTICHOKES POLONAISE

Serves 12

3 packages frozen artichoke hearts (may use canned)
¼ pound butter
1 tablespoon olive oil
½ cup cracker crumbs
2 hard cooked eggs, finely diced
1 tablespoon chopped parsley
¼ clove minced garlic
4 tablespoons dry white wine
2 tablespoons catsup
Salt, pepper, to taste

Cook artichokes as directed on package. Melt butter in skillet. Add other ingredients except artichokes and cook about 5 minutes on low heat. Pour sauce over drained artichokes and serve.

FRESH ARTICHOKE

This is Finger Food

To make 6 servings, you will need:

6 large fresh artichokes, firm and heavy
1 lemon
1 teaspoon oregano
½ teaspoon salt
⅛ teaspoon pepper
1 clove garlic, halved
2 tablespoons vegetable oil

Wash artichokes; trim stems close to base. With a sharp knife, slice an inch from the top and snip off any spiny leaf tips. As you work, rub cut edges with lemon to prevent them from turning brown. Stand artichokes in a deep saucepan or kettle. Slice the lemon and add to pan along with oregano, salt, pepper, garlic, and enough water to make a 2 inch depth. Place 1 teaspoon of the oil in each artichoke. Cover and cook 40 minutes, or until a leaf pulls away easily from the base; drain well.

SAUCE: Melt butter and squeeze the juice of a lemon in it. Give each person a small dish of lemon butter beside the artichoke. As he removes each leaf, dip it in the warm butter sauce and eat only the meaty succulent tidbit at the base. Eventually remove the choke (each person does his own), quarter the base and enjoy to the last bite.

ARTICHOKE CASSEROLE

1 cup cubed ham, chicken, or a pint of oysters
1 can artichoke hearts
1 medium onion, chopped
2 tablespoons chopped parsley
4 tablespoons chopped celery
2 tablespoons flour
1 large can sliced mushrooms and juice
2 chicken bouillon cubes in sufficient juice to make 1½ cups liquid
4 tablespoons dry white wine
4 tablespoons Parmesan cheese, grated
Salt, red and black pepper, to taste

Sauté onion, celery, parsley in olive oil or butter. Add flour and 1½ cups liquid. Cook until sauce is fairly thick. Add artichokes, mushrooms and ham, chicken, or oysters. If too thick, thin with a little stock; add wine and cheese, seasonings and put in casserole. Heat in oven until bubbly.

This is also a great appetizer.

ARTICHOKE RICE

Serves 10

1 package (8 ounce) chicken flavored rice and vermicelli mix
4 green onions, chopped fine
½ bell pepper, chopped fine
12 small stuffed green olives, sliced
2 jars (6 ounce) marinated artichoke hearts, cut up
¾ teaspoon curry powder
½ cup mayonnaise

Cook rice as directed on package. Cool. Drain artichoke hearts and slice (small bite size). Reserve liquid (oil) from one jar of the artichokes. Combine this reserved oil with all ingredients and mix lightly with rice. Serve at room temperature.

Use as a vegetable or serve cold, on lettuce, for a delicious salad.

ASPARAGUS

Asparagus stalks need longer cooking than the tips. The tough ends should cook in boiling water while the tender tips cook in steam. If you don't have an asparagus cooker, tie the stalks together and stand them upright in a large saucepan of simmering salted water. Invert another saucepan and use it for a cover. Cook the asparagus for 12 to 20 minutes, depending upon its age and tenderness.

Serve with melted butter, Hollandaise sauce, vinaigrette, or any sauce you like.

ASPARAGUS SUPREME

Serves 4

1 can asparagus
½ cup slivered almonds
1 cup grated cheese
1½ cups white sauce (medium) (see Sauce section)
3 hard cooked eggs

Cut asparagus in half and place in bottom of casserole. Sprinkle one half of nuts and add sliced, hard cooked eggs. Add another layer of asparagus, nuts and sliced eggs. Pour over this the hot white sauce, into which cheese has been stirred and melted. Season with salt and pepper. Sprinkle cheese on top. Heat in oven until bubbly.

This recipe may be adjusted to serve any number of people.

AVOCADO CASSEROLE

Serves 6 to 8

CREAM SAUCE:

¼ cup butter
2 tablespoons flour
1 cup half and half cream
Salt and pepper

Melt butter, stir in flour, add seasoning and the cream. Stir constantly until medium thick.

Set aside.

Sauté 1 large can mushrooms (sliced) and 1 large can pimentos, chopped, in 2 tablespoons butter. Then add mushrooms and pimentos to sauce.

Peel, seed, and dice 2 large avocados. Fold into sauce. Heat and serve lukewarm in ramekins.

A most unusual dish.

BARLEY CASSEROLE SUPREME

¼ pound butter
2 onions, chopped
¾ pound fresh mushrooms, trimmed and sliced
1½ cups pearl barley
3 pimentos, coarsely chopped
2 cups chicken broth
Salt and pepper

Melt butter in a saucepan. Stir in 2 chopped onions, and the sliced mushrooms and sauté until golden in color and fairly tender. Add 1½ cups pearl barley and cook all until barley is a delicate brown. Transfer this mixture to a casserole. Add the coarsely chopped pimentos and 2 cups chicken broth. Use salt and pepper to taste. Cover the casserole and bake in a 350 degree oven for 50 to 60 minutes until barley is tender and the liquid is absorbed. If the barley seems dry during the baking period, add more broth. However, the final product should be a bit dry. This is a most unusual dish and is used in place of a rice dish. BE SURE TO USE ONLY LITTLE PEARL BARLEY, which is found near the dried soup mix in your supermarket.

BAKED BEANS

Serves 6 to 8

2 large cans pork and beans
2 tablespoons prepared mustard
2 cloves garlic
2 tablespoons Worcestershire sauce
3 tablespoons dark corn syrup
1 big onion, chopped
Juice of 1 lemon
2 tablespoons bottled steak sauce
1 bottle catsup

Mix the above ingredients together. Add 1 bottle catsup. Put in casserole. Strip with bacon. Bake at 325 degrees for 2½ hours. Be sure to remove the buttons of garlic before serving.

BARBECUED BEANS

Serves 10

4 or 5 slices bacon cut in thirds
1 large onion, chopped
5 cups pork and beans
½ bottle catsup
½ box brown sugar
2 tablespoons mustard
2 tablespoons Worcestershire sauce
1 teaspoon liquid smoke

Fry bacon in heavy skillet until crisp. Add onion and sauté it until clear. Add beans and stir. Then add remaining ingredients. Stir well and lower heat to simmer. Let simmer uncovered until cooked down to the consistency desired, about 2 hours or more.

BALES OF GREEN BEANS

Serves 6 to 8

2 cans whole green beans in the vertical pak
1 bottle Italian salad dressing
Bacon strips

Marinate drained green beans in salad dressing for 4 to 6 hours or overnight.

Wrap bacon slices around 6 or 8 beans, covering ends completely. Secure each "bale" with a toothpick.

Place on broiler pan and broil for 10 to 15 minutes or until bacon is done.

Plan for 2 bales of beans per person.

GREEN BEAN CASSEROLE

This is a very special dish, usually served during holidays for our family.

1 pound sliced mushrooms
½ cup butter
1 medium onion, chopped
¼ cup flour
2 cups milk
1 pound Cheddar cheese, grated
⅛ teaspoon hot pepper seasoning sauce
1 teaspoon salt
½ teaspoon pepper
1 teaspoon MSG seasoning
3 cans (#2) French style green beans
1 can sliced water chestnuts
Chopped toasted almonds

Sauté mushrooms and onion in butter. Add flour. Cook and stir until smooth. Add 2 cups warm milk and stir constantly. Add cheese and seasonings and mix well. Add beans and water chestnuts. Mix all and put into casserole dish. Top with chopped toasted almonds. Bake for 35 to 40 minutes at 325 degrees.

This casserole may be made ahead and frozen.

GREEN BEANS INDIA

Serves 8

8 slices bacon, crumbled
½ cup granulated sugar
½ cup vinegar
2 cans French-style green beans, drained
½ medium onion, chopped
3 tablespoons India relish

Preheat oven to 275 degrees. Fry bacon and remove from pan. Sauté onions, sugar, and vinegar in the bacon drippings. Place green beans in casserole and pour sugar mixture over beans. Crumble bacon and mix with relish. Top beans with this mixture and cover. Bake at 275 degrees for 1½ hours.

BROCCOLI CASSEROLE WITH ALMONDS

Serves 6

2 packages frozen broccoli florets
2 tablespoons butter
2 tablespoons flour
2 cups milk
¾ cup grated sharp cheese
1 teaspoon salt
¼ teaspoon pepper
¼ cup chopped toasted almonds
4 slices crisp bacon
½ cup buttered bread crumbs

Cook broccoli until just barely tender. Drain and place in a greased casserole (long, oblong glass).

Make a thick sauce of the butter, flour, milk, cheese, salt, and pepper. Sprinkle broccoli with almonds and bacon. Pour the cheese sauce over all, then sprinkle top with crumbs. Bake in a 350 degree oven for about 20 minutes. It must be bubbly and browned on top. This recipe may be doubled, tripled, etc.

BROCCOLI AND ARTICHOKE CASSEROLE

6 Servings

1 (10 ounce) package chopped broccoli
3 grated carrots (optional)
1 can artichoke hearts, drained and quartered
1 can mushroom soup (not quite all of it)
½ cup mayonnaise
2 eggs, slightly beaten
1 teaspoon lemon juice
1 teaspoon Worcestershire sauce
1 cup shredded Cheddar cheese
¼ cup butter
Garlic salt to taste
Bread crumbs

Butter long glass baking dish. Put artichoke hearts on bottom. Combine all other ingredients except crumbs.

Pour mix over artichoke hearts. Sprinkle with bread crumbs. Pour on remaining butter. Bake at 350 degrees for 25 minutes.

This recipe may be doubled to serve 12.

Mrs. Fred Hulett

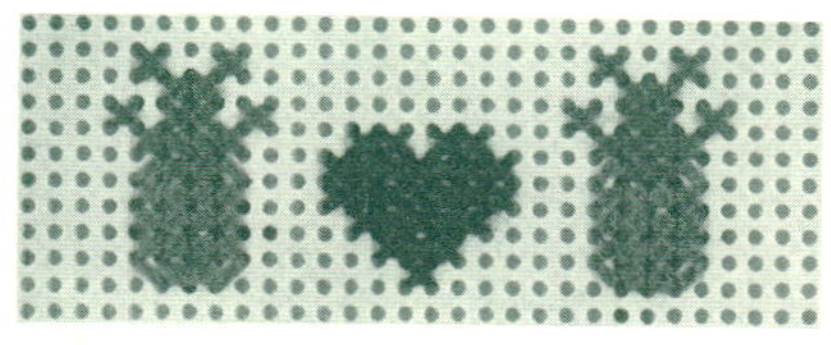

BROCCOLI-RICE CASSEROLE

Serves 12

1 cup onion, chopped
1 cup celery, chopped
1 tablespoon cooking oil
2 packages frozen chopped broccoli
1 can cream of mushroom soup
1 soup can milk
1 jar (8 ounce) pasteurized process cheese spread
2 cups cooked rice
Salt and pepper, to taste

Sauté onions and celery in oil. Cook broccoli according to package directions and drain well. Combine soup and milk and add to cheese, heating to melt. Combine all ingredients. Add buttered bread crumbs on top. Bake at 350 degrees for 30 minutes.

BROCCOLI WITH RIPE OLIVE SAUCE

Cook 1 large bunch of broccoli in salted water until it is barely tender and drain it. OR use frozen broccoli and follow cooking directions on box.

1 garlic clove
1 small can (½ cup) sliced ripe olives
Salt and pepper
½ cup butter
1 teaspoon lemon juice

Steep 1 garlic clove that has been sliced in half in ½ cup hot butter for about 2 minutes. Stir in sliced ripe olives, salt and pepper to taste, and 1 teaspoon lemon juice.

Pour this sauce over the hot, drained broccoli and serve. Don't forget to remove the pieces of garlic before serving.

MINTED CARROTS

Serves 6

12 fresh carrots
½ cup sugar
¼ cup butter
2 tablespoons chopped fresh mint leaves

Peel carrots and cook in boiling salted water. Drain. While hot, pour over the carrots the butter and sugar. Simmer slowly until glazed. Do not brown. Sprinkle mint over carrots just before serving.

JOY'S BROCCOLI WITH SHRIMP SAUCE

Serves 8

2 packages frozen broccoli, cooked
1 can shrimp soup
1 cup cooked, cleaned shrimp
¾ cup light cream
1 tablespoon butter
Salt and pepper
Sharp grated cheese
Paprika

Place well-drained broccoli in shallow buttered casserole. Add ¾ cup cream to the shrimp soup; warm and blend. Add shrimp, butter, salt and pepper.

Pour shrimp mix over broccoli. Sprinkle paprika over top. Cover casserole with grated cheese.

Bake at 350 degrees for 30 minutes.

Mrs. Gerald Mitchell

SYMPHONY CARROTS

12 carrots, cooked until crisp tender and drained (you may use canned Belgian baby carrots, drained)
1 can spiced green grapes (if not available, use fresh, seedless Tompson grapes)

In a saucepan, melt ½ cup butter with 3 tablespoons dark brown sugar, 1 teaspoon cinnamon, and 2 tablespoons or more Brandy.

Pour hot sauce over carrots and grapes and simmer until hot. Serve. Delicious.

CREAMED CELERY

Serves 6

4 cups celery, cut diagonally in ½ inch pieces
2 tablespoons butter
2 tablespoons all purpose flour
2 cups milk
1 teaspoon salt
¾ cup pecan halves
Buttered bread crumbs

Preheat oven to 400 degrees. Grease a 1½ quart casserole. Boil celery until tender in enough water to cover; drain well. Melt butter over medium heat; stir in flour and add milk slowly to make a cream sauce, stirring until thick and smooth. Add salt and celery. Spoon into prepared casserole, top with pecans, and cover with buttered crumbs. Bake for 15 minues at 400 degrees.

FRENCH FRIED CAULIFLOWER

1 head cauliflower
½ cup bread crumbs
1 egg beaten with 1 tablespoon water
Shortening for frying

Par boil cauliflower for 10 minutes. Cool. Separate into flowerettes. Dip each piece in crumbs, then egg, and then crumbs. Fry in fat until golden brown. Sprinkle with salt and pepper. Serve.

This looks pretty on a platter with other vegetables, such as carrots or tiny English peas.

CAULIFLOWER WITH CHEESE SAUCE

Serves 6 to 8

Trim a whole cauliflower and cook it in salted water until it is barely tender and still crisp. Drain well, inverting it on a towel for a few minutes, to be sure it is dry.

Arrange the cauliflower on a serving dish, cover it with hot Mornay sauce, and sprinkle it with ½ cup slivered toasted almonds. Serve immediately.

Mornay sauce is listed in Sauce section.

CORN PIE

Serves 6 to 8

3 to 4 cups of corn (about 8 moderate ears cut from cob

Beat together the following:

5 eggs
1 tablespoon flour
1 pint milk
Salt and pepper to taste

Mix milk mixture well with the corn. Butter a casserole. Add the corn mixture and dot top with butter. Cook in 375 degree oven for about 45 minutes.

CORN FRITTERS

Beat 2 eggs and add 1 generous cup corn cut from cob. Add salt and pepper to taste. Sift 2 cups flour with 1 teaspoon double-acting baking powder and gradually add it to the egg mixture to make a thick batter, adding more flour if necessary.

Drop the batter by spoonfuls into hot fat (about ½ inch in skillet) cooking only a few fritters at a time. Fry them until they are golden brown on both sides. Drain on paper towels and serve hot.

Delicious.

CORN ON THE COB

FOR BOILING: Remove husks. Remove the silks and trim the stems and tips, if necessary. Place in a large kettle of RAPIDLY BOILING WATER that has had a dash of salt and a dash of sugar added to it. Cover tightly and boil from 5 to 10 minutes. Remove from water and serve. It is better not to let corn stand in the water, it becomes water soaked.

FOR THE MICROWAVE OVEN: Corn cooked in the microwave is heavenly. Just follow the cooking directions in your own appliance handbook.

MACARONI AND CHEESE CASSEROLE

Serves 6 to 8

1 medium package macaroni, cooked in boiling, salted water until tender. Drain in collander.
1 package (18 ounce) medium sharp Cheddar cheese, coarsely grated in food processor
Salt and pepper to taste
Milk

Butter a casserole dish. Layer macaroni, cheese, and seasonings, ending with cheese. Pour about 1 inch of milk into casserole.

Bake for 45 minutes to 1 hour in oven at 350 degrees.

Very good with baked ham.

FRESH MUSHROOMS

Wash off or wipe off gently and drain on paper towels any amount of fresh mushrooms. Then slice them lengthwise.

Melt 1 stick real butter in skillet. Add sliced mushrooms. Sauté until the color changes. Keep warm until time to serve.

STUFFED MUSHROOMS TARRAGON

1 pound large mushrooms
2 tablespoons butter
2 tablespoons chopped shallots
1 tablespoon chopped tarragon
1 tablespoon chopped parsley
1 egg, beaten
2 tablespoons brandy
½ cup dry bread crumbs
Salt and pepper to taste

Trim mushrooms and remove the stems. Chop the stems and sauté them in the butter with the chopped shallots for 5 minutes. Add tarragon and parsley, the beaten egg, brandy, bread crumbs, and salt and pepper.

Sauté the mushroom caps in 3 tablespoons butter until they are golden. Place them cap side down on a baking sheet, and stuff them with the bread mixture. Dot each mushroom with butter and broil them for several minutes until they are brown. Serve with garnishes of parsley and lemon wedges. These are divine with a steak.

POPPY SEED NOODLES

3 tablespoons butter
3 tablespoons poppy seeds
½ cup slivered almonds, toasted
1 tablespoon lemon juice
1 (8 ounce) package broad noodles cooked according to package directions
Dash cayenne pepper

Melt butter, add poppy seeds, almonds, lemon juice. Pour this mix over hot drained noodles and toss lightly with a fork. Serve hot.

A good dish to serve with a pot roast.

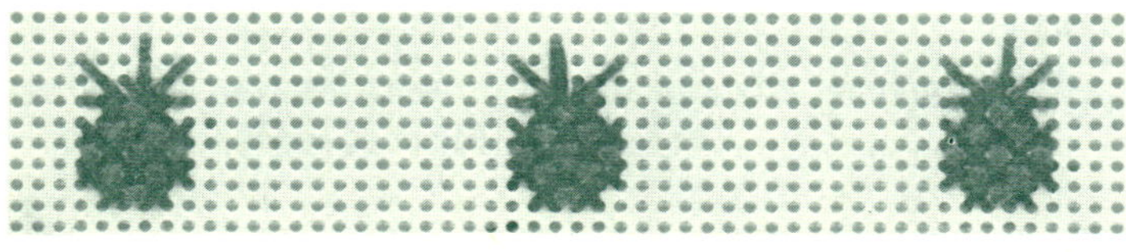

JOANN'S PAPRIKA ONIONS

Serves 6

½ cup salad oil or olive oil
2 tablespoons honey
2 tablespoons white vinegar
½ teaspoon paprika
½ teaspoon dry mustard
½ teaspoon salt
¼ teaspoon sage
4 large onions, cut crossways and parboiled for 10 minutes

Place onion halves in a pyrex dish, cut side up. Mix other ingredients together, blending well. Pour mixture over the onions. Bake, tightly covered with foil, for 30 minutes at 350 degrees. Baste the onions twice during the baking period. These are excellent served with a steak.

NOTE: Onions may be cooked in microwave oven for a few minutes until tender. Follow your own instructions for your microwave. Then finish process in regular oven.

Mrs. James L. Mitchell

BAKED STUFFED ONIONS

Serves 8

8 large Spanish onions
½ pound bulk pork sausage
½ cup chopped onion
1 cup soft bread crumbs
2 tablespoons chopped parsley
1 (7 ounce) can whole kernel corn, drained
2 tablespoons melted butter
½ teaspoon paprika

Peel onions and cut a slice from top. Cook onions in boiling salted water for 12 minutes or until tender but not mushy. Cool; remove center of onions, leaving shells intact. Reserve onion centers for use in other recipes.

Cook sausage until browned, stirring to crumble. Drain and reserve pan drippings. Sauté ½ cup chopped onion in the drippings until tender. Combine sausage, sautéed onion, bread crumbs, parsley, and corn. Fill onion shells with sausage mixture; place in a greased shallow pan.

Combine butter and paprika and brush on onions. This gives them a glazed, pretty look. Cover and bake at 400 degrees for 15 minutes. Remove cover, and bake for 5 more minutes.

GOURMET ONIONS

Serves 6

3 tablespoons butter
½ teaspoon MSG seasoning
½ teaspoon sugar
¼ teaspoon salt
¼ teaspoon pepper
10 to 12 small onions, peeled, cooked, and drained
¼ cup pale dry cocktail Sherry
¼ cup Parmesan cheese

NOTE: If you are in a hurry, use a glass jar of already prepared onions. Just drain them and proceed.

Melt butter in saucepan; stir in MSG, sugar, salt, pepper, and sherry. Add onions and quickly heat for about 5 minutes. Stir occasionally. Put into serving dish and sprinkle with the cheese.

Great with roast beef.

BOBBIE'S ONIONS or ONIONS EN PAPILLOTE

FOR EACH SERVING: Peel and core a large Bermuda or red onion, as you would an apple. Salt and pepper to taste and insert a beef bouillon cube and a pat of butter in center. Wrap in heavy aluminum foil and bake at 400 degrees for 1 to 1½ hours.

Mrs. Everette Crudup

DEVILED GREEN PEA CASSEROLE

Serves 12

1 cup celery, chopped fine
2 boxes frozen tiny English peas
1 can mushroom soup
1 large can sliced mushrooms
½ cup chili sauce
6 hard boiled eggs
1 medium onion, chopped and sautéed
1 tablespoon Worcestershire sauce
1 cup grated Cheddar cheese
Dash hot pepper seasoning
Dash red pepper
Dash paprika
Bread crumbs

Mix everything except hard boiled eggs, bread crumbs and just a little of the cheese.

Put layer of mixture, layer of sliced eggs, then sprinkle a little of the cheese and bread crumbs over top.

Bake at 350 degrees until bubbly.

BLACK EYED PEAS WITH HAM HOCK

Serves 6 to 8

1 quart shelled fresh blackeyed peas
1 quart water
3 pieces ham hock
1 medium onion, minced
1 to 1½ teaspoon salt
¼ teaspoon pepper

Combine all ingredients in a large saucepan. Bring to a boil. Reduce heat, cover and simmer 1 to 1½ hours or until peas are tender. Add more water, if needed.

ENGLISH PEA-ASPARAGUS CASSEROLE

Serves 6 to 8

1 large can asparagus
1 large can tiny English peas
1 small can slivered almonds
1 small jar pimento
1 can mushroom soup
Worcestershire sauce
Grated cheese

Alternate in layers, asparagus, mushroom soup, with Worcestershire sauce sprinkled over each layer, cracker crumbs, cheese, almonds, pimento, peas, and soup. Top with crumbs.

Cook about 20 minutes and then add final layer of cheese.

STEAMED SNOWPEAS WITH NUTMEG

Serves 4

⅓ pound snowpeas
1 tablespoon clarified butter (see Index)
Freshly grated nutmeg
Salt
Pepper

Bring 6 cups water to a boil in a medium saucepan over medium heat. Set snowpeas in steamer or strainer above the water and steam for 1 minute. Drain well.

Heat butter in medium skillet on medium high heat. Add snowpeas and sauté until tender for about 1 to 2 minutes. Season to taste with nutmeg, salt and pepper.

BLEU CHEESE AND BACON STUFFED POTATOES

Serves 4

4 medium baking potatoes
½ cup sour cream
1 ounce bleu cheese, crumbled
½ cup milk
4 tablespoons butter
¾ teaspoon salt
Dash pepper
4 slices bacon, cooked crisp, drained, and crumbled

Rub potatoes with shortening. Bake in hot oven (400 degrees) for 1 hour until done. Remove from oven; cut a lengthwise slice from the top of each potato. Scoop out inside of each and mash. Add sour cream, bleu cheese, milk, butter, salt and pepper to the mashed potatoes and beat with electric mixer or food processor until fluffy. Spoon mixture lightly into potato shells. Place on baking sheet and return to hot oven for 15 minutes or until heated through. Sprinkle each with crumbled bacon.

The potatoes for this recipe do not do well if baked in the microwave. Can also top with grated Cheddar cheese.

STEAMED NEW POTATOES IN THEIR JACKETS

Serves 6

Scrub 18 small potatoes without removing the skin. Then remove a small strip of skin from around the middle of each potato. Put the potatoes on a rack in a large saucepan, cover the pan, and steam the potatoes for 20 to 30 minutes until tender but not soft. Dry the potatoes on paper towels.

Heat 6 tablespoons clarified butter (see Index) in a large skillet and roll the potatoes in the butter until completely coated, then sprinkle with 1 teaspoon ground mace. Then roll in parsley flakes. Serve hot.

JOY'S CREAMY POTATO PUFF

Serves 6 to 8

1 (8 ounce) package cream cheese
4 cups hot mashed potatoes
1 beaten egg
⅓ cup chopped onion
¼ cup pimento
1 teaspoon salt
Dash pepper

Combine softened cream cheese and potatoes. Mix until well blended. Add remaining ingredients and place in a 1 quart casserole and bake at 350 degrees for 45 minutes.

SCALLOPED POTATOES

In a greased casserole, make layers as follows:

Sliced raw potatoes
Sliced raw onions
Salt
Pepper
Grated Cheddar cheese
Milk

Make as many layers as you need but be sure to end with grated cheese. Top with bread crumbs and dot with butter. Then pour in enough milk to be about 1 inch deep in casserole. Bake at 350 degrees for about an hour.

This is a very filling dish and is good for serving a crowd, especially men.

CONSOMMÉ RICE

Serves 6

½ cup margarine or butter
½ medium onion, chopped (may use dehydrated onion flakes)
1 can sliced mushrooms, drained
1 cup raw rice
1 can beef consommé

Sauté onion in butter and add drained mushrooms. Add the raw rice, and stir well. Put in casserole and add consommé. Then add about ½ to ¾ can water. Cover lightly and bake at 350 for 45 minutes or until all broth is absorbed.

This recipe is a good standby for most any occasion and is delicious.

GREEN RICE

Serves 12

2½ cups cooked rice
½ stick butter, melted (¼ pound)
2 cups chopped bell pepper
2 cups chopped parsley
2 green onions (all of them), chopped
2 eggs, beaten
2 cups milk
2 cups grated sharp Cheddar cheese
¼ cup olive oil
Garlic salt or 1 minced clove garlic
Salt, pepper, and red pepper to taste

Cook rice. Sauté garlic and onions in oil but do not brown. Add all other ingredients together. Mix well.

Pour into buttered baking dish and bake for 1 to 1½ hours at 350 degrees.

RATATOUILLE

Serves 6 to 8

3 medium size zucchini
1 medium size eggplant, peeled
4 ripe tomatoes, peeled
2 bell peppers, sliced in lengthwise strips
1 cup thinly sliced onion
¼ cup salad oil or half olive oil
1 clove garlic, finely minced
Salt and pepper to taste
Parmesan cheese
Grated Swiss or Cheddar cheese

Slice zucchini and eggplant into ¼ inch slices. Cut tomatoes in medium dice. Seed the peppers, slice thin and blanch them in a little water in a saucepan. Sauté the onion in the oil until soft; do not brown. Add tomatoes, cook 1 minute. Mix in rest of ingredients, cover, and bring to the boiling point. Cook 5 minutes. Remove cover and cook at simmer heat until all liquid has evaporated. Correct the seasonings; sprinkle with chopped parsley. Can sprinkle on Parmesan cheese or Swiss cheese, or Cheddar cheese or a combination. Or, you don't have to use cheese at all.

NOTE: This is a favorite of my family. It is especially nice in the summer and great with a roast or tenderloin. Also good served in ramekins for a party.

RATATOUILLE IN CREPES

Follow previous recipe for ratatouille.

Put ¼ cup ratatouille in each crepe, roll loosely and place in a buttered shallow casserole. Sprinkle with grated Parmesan cheese or with half Swiss and Mozzarella cheese.

Place in a 350 degree oven until hot and run under broiler to brown. Allow about 2 crepes per person.

NUTTED WILD RICE

Serves 6

1½ cups wild rice
6 cups boiling, salted water
7 tablespoons clarified butter (see Index)
¾ cup coarsely chopped walnuts

Cook wild rice in boiling water for 22 minutes. Drain and mix with 4 tablespoons clarified butter. Sauté walnuts in remaining butter for 3 minutes until golden brown. Mix with rice. You may add a can of drained, sliced mushrooms.

CURRIED RICE WITH PINEAPPLE CHUNKS

Serves 10

2½ cups uncooked regular rice
1 medium onion, chopped
½ cup butter or margarine, melted and divided
2 (10½ ounce) cans consommé
2 (10½ ounce) cans beef broth
1 teaspoon garlic salt
2 (13¼ ounce) cans pineapple chunks, drained. Use the kind in its own juice.
2 teaspoons curry powder

Brown rice in a large heavy skillet, stirring constantly. Place in a 2½ quart casserole. Sauté onion until tender in 2 tablespoons melted butter. Add onion, consommé, broth, garlic salt, and 2 tablespoons melted butter to rice; bake at 350 degrees for 1 hour.

Combine remaining butter, pineapple chunks, and curry powder. Stir well. Add pineapple mixture to rice and bake an additional 15 to 20 minutes.

RICE AND SAUSAGE CASSEROLE

Serves 6

1 pound bulk sausage
1 cup chopped onion
1 clove garlic, minced
1 cup chopped celery
1 chopped green pepper
1 can cream of mushroom soup
2 cans cream of chicken soup
1 cup uncooked rice

Brown sausage in frying pan and pour off grease. Add chopped onion, garlic, celery, and green pepper to sausage and simmer until tender. Wash rice and add to mixture. Then place mixture in pyrex baking dish along with the soups.

Bake for 1½ hours at 350 degrees, stirring occasionally.

HONEY GLAZED VEGETABLES

Cook small white onions in boiling salted water for 20 minutes or until tender. Drain well. Melt ¼ cup honey and stir until mixture is well blended. Add onions and cook slowly until they are glazed. Carrots, sweet potato balls, or tiny beets may be prepared in this way. It is nice to serve a combination of these vegetables.

WILD RICE CASSEROLE

Serves 6

¼ pound butter
1 cup wild rice (can stretch this by adding some white rice)
½ cup slivered almonds
2 tablespoons chopped chives, green onions, or bell pepper
½ pound sliced mushrooms, preferably fresh
3 cups chicken broth

Put all ingredients except broth in a heavy frying pan and cook until rice turns yellow, stirring more or less constantly. Put into a casserole dish with broth, cover tightly and put in oven at 325 degrees for about an hour. Does no harm if it stands a while, which makes it a perfect party dish.

Divine with quail.

RED RICE

Good for a crowd

USE IRON SKILLET:
3 slices bacon
1 pound round steak, cubed
2 (#2) cans red tomatoes
1 can tomato paste
1 medium onion, chopped
1 bell pepper, sliced thin
1 slice lemon
1 tablespoon catsup
1 clove garlic, crushed
½ teaspoon salt
¼ teaspoon each: black pepper, cayenne pepper
½ cup sliced mushrooms
1 cup chopped celery or 1 teaspoon celery seed
1 bay leaf

Fry bacon crisp and drain well. Add meat to fat and brown. Add chopped onion and garlic and cook until yellow. Add all other ingredients, cover, and cook slowly one hour. Crumble bacon and add to sauce last.

If too dry, thin with tomato juice or water.

Sauce may be kept in refrigerator for use next day or frozen for later use.

Serve hot over hot, fluffy, rice.

Use a larger quantity of meat if you want to make it extra hearty.

This sauce is excellent for shrimp. Just omit the meat and add peeled, deveined shrimp about 15 minutes before the sauce is finished.

SYMPHONY SPINACH AND ARTICHOKE AU GRATIN

Serves 8

8 tablespoons milk
3 (16 ounce) jars or cans artichoke hearts
3 (10 ounce) packages frozen chopped spinach
3 (3 ounce) packages cream cheese
4 tablespoons soft butter
1 cup grated cheese

Drain artichokes. Save a few to use for garnish. Distribute on bottom of casserole dish. Squeeze moisture from thawed spinach and arrange over artichokes. Beat cream cheese until smooth and fluffy. Gradually blend milk. Spread mixture over spinach. Sprinkle with Parmesan cheese. Bake uncovered at 350 degrees for 40 to 45 minutes.

SPINACH MADELINE

Serves 6

2 packages frozen chopped spinach
4 tablespoons butter
2 tablespoons flour
2 tablespoons chopped onion
½ cup evaporated milk or plain homogenized milk
½ cup vegetable liquor
½ teaspoon black pepper
¾ teaspoon celery salt
¾ teaspoon garlic salt
Salt to taste
6 ounce roll Jalapeno cheese
1 teaspoon Worcestershire sauce
Red pepper to taste (optional)

Cook spinach according to directions on package. Drain and reserve liquor. Melt butter in saucepan over low heat. Add flour, stirring well until blended and smooth, but not brown. Add onion and cook until soft. Add liquid slowly, stirring constantly to avoid lumps. Cook until smooth and thick; continue stirring. Add seasonings and cheese which has been cut into small pieces. Stir until melted. Combine with cooked spinach.

This may be served immediately or put into a casserole and topped with bread crumbs.

The flavor is improved if the latter is done and kept in the refrigerator overnight. The casserole may be frozen.

Mixture may also be stuffed in tomatoes or onions and baked.

A very versatile dish.

CHEESY SPINACH SOUFFLÉ ROLL

Serves 8

¼ cup plus 2 tablespoons all purpose flour
¼ teaspoon salt
Dash of red pepper
⅓ cup butter or margarine
1¼ cups milk
¾ cup (3 ounce) shredded Cheddar cheese
¼ cup (1 ounce) Parmesan cheese
7 eggs, separated
¼ teaspoon cream of tartar
¼ teaspoon salt
Additional grated Parmesan cheese
Spinach-Mushroom Filling
4 ounces sliced Cheddar cheese, cut diagonally
Fresh spinach (optional) for garnish

Grease bottom and sides of a 15 x 10 x 1 inch jellyroll pan with vegetable oil. Line with waxed paper, allowing paper to extend beyond ends of pan; grease waxed paper with vegetable oil.

Combine flour, ¼ teaspoon salt, and red pepper; stir well.

Melt butter in a large, heavy saucepan over low heat; add flour mixture, stirring with a wire whisk until smooth. Cook 1 minute, stirring constantly with whisk. Gradually add milk; cook over medium heat, stirring constantly with whisk, until very thick and mixture leaves sides of pan. Remove from heat; beat in ¾ cup Cheddar and ¼ cup Parmesan cheese.

Place egg yolks in a large bowl; beat at high speed of electric mixer until thick and lemon colored. Gradually stir in one fourth of hot cheese mixture; add remaining cheese mixture, beating well.

Combine egg whites (at room temperature) and cream of tartar; beat at high speed of electric mixer until foamy. Add salt, and beat until stiff peaks form. Fold one-third of egg whites into cheese mixture; then carefully fold in remaining whites.

Pour cheese mixture into jellyroll pan, spreading evenly. Bake on center rack of oven at 350 degrees for 15 minutes or until puffed and firm to the touch. You must not let it overcook.

Continued on next page

Loosen edges of soufflé with a metal spatula, but do not remove from pan; place on wire rack. Let cool 15 minutes.

Place 2 lengths of waxed paper (cut longer than pan) on a smooth, slightly damp surface; overlap edge of paper nearest you over second sheet. Sprinkle additional Parmesan cheese over the waxed paper. Quickly invert pan onto waxed paper, with long side nearest you; remove pan and carefully peel waxed paper from soufflé. Spoon Spinach-Mushroom Filling over surface, spreading to edges. Starting at long side, roll the soufflé jellyroll fashion; use the waxed paper to help support the soufflé as you roll. Use your hands and gently smooth and shape the roll.

Carefully slide the roll, seam side down onto a large ovenproof platter or cookie sheet. Arrange cheese slices on top. Place 3 inches from broiler element and broil until cheese melts and is lightly browned.

SPINACH-MUSHROOM FILLING:

2 (10 ounce) packages frozen chopped spinach
¼ cup finely chopped onion
¼ cup melted butter
½ cup diced fresh mushrooms
¾ cup shredded Cheddar cheese
¼ cup grated Parmesan cheese
½ cup commercial sour cream
¼ teaspoon salt
¼ teaspoon ground nutmeg

Cook spinach according to package directions. Drain and press dry.

Sauté onion in butter until transparent. Add mushrooms and sauté 3 minutes. Stir in remaining ingredients. Yield: about 1¾ cups.

NOTE: The soufflé is very fragile and may crack during the rolling. Don't worry, the melted cheese will hide the cracks.

SQUASH

2 pounds yellow summer squash, sliced and cooked in boiling salted water until barely tender. Drain.
1 medium onion, chopped and sautéed in 2 tablespoons margarine until tender. Be careful not to burn.
Grate about 1 cup medium Cheddar cheese.

Layer squash, onions, and cheese into a buttered casserole, with cheese on top. Bake in a 350 degree oven for about 20 minutes.

SQUASH CASSEROLE

2 pounds cooked, sliced squash
1 pimento or bell pepper
1 medium onion, grated
1 cup sour cream
2 medium carrots, grated
1 package herb stuffing crumbs
1 stick butter (¼ pound)
Salt, pepper, to taste

Melt butter and stir in herb dressing. Sprinkle in bottom of casserole dish, reserving some to sprinkle on top of casserole.

Pour mixture of ingredients on top of crumbs. Then sprinkle reserved crumbs on top. Bake for 30 minutes at 350 degrees.

This is good placed in ramekins and served for a ladies lunch.

Mrs. Fred Hulett

STUFFED SUMMER SQUASH

Serves 4 to 6

Wash thoroughly and cut stem ends from 4 or 6 small summer squash. Steam them covered over boiling water until tender. Drain and cool. Scoop out centers, leaving a nice shell. Chop up the remaining pulp in a bowl and add the following to it:

¼ teaspoon paprika
½ teaspoon Worcestershire sauce
Minced garlic and minced onion (just a little)
¼ teaspoon salt
1 tablespoon butter
¼ cup grated sharp cheese
Few grains cayenne pepper
⅛ teaspoon curry powder or dry mustard (NOT BOTH)

Stir lightly and refill squash shells with the above mixture. Top each with bread crumbs. Place in buttered pyrex baking dish. Bake in a 400 degree oven until hot for about 10 to 12 minutes.

CHEESE STUFFED ZUCCHINI

Serves 6

Scrub six (8″) zucchini and trim the stem ends. Slice off the top third of the zucchini lengthwise and in a saucepan, blanch the top and bottom sections in boiling, salted water to cover for 10 minutes. Refresh the zucchini under cold running water. Scoop out the pulp from the top and bottom sections with a small spoon, being careful not to tear the bottom of the shells. Invert the bottom shells on paper towels to drain and discard the top shells. Mince the pulp and squeeze out as much moisture as possible.

In a large skillet sauté 1 cup minced onion in 1 stick butter until soft but not brown. Add the minced zucchini and simmer the mixture for 5 minutes.

Make half a recipe of Bechamel Sauce (see Sauce section), replacing ¼ cup of the milk with heavy cream. Remove the skillet from the heat and add the Bechamel Sauce, ¼ cup fine bread crumbs, toasted, 2 tablespoons freshly grated Parmesan cheese, salt and pepper to taste.

Dry the insides of the shells with paper towels. Spoon the mixture into the shells. Sprinkle the tops with freshly grated Parmesan cheese and melted butter. Put the zucchini in a lightly buttered gratin dish.

Bake in a preheated very hot oven (450 degrees) for 10 to 15 minutes, or until the tops are golden and they are hot.

Transfer the squash to a serving tray, sprinkle them with chopped parsley and garnish tray with lemon wedges or slices.

GREEN TOMATO CASSEROLE

A fabulous and unusual dish.

Cut green tomatoes into ½ inch or ¼ inch slices. Arrange over-lapping in a lightly oiled baking dish.

Sprinkle each layer with:

½ teaspoon sugar

Salt and pepper to taste

Lightly brown about ¾ cup bread crumbs in 3 tablespoons butter. Combine with ½ teaspoon oregano, ¼ teaspoon sweet basil, and a small pinch thyme. Shake in a little garlic salt. Sprinkle this mixture over the tomatoes and top with about ⅓ cup or more grated Parmesan cheese.

Bake at 350 degrees for about 45 minutes.

NOTE: Allow about 4 slices per person.

SWEET POTATO BALLS IN NUTS

Yield: about 10

2½ cups mashed sweet potatoes (2 pounds fresh potatoes or 1 can that is 1 pound, 2 ounces)
½ teaspoon salt
Dash pepper
¼ cup or more melted butter
1 cup chopped walnuts, pecans, or almonds OR a combination of nuts
⅓ cup or more honey

Combine potatoes, salt, pepper, and butter. Mix well and then chill for easier handling. Shape into 2 inch balls (about ¼ cup potato mix per ball).

Heat the honey in a small skillet. When hot, dip the potato ball into the honey, coating completely. Use 2 forks. Then roll ball in chopped nuts.

Place balls so they do not touch each other in a greased shallow baking dish.

Bake at 350 degrees for 20 to 25 minutes.

A great winter dish, especially during the holidays.

SWEET POTATOES IN ORANGE HALVES

Serves 8

8 medium sweet potatoes, scrubbed and baked (Microwave is the quickest). Then peel them and put in large mixing bowl of mixer or use food processor.
4 large oranges. Halve and remove all insides.
½ to 1 stick of butter (not more than ½ cup)
¼ teaspoon nutmeg
⅛ teaspoon ground cloves
2 tablespoons dark brown sugar
½ cup white raisins (optional)
1 cup chopped pecans
½ cup pale dry cocktail sherry
48 small marshmallows

Mix all well. Fill orange cups. Top with marshmallows. Place in muffin pans and bake at 350 degrees for 20 minutes.

NOTE: Can do ahead and freeze. Just don't bake until ready to serve.

FRIED GREEN TOMATOES

Serves 4

2 medium size firm green tomatoes
1 egg, beaten
½ cup cracker meal or plain corn meal
½ teaspoon salt
¼ teaspoon pepper
About 3 or 4 heaping tablespoons shortening

Slice tomatoes. Dip each slice in beaten egg and then in the meal to which salt and pepper have been added. Cook in the hot fat until golden brown on both sides, turning once.

Drain well on a paper towel and serve hot.

BROILED TOMATOES

Wash and cut in half or better crosswise, medium size ripe tomatoes. Place on buttered pan. Pile ½ inch high with bread crumbs sautéed in butter until crisp. Season with salt and pepper. Bake at 350 degrees until soft.

VARIATIONS:
a. Mix ½ cup sour cream, ½ cup mayonnaise and ¼ to ½ teaspoon curry powder and put on top of tomatoes before baking.
b. Bread crumbs and Parmesan cheese are good, too.

TOMATO RICE CASSEROLE

Serves 4

½ cup raw rice, cooked
½ to 1 cup sliced mushrooms sautéed in butter

Add mushrooms to rice and then add:

2 or 3 skinned, chopped tomatoes
½ teaspoon brown sugar
½ teaspoon salt
Paprika
2 tablespoons chopped onion
2 tablespoons chopped bell pepper
½ to 1 cup grated hoop Cheddar cheese

Place all in buttered baking dish. Cover with bread crumbs (about ¼ cup). Dot with butter. Bake at 350 degrees for 35 to 40 minutes.

TOMATOES ROCKEFELLER

Serves 8

Cook 2 boxes of frozen chopped spinach until defrosted, not done. Drain well.

Mix with the spinach the following:

1 tablespoon minced onion (can use dried)
1 clove crushed garlic
½ cup melted butter
1 teaspoon MSG
½ tablespoon pepper
½ cup Parmesan cheese
2 eggs
½ cup dry bread crumbs
¼ teaspoon cayenne pepper
Salt to taste

Halve tomatoes and sprinkle with garlic salt. Place on buttered baking dish and top with the spinach mixture. Bake in a 350 degree oven for approximately 15 minutes or until heated through. These are so good that one needs to allow one whole tomato (two halves) per person. The garlic gives the distinctive flavor.

ZUCCHINI-RICE CASSEROLE

Serves 6 to 8

2 pounds zucchini (small)
¼ cup butter
¼ cup salad oil
1½ cups cooked rice
½ cup grated Parmesan cheese
½ cup grated sharp Cheddar cheese
Salt and pepper to taste
2 eggs, slightly beaten
Dry bread crumbs
Melted butter

Wash, slice, and steam zucchini until tender. Cook rice or use left over rice. Combine butter and oil in large saucepan or Dutch oven and melt. Add drained rice and drained zucchini. Sauté until golden, stirring often. Stir in the cheeses, until melted. Add the seasonings. Let cool slightly. Beat eggs and stir in quickly.

Pour into greased baking dish and sprinkle generously with bread crumbs. Drizzle melted butter over top.

Broil until crumbs brown in oven. Watch carefully. Then bake at 350 degrees until bubbly for about 15 minutes.

Breads

ANGEL BISCUITS

Yields: 5 dozen

5 cups flour
¼ cup sugar
3 teaspoons baking powder
1 teaspoon baking soda
1 teaspoon salt
1 cup shortening
1 tablespoon dry yeast (1 package)
2 tablespoons warm water
2 cups buttermilk
½ cup butter, melted

Sift flour, sugar, baking powder, baking soda, and salt together and cut in shortening in a large bowl. (Food processor does fine). In a separate bowl dissolve yeast in warm water. Add dissolved yeast and buttermilk to the dry ingredients and mix well. NOTE: At this stage the dough may be placed in the refrigerator and kept there for nearly a week before using.

Turn out onto a floured board. Add more flour, if necessary to roll out well. Roll to about 3/8 inch thickness. Cut with a biscuit cutter, then dip top in melted butter and fold over. Bake on ungreased baking sheets for 15 minutes in a 400 degree oven.

BISCUITS

Yield: approximately 20

2 cups plain all-purpose flour
1 tablespoon double acting baking powder
½ teaspoon salt
¼ cup cooking oil
½ cup plus 1 tablespoon milk

Mix above ingredients together. Roll out on a lightly floured surface. Cut with biscuit cutter. Bake at 475 degrees for 8 to 10 minutes.

PROPORTIONS FOR 6 TO 10 BISCUITS:
1 cup flour
1½ teaspoons baking powder
¼ teaspoon salt
2 tablespoons cooking oil
⅓ cup milk

PROPORTIONS FOR 28 to 44 BISCUITS:
4 cups flour
2 tablespoons baking powder
1 teaspoon salt
½ cup cooking oil
1¼ cups milk

CHEESE BISCUIT

1 jar Old English Cheese spread
1 package pie crust mix
A few drops of Worcestershire sauce

Mix well. Roll out on a lightly floured surface (waxed paper does fine). Cut with small biscuit cutter. Sprinkle with red pepper or paprika.

Bake at 450 degrees until golden brown, about 8 or 10 minutes.

CINNAMON SUGAR BUTTER

Yield: 2½ cups

½ cup butter, softened
2 cups sugar
2 teaspoons ground cinnamon

Beat until thoroughly blended. Mixture will be crumbly. Store in a glass jar in refrigerator.

This makes divine cinnamon toast. Just sprinkle mixture liberally on bread. Toast in oven on broil. Watch it carefully.

STRAWBERRY BUTTER

Yield: 2½ cups

1 pint fresh strawberries or 1 (10 ounce) package frozen
½ pound unsalted butter
1 cup powdered sugar for fresh berries, ½ cup for frozen

Put ingredients in blender. Blend until smooth and creamy. If it looks curdled, don't worry, just keep blending until smooth and creamy. Chill. Delicious served with all sorts of muffins for a ladies luncheon. Even good with pancakes and waffles. Keeps for a long time.

DELICIOUS HOMEMADE BREAD

(Makes 2 loaves bread and 1 pan rolls)

2 packages active dry yeast
½ cup lukewarm water
⅔ cup shortening
½ cup sugar
1 teaspoon salt
1 cup mashed potatoes
1 cup scalded milk
2 eggs
8 to 10 cups plain flour

Scald the milk and set it aside to cool. In a large mixing bowl put in the salt, sugar, shortening, potatoes, eggs, and mix thoroughly.

Sprinkle the yeast into the warm water and when it is dissolved, add the lukewarm milk and then pour into the potato mixture. Add the sifted flour to make a stiff dough. Toss on floured board and knead well. Put it back into the mixing bowl, cover, and let it rise until double in bulk, in a warm place.

Then turn out on to a floured board and cut to the desired amount for bread and knead well, adding flour as necessary. Shape into loaves and place in greased loaf pans, cover, and let rise for about an hour.

Bake at 350 degrees for about 30 minutes. When brown, remove from pans and place on rack to cool. Brush margarine on the top for a tender crust.

TO MAKE THE ROLLS: It takes less flour when you knead and the dough should be rolled to a medium thickness. Cut with a biscuit cutter and dip one side in melted butter and fold over, place in a greased pan, cover, and when ready to bake, put in a 400 degree oven for about 15 minutes.

VARIATIONS:

ORANGE ROLLS: Roll dough into a rectangular shape and spread with the following:

½ cup sugar
2 tablespoons margarine
1 tablespoon grated orange rind

Cut into 1½ inch slices and place in a greased cake pan. Let rise about 1 hour and bake at 375 degrees for about 25 minutes. Remove from oven and frost immediately with an orange icing. Combine and drizzle one cup of confectioners sugar and 1½ tablespoons orange juice over the orange rolls.

Continued on next page

CINNAMON ROLLS: Spread dough rectangle with cinnamon, granulated sugar and chopped pecans. Spread white icing over these. (Confectioners sugar and milk).

SPOON BREAD

⅓ cup corn meal
1 cup buttermilk
1 cup plain milk
2 tablespoons flour
2 eggs
½ teaspoon soda
½ teaspoon salt
1 teaspoon baking powder
1 tablespoon sugar
2 tablespoons butter, melted

Sift dry ingredients twice. Beat eggs until light. Add buttermilk and ½ cup milk. Mix well and then add dry ingredients.

Grease baking dish with the melted butter and pour excess into batter. Stir. Then pour batter into hot dish. Gently pour other ½ cup milk over batter. DO NOT STIR.

Bake in pan of water (pain Marie) for 20 minutes in hot oven (about 425 degrees).

STRAWBERRY BREAD

Yield: 2 loaves

3 cups flour
2 cups sugar
1 teaspoon baking soda
1 teaspoon salt
1 teaspoon cinnamon
1¼ cups cooking oil
4 eggs, well beaten
2 (10 ounce) packages frozen strawberries

Mix all dry ingredients together. Make a well in center and pour in all liquid ingredients. Mix well.

Line 2 loaf pans with brown paper. Be sure to grease paper on both sides. Pour in batter and bake at 350 degrees for 1 hour. Delicious sliced for a morning coffee.

Mrs. John DeMarines

FAYE'S BANANA NUT BREAD

½ cup shortening
¾ cup sugar
1 egg
1 teaspoon lemon juice
2 cups flour
1 teaspoon soda
½ teaspoon salt
1 cup bananas (3)
1 cup nuts, chopped

Cream shortening and sugar. Add egg and lemon juice. Add dry ingredients, then mashed bananas and the nuts.

Fill loaf pan about ½ full. Bake at 350 degrees for 60 to 70 minutes.

Mrs. Brock O'Leary

COFFEE CAKE

So divine served hot in the mornings

Yield: 4 to 6 coffeecakes

1 stick (¼ pound) butter
½ cup sugar
3 eggs
3 packages yeast
½ cup warm water
1½ cups milk, scalded
3 cups plain flour
1 teaspoon salt
3 or 4 additional cups flour
Dark brown sugar
Sliced apple
Raisins
Cinnamon
Chopped pecans

Cream butter and ½ cup sugar together. Add eggs, one at a time. Dissolve the yeast in ½ cup warm water. Scald milk and let it cool to lukewarm. Take dissolved yeast and put in the cooled milk. Sift together 3 cups flour and 1 teaspoon salt. Add to milk and yeast. Stir well. It looks like batter. Add egg mixture. Then add 3 or 4 cups more flour (a total of 6 to 8 cups). Let rise for 2 hours. It must be stretchy.

Take a big ball of dough. Roll out on a floured surface. Brush with melted butter. Sprinkle on brown sugar. Slice ½ an apple on top. Sprinkle on raisins, cinnamon, and chopped pecans. Roll up into a long roll. Twist ends around to form a circle. Cut about 5 deep slits and twist slightly. Brush top with butter. You may put pecan halves and candied cherry halves in the slits. Butter pie pan well. Let finished coffee cake rise ½ hour before baking for 15 minutes at 375 degrees.

FOR GLAZE: Mix powdered sugar and milk.

GOLDEN CORN STICKS

Yield: 10 or 12

⅓ cup sifted all purpose flour
1 tablespoon sugar
1 teaspoon baking powder
½ teaspoon soda
½ teaspoon salt
1⅓ cups yellow corn meal
1 beaten egg
1 cup dairy sour cream
2 tablespoons salad oil or melted shortening

Sift flour, sugar, baking powder, soda and salt. Stir in meal. Combine egg, sour cream, and salad oil, add to dry ingredients and stir until just blended.

Preheat corn stick pans, then oil generously. Fill pans ⅔ full. Bake corn sticks in 400 degree oven for about 25 minutes.

NOTE: If you do not have corn stick pans, you may use muffin tins.

HUSH PUPPIES

Serves 4 to 6

1 cup yellow corn meal, plain
1 onion, chopped
¾ tablespoon salt
¼ teaspoon pepper
2 teaspoons baking powder
1 egg, beaten
¾ cup milk
2 tablespoons melted fat

Mix dry ingredients thoroughly and gradually add milk, blending well. Add beaten egg, then chopped onion.

Drop from spoon into hot, deep fat and fry until golden brown. Makes about 16 when dropped from a tablespoon. These are usually served with fried fish and are cooked right along with the fish.

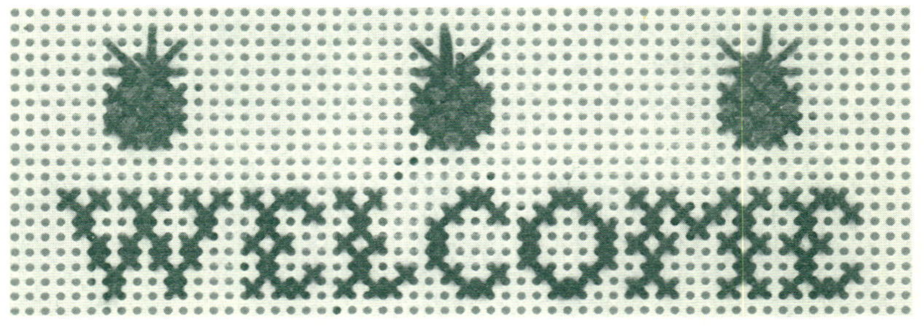

APPLESAUCE MUFFINS

Yield: 3½ dozen muffins

½ cup butter or margarine, softened
½ cup sugar
2 eggs
¾ cup applesauce
1¾ cups all purpose flour
1 tablespoon baking powder
½ teaspoon salt
¼ cup butter melted
¼ cup sugar
1/8 teaspoon ground cinnamon

Cream butter; gradually add ½ cup sugar, beating until light and fluffy. Add eggs, one at a time, beating well after each addition. Stir in applesauce.

Combine flour, baking powder, and salt; add to creamed mixture, and stir just until moistened.

Spoon batter into lightly greased miniature muffin pans, filling ⅔ full. Bake at 425 degrees for 15 minutes or until done. Remove from pan immediately and dip muffin tops in melted butter. Combine ¼ cup sugar and cinnamon; sprinkle sugar mixture over top of each muffin.

BRAN MUFFINS

(Uncooked batter will keep 6 weeks in refrigerator)

2 cups boiling water
2 cups 100% bran cereal
1 cup shortening
3 cups sugar
4 eggs, beaten
1 quart buttermilk
5 cups flour
5 teaspoons soda
1 teaspoon salt
4 cups all bran cereal

Pour water over the 100% bran. Set aside. Cream shortening and sugar; add eggs and milk. Add water-bran mixture. Sift together flour, soda, and salt. Add all bran. Fold all ingredients together only until all dry ingredients are moistened.

Bake in greased muffin tins for 20 minutes at 400 degrees.

Delicious with butter and honey. Muffins will freeze. A great treat to send your neighbors—just send a jar of the mix with directions for baking.

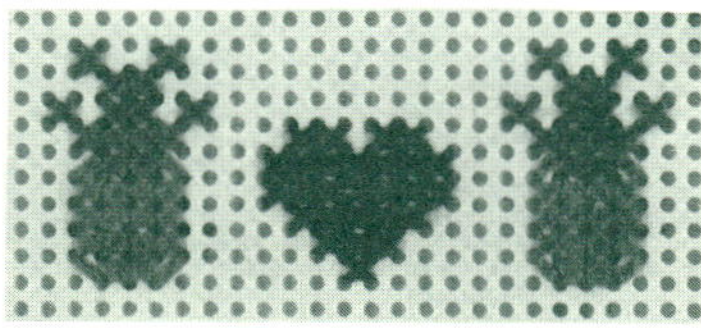

LEMON MUFFINS

1 cup butter
1 cup sugar
4 eggs, separated
2 cups flour
2 teaspoons baking powder
1 teaspoon salt
½ cup lemon juice, fresh
2 teaspoons lemon rind, grated

Cream butter, add sugar, add egg yolks; beat until light. Sift flour with baking powder and salt, and add alternately with lemon juice. DO NOT OVER MIX.

Fold in stiffly beaten whites and the lemon rind. Fill buttered muffin tins ¾ full.

Bake at 375 degrees for 20 minutes.

ORANGE MUFFINS

Yield: about 5 dozen tiny muffins

½ cup butter or margarine
1 cup sugar
3 eggs
½ cup milk
2 cups flour
2 teaspoons baking powder
1 teaspoon vanilla

Cream butter and sugar; add eggs and beat. Sift flour and baking powder together and add alternately with milk. Add vanilla.

Bake in very small greased muffin tins at 350 degrees for 10 minutes. Do not let them brown on top. Frost with the following icing.

ICING:

Juice and grated rind of 1 orange
Juice and grated rind of 1 lemon
2 cups confectioners sugar

Combine and stir until smooth.

Dip HOT muffins into icing as soon as they are removed from the oven. Dry on rack. Serve warm.

These may be frozen.

WILLIAMSBURG SWEET POTATO MUFFINS

Yield: 24 small

1 stick butter (¼ pound)
1 cup sugar
1¼ cups mashed cooked sweet potatoes
2 eggs
2½ cups flour
1½ tablespoons double acting baking powder
1 teaspoon nutmeg
1 teaspoon salt
½ teaspoon cinnamon
1¼ cups milk
½ cup chopped pecans
1½ teaspoon lemon extract

Cream butter and sugar. Add eggs one at a time. Add sifted dry ingredients alternately with the milk. Add extract and mashed sweet potatoes. Add chopped pecans. You may also add ½ cup raisins. Be careful and do not over mix.

Bake in a 400 degree oven for about 25 minutes.

FOR A FINISHED TOUCH: Mix ¼ cup sugar with 1 tablespoon cinnamon and shake over the top of the hot muffins before serving.

SOFT PRETZELS

Yield: 1½ dozen

1 package dry yeast
1½ cups warm water (105 to 115 degrees)
4 cups all purpose flour
1½ teaspoons sugar
¾ teaspoon salt
1 egg white
Kosher salt
Mustard (optional)

Dissolve yeast in warm water. Combine flour, sugar, and salt; add yeast mixture, and mix until well blended. Turn out onto a lightly floured surface, and knead until smooth and elastic (about 5 minutes).

Using kitchen shears dipped in flour, cut dough into 18 pieces; roll each into a ball.

With floured hands, roll each ball between your hands to form a rope about 14 to 16 inches long and about ½ inch in diameter; twist each into a pretzel shape, and place on a lightly greased baking sheet.

Beat egg white until frothy, and brush on each pretzel; sprinkle with salt. Bake at 400 degrees for 15 minutes or until lightly browned. Serve warm or cold with mustard, if desired.

ALEXA'S FAVORITE PANCAKES

Yield: about 18

2 cups all-purpose flour
½ teaspoon salt
2¼ teaspoons baking powder
1 tablespoon sugar

Sift the above dry ingredients.

Combine, beat until blended, and then add to flour mixture the following:

1 beaten egg (2 eggs, if small)
1 cup milk
2 tablespoons cooking oil

Stir the batter with a few swift strokes until the flour is well dampened. Ignore the lumps.

Heat skillet (I use an electric skillet) and butter it. Cook the pancakes on both sides. Serve with lots of butter and assorted syrups.

Easy and good.

VARIATION: BLUEBERRY PANCAKES. Add 1 cup fresh blueberries that have been sprinkled with 2 tablespoons sugar and a little cinnamon, 2 tablespoons commercial sour cream and 2 tablespoons dark brown sugar and blend gently into the batter.

POP OVERS

1 cup flour, sifted
¼ teaspoon salt
2 eggs
1 cup milk, less 1 tablespoon
1 tablespoon melted butter

Beat eggs, add milk and butter. Then add slowly to flour. Stir until blended (1 minute with electric mixer).

Butter muffin tins or custard cups and heat in oven. Fill hot cups one-third full.

Bake for 20 minutes at 450 degrees, then reduce heat to 350 degrees for 15 more minutes. DO NOT PEEP.

Serve hot with more butter and homemade preserves.

BEER ROLLS

3 cups biscuit baking mix
1 can beer (12 ounces)
¼ cup sugar

Mix together. Put in two greased muffin tins. Bake at 400 degrees and serve hot.

CINNAMON ROLLS

Yield: 1 dozen

½ cup milk
¼ cup sugar
½ teaspoon salt
⅓ cup shortening
¼ cup warm water
1 package dry yeast
2 eggs
2½ to 3 cups sifted all purpose flour
¾ cup brown sugar, firmly packed
⅓ cup raisins
1 teaspoon ground cinnamon
2 tablespoons melted butter

Combine milk, sugar, salt, and shortening in a small saucepan. Place over low heat until it almost scalds. Remove from heat and cool to lukewarm.

Put warm water in bowl and sprinkle yeast in. Stir to dissolve. Add yeast to milk mixture. Then add eggs and 1½ cups flour. Beat until smooth. Add enough of the remaining flour to make a dough that is easy to handle.

Turn on to floured surface. Shape into a rounded ball. Knead until smooth and elastic. Put dough into large greased bowl, bringing greased side of dough to the top. Cover. Set bowl in a warm place and let rise until double in bulk (about 1 to 1½ hours).

Turn dough on to floured surface. Roll out to a rectangle 15 x 8. Brush with melted butter. Sprinkle with brown sugar-raisin mixture. Roll up jellyroll fashion from the long side. Seal by pinching edges. Cut into 12 slices. Place cut sides down in greased 9 x 1½ inch pan. Cover with towel and let rise about an hour.

Bake at 375 degrees for 20 to 25 minutes or until done.

Remove from oven. Remove buns from pan and place on wire rack to cool. Makes 1 dozen.

GLORIA'S ICE BOX ROLLS

This is a Never-Fail Recipe

4 cups milk
1 cup sugar
1 cup shortening
1 tablespoon salt
1 teaspoon soda
1 teaspoon baking powder
2 packages dry yeast
Flour (all-purpose)
(approximately 7 cups)

Mix sugar, milk and shortening in a saucepan. Heat on medium until fat is almost melted. Remove from heat and cool until likewarm. Put 4 tablespoons warm water in a large bowl. Sprinkle yeast over water and dissolve. Add lukewarm milk to yeast alternately with flour, beating well after each addition. Add enough flour (about 6½ to 7 cups) to make a batter just a little more stiff than a cake batter. Cover and let rise for 2 hours. AFTER THIS FIRST RISING, ADD SALT, SODA, AND BAKING POWDER with about ½ cup more flour. Mix well, but do not beat. Put in refrigerator until ready to use.

Make into rolls and let rise 2 hours before baking. Bake at 425 degrees. Rolls are better if dough is left overnight in refrigerator.

These rolls may be baked and then frozen for later use.

Mrs. Mack Emmons

FRENCH TOAST

A family favorite and a quick breakfast.

1 or 2 eggs
Salt and pepper
1 teaspoon granulated sugar
Milk

Beat egg and seasonings in large bowl with a fork. Add about 1 cup milk and stir well.

Melt butter in skillet. Be careful and don't scorch.

Dip slices of plain white bread into batter and then place in hot butter. Fry on both sides until lightly brown. Serve hot.

We sprinkle powdered sugar on before eating. Other options are syrup, fresh strawberries, cinnamon sugar.

SESAME SEED TOAST FINGERS

Cut crusts from slices of bread and cut each piece in half or in thirds, making nice sized fingers.

Dip each piece in melted butter and place on a cookie sheet. Sprinkle Sesame seeds on top, almost solidly.

Bake at 250 degrees for 1 to 2 hours. Bread will become very dry and crisp.

Delicious passed at a ladies luncheon or served with a seafood appetizer.

VARIATION: Cut bread into 4 sticks, and place on ungreased cookie sheet. Brush with butter, sprinkle evenly with Parmesan cheese and sesame seeds and bake.

WAFFLES

Sift together the following ingredients:

3 cups sifted all purpose flour
4 teaspoons double acting baking powder
1 teaspoon salt
2 teaspoons sugar

Melt and cool:

⅔ cup butter or margarine

Put into small bowl of mixmaster:

4 egg whites and beat until stiff (about 1 minute) on No. 10 speed.

Place into large bowl of mixmaster the 4 egg yolks. Beat on No. 10 speed about 1 minute. Add 2 cups milk. Then add sifted dry ingredients. Beat on No. 4 speed until blended. Scrape bowl while beating. Add melted and cooled butter. Beat only until blended. Fold in beaten egg whites on No. 1 speed. Bake in a pre-heated waffle baker.

Recipe makes about 3 full size waffles in an electric waffle baker or 8 smaller waffles.

NOTE: Can add chopped pecans to mix.
DELICIOUS.

Sauces

CLARIFIED BUTTER

To obtain clarified butter:

Melt creamery butter over very low heat. Skim off the foam which rises to the top. The remainder will be separated into two parts, a clear yellow liquid and a white residue which sinks to the bottom of the pan. Strain off the clear yellow (clarified) butter into a bowl. Discard the residue.

Clarified butter is used for sautéing delicate foods and for making brown butter. It does not burn as fast as ordinary butter and because of its clarity, it leaves no residue in the dish in which it is used.

HOW TO MAKE A ROUX

A foundation for many sauces, gravies, etc.

2 tablespoons butter, shortening or bacon drippings
2 tablespoons flour

Melt the butter, shortening or bacon drippings in an iron skillet. Add the flour and stir constantly until dark brown. BE CAREFUL AND DO NOT BURN. If you do over-brown it or burn it, throw it away and begin again. This process takes or seems to take a long time.

To this basic roux, add seasoning and stock to make other sauces, etc.

BARBECUE SAUCE I

3 tablespoons catsup
2 tablespoons vinegar
1 tablespoon lemon juice
2 tablespoons Worcestershire sauce
4 tablespoons water
2 tablespoons butter
3 tablespoons dark brown sugar
1 teaspoon salt
1 teaspoon mustard
1 teaspoon chili powder
1 teaspoon paprika
½ teaspoon cayenne pepper

Mix above ingredients and heat thoroughly. This is enough sauce for about 3 pounds of chicken or other meat. I usually double the recipe to be sure there is enough.

Delicious.

BARBECUE SAUCE II

3 tablespoons catsup
2 tablespoons Worcestershire
2 tablespoons vinegar
3 tablespoons water
1/8 teaspoon salt
2 tablespoons butter
2 tablespoons lemon juice
2 teaspoons sugar

Mix altogether. Cook until butter is melted. Add 2 or 3 drops hot pepper seasoning sauce. Good over chicken, roast, or whatever.

BEARNAISE SAUCE

Beautiful and tart and good with steak, chicken, lamb chops...

2 egg yolks
1 tablespoon lemon juice
¾ cup melted butter
1 tablespoon drained capers
2 tablespoons chopped parsley
1½ teaspoons tarragon vinegar
Salt and pepper

In top of double boiler, beat yolks with lemon juice until blended. Place over hot, not boiling, water. Do not allow water in bottom pan to touch top pan. Slowly add melted butter, stirring constantly with a wooden spoon. Cook and stir just until mixture thickens. Remove from heat and add capers, parsley, vinegar, salt and pepper. Stir to mix. Makes 1 cup sauce.

BECHAMEL SAUCE

Yield: about 2 cups

1 tablespoon onion, finely chopped
3 tablespoons butter
¼ cup flour
2 cups scalded milk
¼ teaspoon salt
¼ teaspoon white pepper
1 tablespoon dry white wine (optional)

In a saucepan, sauté the finely chopped onion in 3 tablespoons butter until it is soft. Add ¼ cup flour, mix well, and cook the roux over low heat, stirring for 3 minutes (use a spiral wire whisk for stirring). Remove the pan from the heat and pour in 2 cups scalded milk, stirring vigorously with a whisk until the mixture is thick and smooth. Add ¼ teaspoon salt and ¼ teaspoon white pepper to taste and simmer the sauce for 10 minutes. Strain the Bechamel Sauce through a fine sieve and cover it with a buttered round of waxed paper.

CECIL'S COCKTAIL SAUCE FOR SHRIMP

½ cup catsup
¼ cup chili sauce
½ lemon cut in pieces
½ tablespoon horseradish
½ teaspoon Worcestershire sauce

Put all ingredients in blender and blend on medium to high speed until lemon is very finely chopped. One recipe makes ¾ cup. I always double the recipe.

This is the best cocktail sauce ever.

William Cecil Brunson

CUMBERLAND SAUCE

Serve with ham, lamb, or turkey

Yield: ½ cup

3 tablespoons red currant jelly
2 tablespoons port wine
2 tablespoons orange juice
1 tablespoon lemon juice
1 teaspoon dry mustard
½ teaspoon ground ginger
1 teaspoon paprika
3 tablespoons orange rind finely shredded, covered with cold water, brought to a boil and drained

Melt jelly over low heat until liquid. Cool and add remainder of ingredients. Blend well.

Just before serving sauce, add ½ cup brandy and 1 lump of sugar and ignite.

HOLLANDAISE SAUCE

Yield: 1 cup

4 egg yolks
1 to 2 tablespoons lemon juice
½ pound butter, melted
¼ teaspoon salt

In top of double boiler, beat yolks slightly and stir in lemon juice. PLACE OVER HOT, NOT BOILING WATER. Don't allow water in bottom of pan to touch top pan. Add butter a little at a time, stirring constantly with a wooden spoon. Add salt and pepper to taste. Continue cooking slowly just until mixture thickens, stirring all the time.

CREAM SAUCE OR WHITE SAUCE

THIN:

1 tablespoon butter
1 tablespoon flour
¼ teaspoon salt
1 cup milk

MEDIUM:

2 to 3 tablespoons butter
2 to 3 tablespoons flour
¼ teaspoon salt
1 cup milk

THICK:

3 to 4 tablespoons butter
4 tablespoons flour
¼ teaspoon salt
1 cup milk

Melt butter in saucepan; blend in flour and salt and let bubble up together. Take off heat, add milk all at once; cook over low to medium heat, stirring constantly until thickened.

USES:

Thin: Creamed vegetables, scalloped potatoes.
Medium: Creamed vegetables, scalloped dishes, creamed chicken and seafoods.
Thick: Croquettes.

OTHER VARIATIONS:

CHEESE SAUCE: Add ½ to 1 cup grated cheese to 1 cup medium cream sauce while hot.

QUICK MUSTARD SAUCE: Add 1 tablespoon prepared mustard.

CURRY SAUCE: Add ¼ to ½ teaspoon curry powder and a little minced onion to the butter.

EGG SAUCE: Add 2 cut up hard cooked eggs. Correct the seasonings.

MARCHAND DE VIN SAUCE
(A deep brown butter sauce)

Yield: 1½ cups

½ cup butter
⅓ cup finely chopped mushrooms
½ cup minced ham
⅓ cup finely chopped green onions
½ cup finely chopped onion
2 or 3 cloves garlic, minced
2 tablespoons flour
⅛ teaspoon pepper
Dash cayenne pepper
¾ cup beef stock
½ cup claret

In a 9 inch skillet melt butter, sauté mushrooms, ham, shallots, onion, and garlic. When onion is tender, add flour, pepper, and cayenne. Brown nicely about 7 to 10 minutes, stirring constantly. Blend in the stock and wine. Cover and simmer over low heat about 15 minutes, stirring now and then.

NOTE: For beef stock you may use ½ cup canned condensed beef broth and ¼ cup water.

MINT SAUCE
(For lamb)

½ cup fresh mint leaves, crushed
¼ cup sugar
½ cup water
½ cup vinegar

Let stand overnight. Cook over very low heat for about 2 hours. Thin, if necessary, with equal parts water and vinegar. Cool for 1 hour. So very good.

MORNAY SAUCE

Yield: about 2 cups sauce

2 cups Bechamel Sauce
2 tablespoons grated Parmesan cheese
2 tablespoons grated Gruyere cheese
2 tablespoons butter

To 2 cups Bechamel Sauce, add 2 tablespoons freshly grated Parmesan cheese, 2 tablespoons grated Gruyere cheese, and 2 tablespoons butter. Stir the sauce until the cheeses and butter are melted. Remove from heat.

RICH MORNAY SAUCE

Yield: about 2½ cups sauce

To 2 cups Bechamel Sauce, add the following:

2 egg yolks, lightly beaten with ½ cup heavy cream
2 tablespoons grated Parmesan cheese
2 tablespoons grated Gruyere cheese
2 tablespoons butter

Stir sauce until cheeses and butter are melted and remove from heat.

RAISIN SAUCE FOR HAM

Yield: 2 cups

¼ cup sugar
1 tablespoon flour
1 cup boiling water
Juice and rind of one orange
½ cup seeded raisins
1 tablespoon butter

Mix flour and sugar. Add boiling water and cook in double boiler until thick. Add orange juice, grated rind, raisins, and butter. Simmer for a few minutes. Serve hot.

WEIDMANN'S SHRIMP REMOULADE SAUCE

1 tablespoon minced garlic, heaping
½ cup salad oil or olive oil
2 tablespoons finely chopped celery
1 drop oil of mustard
1 cup creole mustard
½ cup white vinegar
1 tablespoon green onion tops, chopped

Season to taste with salt and pepper. Add a dash of Worcestershire sauce and ½ cup dry sherry wine. Mix well the garlic, paprika, mustard. Alternately add oil and vinegar, until well blended. Add celery, onions, and a little parsley.

This is enough sauce for about 2 pounds of boiled shrimp. You can marinate the cooked, peeled shrimp in the sauce for several hours and serve on shredded lettuce. This makes about 6 servings. Or the sauce may be used as a dip for the shrimp at a cocktail party.

Weidmann's is a very famous restaurant in Meridian, Mississippi, since 1870.

BLACKBERRY SAUCE

Yield: about 3 cups

⅔ cup butter, melted
3 tablespoons all purpose flour
1¼ cup sugar
¼ to ½ teaspoon ground nutmeg
Dash of salt
¼ cup water
2 cups fresh blackberries

Combine butter and flour in a saucepan. Add sugar, nutmeg, salt, water, and blackberries. Cook over low heat, stirring constantly, until thickened.

Heavenly served over vanilla ice cream.

M'S CHOCOLATE SAUCE

Yield: ¾ cup sauce

½ package (4 squares) semi-sweet chocolate
6 tablespoons water
¼ cup sugar
2 tablespoons butter
½ teaspoon vanilla extract

Melt chocolate in water over low heat, stirring until blended. Stir in sugar. Boil gently 4 minutes, stirring constantly. Remove from heat; add butter. Serve hot.

Delicious served over vanilla ice cream.

HOT FUDGE SAUCE

Yield: 1½ cups

This kind of sauce slides down the ice cream and hardens. Very old fashioned.

6 tablespoons unsalted butter (¾ stick)
½ cup water
3 ounces unsweetened chocolate
1 cup sugar
2 tablespoons light corn syrup

Melt butter with water in small saucepan over medium heat; then bring to boil, stirring constantly. Add chocolate and let melt, stirring occasionally. Don't worry if there are lumps. They will melt. Add sugar and corn syrup and let boil gently for 5 minutes. Serve hot.

MAGIC CHOCOLATE SAUCE

Yield: 2 cups

1 can sweetened condensed milk
2 squares (2 ounces) unsweetened chocolate
1/8 teaspoon salt
½ to 1 cup hot water
½ teaspoon vanilla extract

In top of double boiler put condensed milk, chocolate, and salt. Cook over rapidly boiling water, stirring often until thickened. Remove from heat. Slowly stir in hot water until sauce is the desired thickness. Stir in vanilla.

May be served hot or chilled.

HOT LEMON DESSERT SAUCE

¾ cup sugar
2 tablespoons cornstarch
1¼ cups boiling water
3 tablespoons lemon juice
Rind of 1 lemon, grated
2 tablespoons butter
Pinch of salt
¼ teaspoon vanilla

Combine and mix thoroughly the sugar and cornstarch. Slowly add the boiling water. Cook, stirring constantly, until thickened. Add remaining ingredients and blend well.

Serve hot. Delicious over pound cake.

PRALINE PARFAIT SAUCE

Yield: 2½ cups

2 cups dark corn syrup
⅓ cup sugar
⅓ cup boiling water
1 cup chopped pecans, toasted

Combine syrup, sugar, water in saucepan. Bring to a boil over medium heat, stirring constantly. As soon as mixture reaches boiling point, remove from heat. Cool. Add nuts. Serve over vanilla ice cream.

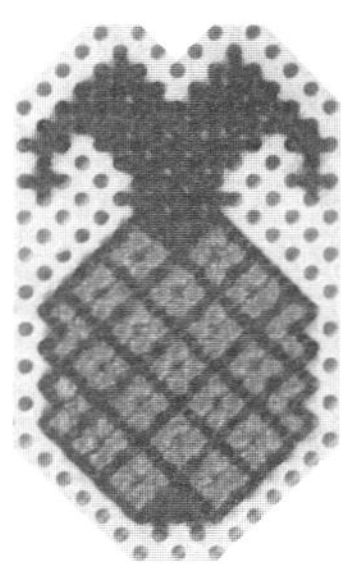

RUM BUTTER SAUCE

2 cups sugar **1 cup water**

Boil sugar and water to make a simple syrup.

ADD:
2 tablespoons butter and cool.

ADD:
3 tablespoons light rum

Keeps indefinitely in a covered jar in refrigerator.

TO SERVE: Warm in a saucepan or double boiler. Delicious served hot over pound cake.

FRUIT MARINADE (MINT)

¼ cup crushed fresh mint leaves
½ cup sugar
1 tablespoon lemon juice
1 tablespoon lemon rind, grated
1½ cups orange juice

Bring the above ingredients to a boil and then cool. Pour over fresh, canned or any mixture of fruit. Let marinate overnight.

Mrs. H. Wingfield Glover

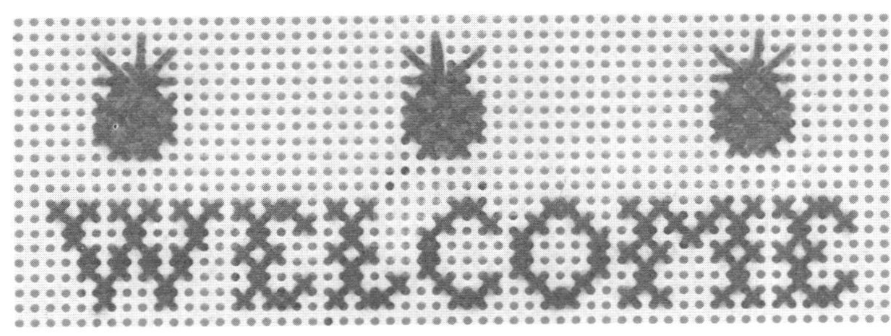

Desserts

ALMOND RUM CREAM DESSERT

Serves 8 generously

1 package Zwieback
⅔ cup sugar
8 tablespoons light rum
½ cup currant jelly (red)
½ cup almonds, chopped
3 eggs
2 tablespoons flour
2 cups milk
1 pint whipping cream
Strawberries for garnish

Make bowl of Zwieback crumbs as for pie shell. Set aside.

Beat eggs until thick. Add sugar sifted with flour and 3 tablespoons of the rum. Mix well. Scald milk with 5 tablespoons of rum. Add hot milk to egg mixture slowly, stirring constantly. Cook over hot water until mixture thickens. Cool.

Put small amount of Zwieback crumbs in bottom of sherbet glass. Brush with melted currant jelly and sprinkle with a few toasted almonds. Fill sherbet glass with rum cream. When ready to serve, cover with rum flavored whipped cream and garnish with strawberries that have been dipped in melted red currant jelly. Serve chilled.

NOTE: Do not dip strawberries until just before serving. Elegant dessert for spring dinner party.

Recipe could serve 12 if made in oblong glass baking dish.

Mrs. Lawrence Paine

EASY BANANAS FOSTER

Serves 6

½ stick butter (4 tablespoons)
6 heaping tablespoons dark brown sugar
4 bananas
1 tablespoon banana liqueur, overflow a bit
1 tablespoon light rum
2 tablespoons brandy
Vanilla ice cream

Mix butter and brown sugar in skillet. Cook over medium heat until sugar is melted. Slice bananas in halves or quarters and add to butter mixture, cooking until tender. Add banana liqueur and stir.

At this point, can hold rest of preparation until just before serving. When ready to serve, heat. Sprinkle rum and brandy over top. Ignite. Spoon gently a few times. Serve warm over vanilla ice cream. The last step can be done at the table in a chafing dish with great flair.

BANANA PUDDING

1 cup sugar
3 tablespoons all-purpose flour
Dash of salt
4 eggs
2 cups milk
1 teaspoon vanilla extract
Vanilla Wafers
5 or 6 bananas, sliced as you go

Combine ¾ cup of the sugar, flour and salt in the top of a double boiler. Mix in 1 whole egg and 3 egg yolks. Stir in the milk. Cook, uncovered, over boiling water, stirring constantly, until thickened. Remove from heat. Add the vanilla.

Line custard cups with vanilla wafers, then a layer of sliced bananas, then a layer of custard. Repeat, ending with custard.

Beat remaining 3 egg whites stiff, but not dry. Gradually add remaining ¼ cup sugar and beat until mixture forms stiff peaks. Pile on top of each pudding, covering entire surface. Place all custard cups on a baking sheet and bake in a preheated hot oven (425 degrees) for 5 minutes or until delicately brown. Watch them closely. You may serve them warm or chilled. Our family likes them chilled.

You may also prepare this pudding in a 1½ quart casserole.

BRANDY FREEZE

1 cup macaroons, crumbled
½ cup brandy (or until it tastes good
1 gallon good quality ice cream, softened a bit

Mix above ingredients together well and freeze overnight or until ready to serve. Serve in sherbet glasses. Top each serving with toasted almonds.

Mrs. Richard Wilbourn

CHARLOTTE RUSSE

A Delicious Old Timey Dessert

½ box unflavored gelatin
6 egg whites
1 scant cup sugar
1 pint milk
1 quart heavy cream
2 tablespoons vanilla extract or flavor with dry sherry

Heat milk and dissolve gelatin in milk. Cool. Whip egg whites stiff so that when bowl is turned upside down the eggs will not fall out. Whip cream. Combine beaten egg whites with whipped cream, folding gently and well. Then pour cold milk and gelatin into egg and cream mix, holding milk HIGH and pouring a very thin stream slowly. Continue folding until blended.

Cover bowl with plastic wrap and refrigerate until set.

Serve in crystal sherbets with a delicious cookie.

CHERRIES JUBILEE

Serves 6

½ cup cognac
1½ quarts vanilla ice cream
¾ cup red currant jelly
1 large can (16 ounce) pitted Bing cherries
½ cup blanched almonds

Drain cherries and stuff with almonds. Refrigerate. This step can be done in advance. Put jelly in chafing dish and stir over direct heat until jelly melts. Add cherries and simmer slowly. Add cognac and heat. When heated, ignite cognac and spoon cherries and sauce over individual servings of ice cream.

CHOCOLATE ECLAIRS OR CREAM PUFFS

This is Ricki's good recipe.

PASTRY:

¼ cup butter
½ cup boiling water
½ cup flour
2 eggs

Add butter to water and heat until butter melts. Add flour all at once and stir vigorously until ball forms in center of pan. Remove from heat and add eggs one at a time, beating after each addition. Using pastry bag, make 6 large puffs or 18 tiny ones. Shape like cream puffs or like eclairs. Shape on buttered cookie sheet and bake 15 minutes at 450 degrees, then lower heat to 375 degrees and bake 20 minutes.

FRENCH CREAM FILLING:

4 egg yolks
¾ cup plus 2 tablespoons sugar
⅓ cup flour
2 cups scalded milk
1 tablespoon sugar
Vanilla, rum, or brandy, to taste

Beat yolks, sugar and flour. Pour scalded milk over the egg mixture and cook in a double boiler, stirring constantly until mixture is thick. Add flavoring, cool and put in refrigerator. To keep skim from forming, sprinkle 1 tablespoon sugar over top.

ICING:

2 tablespoons butter
3 tablespoons milk
Melted chocolate
½ teaspoon vanilla
2 cups confectioners sugar (you may need more)

Heat butter and milk. Add vanilla and enough sugar to form the right consistency. Add melted chocolate to part of it. Do not make icing until ready to use.

VARIATION: Eliminate icing. Dust eclairs or puffs with powdered sugar. Pass pitcher of rich, thick, warm, chocolate sauce to pour over pastries.

Mrs. Frank Tucker

CHOCOLATE MOUSSE

Serves 4

¼ pound sweet chocolate
3 large or 4 small eggs, separated
Whipping cream

Soak chocolate in warm water to cover, on top of stove in a covered small saucepan. After about 4 minutes on very low heat, the chocolate will be soft. Pour off water.

Beat chocolate with egg yolks over low heat. Beat constantly until it is like a thick sauce. Remove from heat. Beat egg whites, slowly at first, increasing speed as you go. Beat until very stiff. Slowly add a little of the whites at a time to the chocolate mixture. Mix with a wooden spoon, not vigorously but mix well. Pour into serving dish. Refrigerate for at least 1 hour, preferably 4 hours. Serve with whipped cream.

This is a heavier mousse because it is made with all eggs and not cream.

FROZEN CHOCOLATE MOUSSE

Very light and delicious

Makes 16 (3 ounce) servings

¾ cup butter, softened
1½ cups sugar
3 eggs, separated
1 tablespoon brandy
½ teaspoon almond extract
¼ cup toasted slivered almonds
½ pound semisweet chocolate chips, melted
2 cups heavy cream, whipped
Shaved chocolate for garnish

Cream butter until light and fluffy. Add sugar. Add egg yolks, brandy and almond extract. Add chocolate and almonds.

Beat egg whites until stiff and fold them into chocolate mixture. Fold in whipped cream. Freeze in individual soufflé dishes or in paper lined muffin tins.

Garnish with a dab of whipped cream, shaved chocolate, and a cherry. A grand dessert after a heavy dinner.

MOUSSE AU CHOCOLAT

Rich and very fattening, but Oh, so heavenly...

Serves 8 to 10

4 eggs (large)
1½ tablespoons instant coffee dissolved in ¼ cup hot water in a small saucepan
¾ cup sugar
¼ cup dark Jamaican rum, cognac, or orange liqueur
Chocolate: use EITHER 4½ ounces semisweet baking chocolate and 1½ ounces unsweetened baking chocolate OR use 6 ounces semisweet baking chocolate
1½ sticks unsalted butter (6 ounces)
Pinch of salt
¼ teaspoon (scant) cream of tartar for egg whites

Separate the eggs. Set whites aside. Beat the yolks for 2 or 3 minutes until pale and lemon colored and thick. Stop beating while you make the sugar syrup.

Set pan with coffee over high heat, blend in sugar, and bring to a boil. Liquid will be clear. All at once, bring hot liquid over to yolks. Begin beating yolks again at medium speed while you slowly dribble in the hot syrup. Set aside and prepare chocolate.

Stir the ¼ cup rum or other liquid into the now empty sugar-boiling pan. Break the chocolate into it. Place chocolate pan into pan of simmering water. Stir once, cover pan, and let chocolate melt while you continue with the yolks.

Set egg yolk pan into 2nd pan of water and keep temperature of water at just below the simmer. Beat yolk mixture slowly for 5 or more minutes until it doubles in volume. (It becomes like a hot, thick, cream).

Pour and scrape egg mix into big bowl of electric mixer. Beat at moderate speed until cool for about 5 minutes. It is ready when you can lift a bit on a spatula and it dribbles off in a thick ribbon.

Stir up chocolate. Be sure it is melted, smooth and shiny. Remove pan from hot water. Cut butter into 1 inch pieces and quickly beat it into the chocolate. Scrape chocolate over yolk mix. Combine with spatula rapidly.

Beat egg whites. When foamy, add salt and cream of tartar. Beat until stiff but not dry. They will be shiny. Fold whites into chocolate mixture by rapid scoops with your spatula. Be fast so whites will hold their volume.

Pour into serving dish. Chill or freeze. Will keep 3 or 4 days in refrigerator. You may wrap mousse airtight and freeze.

COFFEE TORTONI

Serves 6

1 egg white
1 tablespoon instant coffee
1/8 teaspoon salt
2 tablespoons sugar
1 cup heavy cream, whipped
1/4 cup additional sugar
1 teaspoon vanilla extract
1/2 teaspoon almond extract
1/4 cup toasted chopped almonds

Combine egg whites and instant coffee. Beat with mixer until stiff. Gradually add 2 tablespoons sugar. Beat until it looks satiny. In another bowl, combine heavy cream with additional sugar. Beat until stiff. Add flavorings. Fold mixtures together. Put in paper baking cups in muffin tins and freeze. (You may sprinkle almonds on top before freezing or you may blend them in to mixture.)

You may also put this mixture into parfait glasses and freeze. Garnish with a cherry before serving.

I always double this recipe. Serves 8 or 10 when doubled.

CARAMEL CUP CUSTARD

Serves 6

3 eggs
2 cups milk
1/4 teaspoon salt
1/4 teaspoon sugar
2 teaspoons butter
1 teaspoon vanilla

Beat the eggs, yolks and whites together. Add sugar, salt, and milk. Beat well. Brush 6 small custard cups with the butter. Put into each cup about a teaspoon of caramel and shake the cups. Then pour in the custard. Place cups in pan of warm water and bake for 30 minutes, or until you can insert a silver knife in center and have it come out dry.

TO MAKE CARAMEL: Put 4 tablespoons granulated sugar into a small heavy skillet and let melt until light brown. You might have to stir it a little. It will be completely melted.

TO SERVE: Invert on dessert plate. Can be served with or without sweetened whipped cream.

Our family prefers this dessert cold.

STRAWBERRY CREPES

Serves 8

1 package (8 ounces) cream cheese, softened
6 tablespoons sugar
2 teaspoons grated orange rind
½ teaspoon ground cinnamon
1 pint strawberries, washed, hulled and sliced
4 tablespoons (½ stick) butter
¾ cup sifted all-purpose flour
¼ teaspoon salt
3 eggs
1 cup milk
½ cup orange juice
¼ cup orange flavor liqueur

Blend cream cheese, 2 tablespoons sugar, rind and cinnamon in small bowl; stir in ½ cup sliced berries and set aside.

Melt 1 tablespoon butter and reserve.

Measure flour, 1 tablespoon remaining sugar, and salt into a sifter. Beat eggs until thick in a medium size bowl. Sift dry ingredients over, beat just until smooth. Stir in milk and reserved melted butter. Heat an 8 inch heavy skillet slowly; grease pan lightly with butter.

Pour batter, ¼ cup at a time, into skillet, tilting to cover bottom completely. Cook over medium heat, 1 to 2 minutes, until underside is golden. Turn and brown on other side. Stack crepes with aluminum foil between each. (Can freeze).

Spoon 2 generous tablespoons cream cheese filling into center of each crepe. Roll up and fold ends under. Place seam side down in a shallow baking dish. Keep warm in a slow oven (250 degrees).

Melt remaining butter in medium saucepan. Stir in remaining 3 tablespoons sugar, remaining strawberries, and orange juice. Heat until bubbly. Remove from heat. Stir in liqueur. Pour over crepes and serve at once.

LEMON CUP CUSTARD

Serves 16

A delicious light dessert...more like a soufflé than a true baked custard.

6 tablespoons flour
¼ pound butter
1¾ cup sugar
½ teaspoon salt
8 egg yolks
8 egg whites
Grated rind of two lemons
2 cups milk
1 cup fresh lemon juice

Beat butter until fluffy, slowly add sugar, and beat for 3 minutes with electric mixer. Add egg yolks and beat 3 more minutes. Fold in flour. Stir in lemon juice. Gradually add milk, salt, and lemon rind. Fold in medium stiff egg whites.

Fill custard cups. Set in pan with hot water and bake in 350 oven until the custard is set and slightly golden brown on top.

May be served warm or chilled.

NOTE: This recipe was given to us by Mr. Christof Weihs, of The Colony House Restaurant in Charleston, South Carolina.

POTS DE CREME AU CHOCOLAT

Serves 6

½ cup cream
½ cup sugar
½ grated orange rind
4 egg yolks
3 tablespoons cocoa

Mix sugar and cocoa and cream. Bring to a boil. Remove from heat and cool a little. Add 4 beaten egg yolks.

Return to heat in top of a double boiler and cook until slightly thick. DO NOT LET IT BOIL. Cool.

Spoon into pots de creme cups or wine glasses. Only fill cup or glasses half full because it is too rich for large servings. Top with a little whipped cream.

NOTE: For Coffee Pots de Creme: Add 2 tablespoons powdered instant coffee instead of chocolate and substitute 1 tablespoon brandy for the grated orange peel. This version is wonderful in the winter.

FLOATING ISLANDS

A delicious favorite

Separate 4 large eggs and reserve 3 of the whites. Combine the yolks with 5 tablespoons sugar and a pinch of salt and set aside. Beat the whites until they form soft peaks, gradually adding 5 tablespoons sugar, beating until well blended.

Heat 2½ cups milk in a large skillet (stainless steel) until just below the boiling point. It will be like a very very gentle simmer, Form the egg white mix into ovals. Drop the ovals into the simmering milk a few at a time and simmer them for about 3 minutes, poaching on each side. Drain on paper towels.

Strain the hot milk into the reserved yolk and sugar mixture. Add 2 teaspoons vanilla and stir the mixture well with a wire whisk or wooden spatula. Pour the custard into a saucepan and cook it over medium heat, stirring until it coats the spatula. Pour the custard into a flat serving dish and arrange the meringue ovals on top. Chill.

Before serving, cook ½ cup sugar until it caramelizes and drizzle over the meringues.

BASIC ICE CREAM

For use in electric freezer

5 or 6 eggs
1½ cups sugar
1 quart milk, almost scalded
1 teaspoon vanilla extract
1 teaspoon almond extract
1 pint half and half cream
4 half pints whipping cream

Beat eggs with a wire whisk in a very large stainless steel boiler. Don't use aluminum because the custard will turn a gray color. Stir in sugar. Add hot milk, stirring constantly. Cook on low until mixture "coats the spoon." Add flavorings and cool. Add cream and refrigerate until ready to freeze.

PEACH ICE CREAM: Add 2 or 3 cups peaches pureed in food processor or blender plus ½ cup sugar.

STRAWBERRY ICE CREAM: Add 2 cups pureed strawberries and ½ cup sugar.

PEPPERMINT ICE CREAM: Add crushed peppermint stick candy to hot custard.

AMARETTO ICE CREAM

Yield: 1½ quarts of ice cream

1 quart heavy cream
2 cups sugar
2 cups Amaretto liqueur
8 egg yolks

Heat sugar and Amaretto until thick and syrupy. Set aside. Beat yolks until light, ribboned and lemon colored. Then pour sugar mixture VERY SLOWLY into the egg yolks while beating until thick.

Whip cream until peaks form. Fold egg yolk mixture, when cooled, into the whipped cream. Blend well. Place in tightly covered plastic containers and freeze. Can also freeze in electric freezer.

APRICOT ICE

Yield: about 2 quarts

1 cup sugar
½ cup white corn syrup
2 cups water
4 tablespoons lemon juice
2 cups apricot pulp and juice (1 large can peeled apricots or 2 smaller ones)

Cook to 240 degrees the sugar, corn syrup and 1 cup water. Remove. Cool. Add lemon juice, 1 cup cold water, and apricots. Cool and freeze. Does great in an electric ice cream freezer.

Delicious served with fudge cake.

BLACKBERRY ICE CREAM

Yield: about 3½ quarts

2½ cups sugar, divided
3 cups fresh blackberries
3 eggs, beaten
¼ teaspoon salt
1 tablespoon vanilla extract
6 cups milk
1 (13 ounce) can evaporated milk

Sprinkle ½ cup sugar over blackberries. Crush them lightly. Puree berries in blender. If desired, put through a sieve to remove seeds.

Combine eggs, salt and remaining 2 cups sugar. Beat well. Stir in vanilla, milk, and blackberry mixture. Pour into freezer can of a 1 gallon ice cream freezer. Freeze according to manufacturer's instructions.

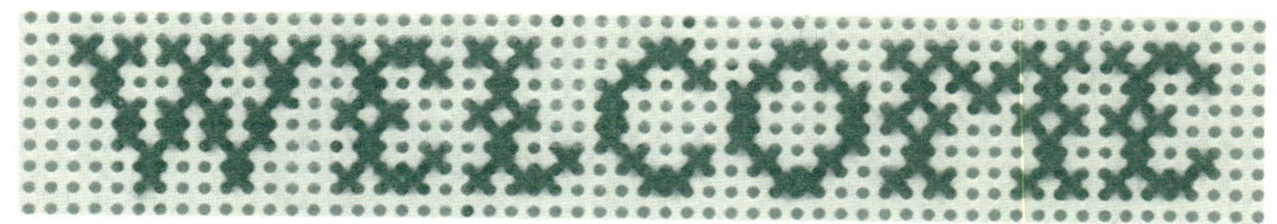

CHOCOLATE ICE CREAM

Yield: 1½ quarts

¼ cup cold water
⅓ cup sugar
12 ounces dark sweet chocolate (preferably imported) broken into pieces
4 tablespoons (½ stick) unsalted butter, cut into pieces
3 cups whipping cream
6 egg yolks
⅓ cup sugar

Combine water and ⅓ cup sugar in small saucepan and bring to boil over medium heat. Remove from heat and add chocolate and butter. Cover and let stand several minutes. Remove lid and stir until mixture is smooth.

Scald cream in medium saucepan but do not let it boil.

Beat yolks with remaining sugar in large bowl until thick and lemon colored. Beat in chocolate mixture. Add cream, beating constantly until blended. Let cool, stirring occasionally.

Transfer to ice cream freezer and freeze, following manufacturers instructions.

MOT'S PINEAPPLE SHERBET

1 cup fresh grated pineapple or canned crushed pineapple
1 cup pineapple juice
1 cup water
1 cup sugar
Grated rind and juice of 1 lemon
1 cup heavy cream
3 tablespoons Kirsch

Combine pineapple, juice, water, sugar and lemon rind in saucepan. Bring mixture to a boil. Cook for 5 minutes, then strain. Add the lemon. Freeze the mixture in an electric or crank freezer. Just before it freezes hard, add whipped cream and Kirsch.

Delicious.

Mrs. Fred Hulett

LEMON ICE CREAM

Yield: 1½ gallons

1 quart whipping cream
1 quart half and half cream
1 pint milk
4 cups sugar
Juice of 8 lemons (about ¾ cup of juice)
1 tablespoon grated lemon rind
2 teaspoons lemon extract

Combine all ingredients and mix well. Pour mixture into container of a 1½ gallon ice cream freezer and follow the manufacturers instructions.

Be sure to let it ripen at least 30 minutes before serving. Delicious.

PHILADELPHIA ICE CREAM

Rich and easy

Yield: 1 quart

1 quart (4 cups) heavy cream
¾ cup sugar
¼ teaspoon salt
2 tablespoons vanilla extract

Combine 2 cups cream, sugar and salt in a saucepan. Heat, stirring often until sugar dissolves. Remove from heat. Add remaining 2 cups cream and vanilla.

Follow manufacturers instructions on your ice cream freezer.

MELBA MINIATURES

Serves 16

1 package (10 ounce) frozen red raspberries
2 tablespoons light corn syrup
1 cup milk
2 cups miniature marshmallows
½ teaspoon lemon juice
1/8 teaspoon salt
1 tablespoon lemon juice
1 can (14 ounce) crushed pineapple, drained
1 cup heavy cream, whipped
½ cup toasted slivered almonds
Paper cupcake shells

Defrost raspberries. Add corn syrup and ½ teaspoon lemon juice. Spoon raspberry mix into paper baking cups that have been set into muffin tins. Place pans in freezer and chill until raspberries are partially set. Then scald milk, add marshmallows and stir until melted. Cool. Add salt and 1 tablespoon lemon juice. Fold in pineapple, whipped cream and almonds. Spoon mix over raspberries. Freeze until firm.

TO SERVE: Remove paper cup and invert into sherbets.

FROZEN LEMON PIE

Serves 8

3 egg yolks, well beaten
Juice and rind of 1 lemon
⅔ cup sugar
½ teaspoon salt
1 cup heavy cream, whipped
¾ cup crushed vanilla wafers
3 egg whites, beaten stiff

Combine in the order given, the first four ingredients and cook in saucepan until the consistency of custard, stirring constantly. Cool. Fold in beaten egg whites and then whipped cream.

Sprinkle vanilla wafer crumbs in long pyrex dish. Pour mixture on top of crumbs. Then sprinkle light coating of crumbs on top. Cover with plastic wrap and freeze. Cut in squares to serve.

Garnish with fresh strawberries, fresh sliced peaches, or a cherry.

LEMON CHIFFON RING

Serves 12

A very delicate, light dessert and beautiful for a dinner party.

4 teaspoons unflavored gelatin
½ cup cold water
⅔ cup lemon juice
⅔ cup sugar
6 eggs, separated
Pinch of salt
2 teaspoons lemon rind, grated
3 tablespoons sugar
½ pint heavy cream, whipped
Fresh grated coconut

Dissolve gelatin in cold water. Mix lemon juice and ⅔ cup sugar together. Add salt to egg yolks and beat until thick and lemon colored. Add lemon juice and sugar mixture to the yolks, stirring while you add. Cook in top of double boiler until mixture coats the spoon.

Remove from heat and add softened gelatin. Stir until dissolved. Add grated lemon rind. Chill in the refrigerator until it begins to thicken.

Beat the egg whites until stiff with 3 tablespoons sugar. Add to the other mixture, folding together well. Pour into ring mold and chill until firm.

Take out of mold onto serving platter. Frost with whipped cream and cover top and sides with freshly grated coconut.

Can serve as is or with fresh fruit such as strawberries or peaches. Garnish platter with fresh mint and lemon slices.

GREEN CITRUS MERINGUES

Very delicate and good

Serves 12

MERINGUES:

4 egg whites
Pinch salt
½ teaspoon fresh lime juice
¾ cup sugar
¼ cup sugar

Beat egg whites with a pinch of salt until stiff but not dry. Beat in ½ teaspoon lime juice and gradually add ¾ cup sugar about a tablespoon at a time, beating constantly until the meringue is thick. Fold in ¼ cup sugar very lightly.

Oil and flour lightly a baking sheet. Fit a pastry bag with a small fluted tube and fill bag with meringue. Press out about 1 tablespoon meringue for each and spread in a circle about 2 inches in diameter with back of spoon to form base for nest. Press out small kisses of the meringue around the edge of each circle, each touching the other, forming small nests. Sprinkle meringues with finely granulated sugar and bake in a slow oven 250 degrees, for 30 minutes, watching them carefully. They must not color. While they are still warm, remove them from baking sheet to rack to dry.

FILLING:

3 egg yolks
¼ cup fresh lime juice
¼ cup sugar
Pinch of salt
2 cups heavy cream, whipped

Combine 3 egg yolks beaten, ¼ cup fresh lime juice, ¼ cup sugar and a pinch of salt. Cook in double boiler over simmering water, stirring constantly, until custard is thick. Cool it and fold in 2 cups heavy cream, whipped. Tint the custard a very pale green. Fill meringue nests with the cream and chill well before serving.

Garnish side of nest with a twisted thin slice of lime. A good dessert for a ladies spring luncheon.

MILE HIGH PIE

Serves 8 to 12

CRUST:
1½ cups sifted flour
½ teaspoon salt
½ cup shortening
4 or 5 tablespoons cold water

FILLING:
1 pint vanilla ice cream
1 pint chocolate ice cream
8 egg whites
½ teaspoon vanilla
¼ teaspoon cream of tartar
½ cup sugar

CRUST: Sift together flour and salt. Cut in shortening until pieces are the size of small peas. Sprinkle 1 tablespoon cold water over flour mixture and gently toss with fork. Repeat until all is moistened. Form into a ball with fingers and roll out to 1/8 inch thickness on lightly floured surface. Fit loosely into a 9 inch pie pan, pricking well. Bake 10 to 12 minutes at 450 degrees. Cool.

FILLING: Layer the ice cream in pie shell. Beat egg whites with vanilla and cream of tartar until soft peaks form. Gradually add sugar, beating until stiff and glossy and sugar is dissolved. Spread meringue over ice cream to edges of pastry. Broil for 30 seconds to 1 minute to brown meringue. Then freeze at least several hours.

TO SERVE: Drizzle chocolate sauce over each serving.

CHOCOLATE SAUCE:
2 squares sweet chocolate
2 squares bitter chocolate
¼ pint cream
½ cup sugar

Cook all ingredients in double boiler until thick, using ½ of the cream to start with. Add the balance to achieve pouring consistency.

EASY LEMON PARFAIT

1 (10 ounce) package frozen strawberries
1 tablespoon orange liqueur
1 pint lemon sherbet

Thaw fruit. Put in bowl and add orange liqueur. Stir well.

TO MAKE PARFAIT: Alternate in parfait glass, fruit, then sherbet, in layers. Garnish with whipped cream. Put back in freezer until ready to serve.

CHERRY PARFAIT

Serves 6

½ tablespoon unflavored gelatin
½ cup sugar
½ cup water
2 egg whites
1 cup heavy cream
1 teaspoon almond extract
¼ teaspoon salt
½ cup maraschino cherries, chopped
½ cup chopped almonds

Sprinkle gelatin over 2 tablespoons cold water to soften. After about 5 minutes, set container with gelatin in a pan of boiling water and stir until dissolved.

Cook sugar and ½ cup water until a drop tested in cold water forms a soft ball (238 degrees on candy thermometer). While syrup cooks, beat egg whites until they hold a point. Pour a thin stream of the hot syrup into the beaten egg whites and beat constantly until mixture cools. Stir in melted gelatin and cool completely.

Beat heavy cream until it holds a shape; then beat in almond extract and salt. Gently mix in egg white-gelatin combination along with well drained chopped cherries and toasted chopped almonds.

Spoon into 6 parfait glasses and freeze until firm. Garnish with a little whipped cream and a long stemmed cherry. It is also nice to serve a cookie with a parfait, such as a macaroon.

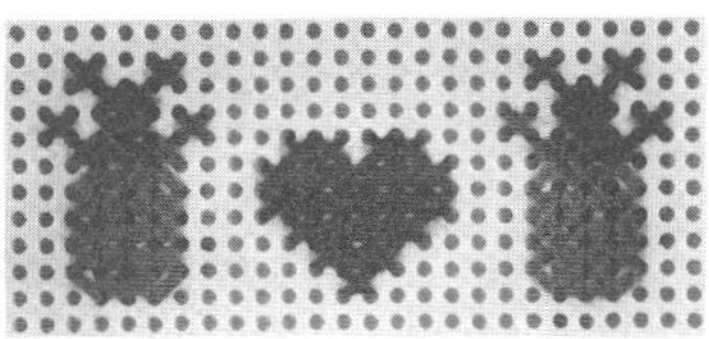

LIME STRAWBERRY PARFAIT

Serves 8

1 pint lime sherbet
1 pint peach ice cream
1 cup sliced sugared strawberries

Chill 8 parfait glasses. Soften sherbet and ice cream so they can be layered easily.

Start with ice cream, then strawberries, and sherbet in layers. Refreeze. To serve, garnish with a dab of whipped cream.

RASPBERRY PARFAIT

Serves 8

2 cups heavy cream, whipped
18 coconut macaroons
1 cup pecans, chopped fine
1 pint raspberry sherbet
½ cup grated coconut (use frozen)

Whip 1½ cups cream. Add crushed macaroons and pecans into whipped cream.

Scoop raspberry sherbet and layer it into parfait glasses, then put a layer of cream mixture. Then whip the remaining ½ cup cream. Add red food coloring. Dab on top of each parfait, then sprinkle with coconut. Return parfaits to freezer.

LETA'S STRAWBERRY PARFAIT

Serves 4

1 pint softened vanilla ice cream
½ cup crushed vanilla wafers
¼ cup ground pecans
½ teaspoon grated lemon peel
½ cup sliced strawberries
½ cup sugar
1 egg white
½ cup dairy sour cream

Mix wafers, nuts and lemon peel together and set aside. Beat egg whites, add sugar. Beat about 10 minutes. Then fold in sour cream and strawberries.

TO PREPARE FINISHED PARFAITS:
Make in layers...
1. Layer of ice cream
2. Layer of combined wafer, nut and peel mix
3. Layer of strawberry mix

Freeze. Garnish with a sprig of mint and a fresh strawberry when ready to serve.

NAPOLEONS

Serves 8

Considered to be an Imperial Dessert. This flaky dessert is named for Naples.

5 cups sifted all purpose flour
1 pound butter
Water
1 tablespoon vinegar
1½ cups milk
5 egg yolks
6 tablespoons granulated sugar
1½ tablespoons vanilla extract
1 cup confectioners sugar
¼ cup semisweet chocolate pieces
1 teaspoon white corn syrup

STARTING THE PASTRY: Sift 4½ cups flour into large bowl. Add ½ pound butter in small pieces. With pastry blender, cut it in until it looks like corn meal. Mix 1 cup cold water with vinegar and pour over flour. Mix well with pastry blender. Shape into a ball and let rest for 20 minutes.

Then on lightly floured surface, with stockinet covered rolling pin, roll pastry into a rectangle that is ¼ inch thick.

ROLLING IN BUTTER: Starting at narrow end of pastry dough, dot ⅔ of it with butter. Then fold unbuttered third over center third, then last third on top, making 3 layers. Next, fold opposite ends so they completely overlap, making equal thirds. Wrap in plastic wrap. Chill for 30 minutes.

THEN: Roll out, fold, wrap, and refrigerate three more times.

THEN: Roll it into a rectangle 17″ x 12″ x ¼ inch. Let it and you rest for 30 minutes. And smile, for you have just made the puff pastry that is supposed to be so difficult.

BAKING PASTRY: Cut rolled out dough into three lengthwise strips, 4 inches wide. Fold each in thirds and place on an ungreased cookie sheet and unfold into original length. With a fork, prick the top of each. Refrigerate for 30 minutes. Bake at 400 degrees for 50 to 55 minutes. Cool on rack.

Split each piece lengthwise into 2 strips.

MAKE THE FILLING: Scald the milk. Into the egg yolks, beaten well with granulated sugar, stir in ½ cup flour and milk. Heat all in a saucepan, stirring until thick. Add vanilla. Refrigerate.

Continued on next page

COMPLETING THE NAPOLEONS: About 1 hour before serving: Stir confectioners sugar well with 1 tablespoon water for icing. Over warm water, melt chocolate with 1 teaspoon water and corn syrup while stirring, for glaze.

Complete the top strip first. Ice the strip. Then with the glaze, make crosswise, zigzag lines about ½ inch apart from one end to the other; next, with tip of spatula, make lengthwise zigzag lines ½ inch apart. Set aside.

Cover second strip with half of filling. On it place third strip. Cover this with rest of filling. Top with glazed, iced strip.

Just before serving, cut the Napoleon into 8 equal pieces. This is the hardest part. You must use a very sharp knife and have lots of patience. DELICIOUS.

FRENCH PINEAPPLE DESSERT

Serves 8 to 12

1 pound vanilla wafers
½ cup butter
2 cups powdered sugar
4 eggs
½ pint whipping cream
1 cup pecans
1 cup crushed pineapple
1 small bottle maraschino cherries

Crush wafers and put half of crumbs in a 9 x 13 inch pan. Cream butter with powdered sugar. Add eggs one at a time. Beat well. Pour mixture over wafer crumbs and smooth out. Whip cream. Drain pineapple. Chop cherries and nuts. Mix fruit and nuts with cream and pour over sugar and egg mixture. Sprinkle wafer crumbs over top.

Refrigerate for 24 hours. Serve in squares.

BOBBIE'S PEARS ELLE HELENE

3 cups water
2 cups sugar
1 tablespoon vanilla
8 pears

Boil 3 cups water, sugar, and vanilla for at least 5 minutes. Then peel, halve, and core pears. Add them to the hot syrup and simmer until tender.

This is a very bland dessert plain. It is great served with a scoop of vanilla ice cream and pass chocolate sauce to spoon over the pears.

Mrs. Everett Crudup

KIRSCH TORTE

Serves 10 to 12

1½ cups Jelly Filling*
2 Meringue Layers*
1 (9″) Sponge Cake*
Kirsch Solution*
Buttercream Frosting*
⅓ cup chopped toasted almonds
Red jelly (optional)
***instructions given for preparation**

Spread ½ of the filling on one of the meringue layers. Put the sponge cake on top. Pour the Kirsch solution over the sponge cake. Spread the remaining jelly filling over the sponge cake and top with the second meringue layer. Frost the torte with the buttercream frosting over the top and around the sides. Cover the sides of the torte with the chopped almonds. If desired, make a design on top of the torte with the red jelly that has been well beaten. Note: This torte tastes best if made at least 24 hours before serving. Makes 10 to 12 servings.

SPONGE CAKE:

4 eggs
¾ cup granulated sugar
½ teaspoon baking powder
¾ cup sifted cake flour
¼ teaspoon salt

Preheat oven to 325 degrees. Place the eggs and sugar in a bowl and warm very gently over warm water, stirring occasionally to prevent drying. When the mixture is lukewarm, beat with an electric mixer til very thick and pale lemon colored. Sift together the baking powder, flour, and salt and fold into the egg mixture. Turn into a 9″ springform pan that has been lightly greased and floured on the bottom only. Bake 50 to 60 minutes, or until the cake rebounds to the touch when pressed gently in the center. Turn upside down in the pan to cool.

MERINGUE LAYERS:

3 egg whites
⅛ teaspoon cream of tartar
⅞ cup superfine granulated sugar
1 tablespoon vanilla sugar (see note)
1 cup finely ground almonds

Preheat oven to 250 or 275 degrees. Beat the egg whites and cream of tartar til the mixture forms peaks. Gradually beat in the sugar, a tablespoon at a time, mixed with the vanilla sugar, until all graininess disappears from the mixture. Fold in the nuts. Turn the mixture into 2 (9 inch) greased Teflon-lined pans, preferably lined on the bottom with a layer of parchment paper. Bake 1 hour. Turn oven off and leave layers in oven with the door closed for another hour.

Cool on rack.

continued on next page

NOTE: Vanilla sugar is available in the spice section of most specialty stores. Do not attempt to make these layers on a damp or humid day.

JELLY FILLING:

3 tablespoons cornstarch
½ cup granulated sugar
1 cup milk
4 tablespoons red currant jelly
¾ cup butter
2 drops red food coloring (optional)

Blend together the cornstarch, sugar and ¼ cup of the milk. Heat the remaining milk to boiling. Remove from the heat and add to the above mixture. Bring the mixture to a boil once, stirring. Remove from heat and add the jelly. Cool to barely lukewarm. Blend the butter until creamy. Add the jelly mixture to the butter a tablespoon at the time, blending continuously. If a deeper color is desired, add the food coloring. Refrigerate until spread consistency is reached.

KIRSCH SOLUTION:

6 tablespoons water
3 tablespoons granulated sugar
6 tablespoons Kirsch

Bring the water and sugar to a boil. Stir until sugar is dissolved. Cool, then stir in the Kirsch.

BUTTERCREAM FROSTING:

⅔ cup granulated sugar
⅓ cup water
⅛ teaspoon cream of tartar
5 egg yolks
1 cup soft butter
1 teaspoon vanilla extract

Combine the sugar, water and cream of tartar in a small saucepan. Bring to a boil, stirring until the sugar dissolves. Continue to beat without stirring until mixture registers 238 or 240 degrees on a candy thermometer or forms a soft ball in cold water.

Beat the egg yolks until very thick and light. Pour the hot syrup in a fine stream into the egg yolks, beating all the time. Beat until the mixture starts to thicken. Cool to room temperature, then beat in butter and vanilla. Chill until firm enough to spread.

SPANISH WINDTORTE

One of the most fragile, tender and delicate of desserts.

12 egg whites, at room temperature
1/8 teaspoon salt
3/4 teaspoon cream of tartar
3 cups superfine granulated sugar
3 tablespoons confectioners sugar
1 quart strawberries
4 cups heavy cream, whipped
Parchment paper or unglazed brown paper

Preheat oven to 250 degrees.

Place 8 of the egg whites in large mixer bowl. Add half the salt. Beat until frothy, add 1/2 teaspoon cream of tartar. Continue to beat and gradually add a tablespoon at a time, 1 3/4 cup of superfine sugar. Beat until smooth and glossy and there is no hint of graininess when the mixture is felt with the fingers. Fold in 1/4 cup more of the superfine sugar.

DIRECTIONS: You are going to make 5 eight inch circles of meringue on the parchment paper.

1. Using a piping bag fitted with #8 plain tube, start in center of circle and make a snail-like pattern going round and round until completely covered.
2. On next 3 circles, make a ring of piped meringue, two layers high round the outside edge. These will form the sides for the cake.
3. On the last circle, using a No. 6 star tube, pipe the meringue into a fairly thick single layer ring around the edge. Fill the center with crisscrossed lattice work substantial enough to enable this layer to be lifted off and used for top of cake.
4. Bake all 5 circles of meringue for 2 to 3 hours until crisp but having no color.

TO COMPLETE: Beat the remaining 4 egg whites with other half of salt until frothy. Add remaining cream of tartar and beat until peaks form. Gradually add 3/4 cup of sugar, until smooth and glossy. Add remaining sugar.

1. Place solid meringue circle on serving platter. Dot around the edges with the fresh meringue and put on the first ring. Dot the top of this ring and position the second ring. Repeat with the third.
2. With a spatula, use meringue to frost all around the outside of the cake shell to make a smooth surface. Using the decorating bag and #6 star tube, decorate the cake around the bottom and on sides. Bake at 200 degrees for several hours or overnight.

Continued on next page

TO SERVE: Combine whipped cream with confectioners sugar and strawberries, sliced, except for a few left whole to use for garnish. Pile strawberries into the cake shell very carefully. Top with the lattice meringue top and garnish with whole strawberries.

NOTE: For best results, do not attempt on a damp or humid day. If baked meringue breaks, mend it together with unbaked meringue. If you don't have decorator tubes, ad-lib with a spoon.

JANE ELLEN'S PECAN TORTE

1/3 pound sifted dark brown sugar, packed
1/3 pound confectioners sugar, sifted
1 whole egg
1/3 pound softened butter
1/3 teaspoon vanilla
1/6 quart chopped pecans
5 ounces coconut macaroons, crumbled (you can add 1 can flaked coconut to plain macaroons for the same or similar result)

Mix well and refrigerate. When hardened, roll into logs that are 2½ inches in diameter. Wrap in foil. Freeze. Slice to serve.

Garnish with one scoop of vanilla ice cream and a cherry.

It's so good, you should triple the recipe.

Keeps indefinitely, however, it's too good to last long.

Mrs. Woodie Davis

FROZEN RASPBERRY PIE

Serves 8

1 stick soft butter (½ cup)
¼ cup brown sugar
1 cup all purpose flour
½ cup chopped almonds
10 ounces frozen raspberries
1 cup sugar
3 unbeaten egg whites
1 cup whipping cream

Mix and spread first four ingredients in an 8 inch square pan and bake at 400 degrees for 15 minutes. Cool, crumble and press into pie pan.

Beat next three ingredients at high speed for 15 minutes. Fold in whipped cream. Pour into pie shell and freeze overnight.

ENGLISH TRIFLE

Serves 8 to 10

2 cups custard sauce
1 teaspoon unflavored gelatin
2 dozen ladyfingers or 1 layer of sponge cake cut in fingers, divided
1 cup strawberry jelly or jam, divided
Rind of 1 lemon, grated and divided
1 cup dry sherry
3 tablespoons brandy
Fresh fruits in season (strawberries, bananas, blueberries, peaches)
1 dozen macaroons, crushed
2 cups heavy cream, whipped
½ cup slivered almonds, toasted

CUSTARD SAUCE:
1½ tablespoons cornstarch
2 cups light cream
4 egg yolks
½ cup sugar
1 teaspoon vanilla

Dissolve cornstarch in ¼ cup cream. Beat yolks until light, then combine with cornstarch. Heat remaining cream, taking care not to boil, and add sugar. Pour 1 cup hot cream and sugar over egg mixture, stirring constantly.

Return cream to low heat, stir in egg-cream mixture, and continue to stir and cook 5 minutes until sauce is slightly thickened. Add vanilla, blend thoroughly, and cool.

DIRECTIONS FOR PUTTING TRIFLE TOGETHER: Prepare custard sauce. Add 1 teaspoon unflavored gelatin, softened, to custard while cooking, if desired.

Coat ½ of the ladyfingers with ½ cup strawberry jelly or jam, place in the bottom of a crystal bowl 8 inches in diameter and 3½ inches deep and sprinkle with ½ of the lemon rind.

Sprinkle liberally with ½ cup sherry and half of the brandy.

Cover with a layer of half the fresh fruit and half the macaroons. Allow to set about an hour.

Pour half of the custard sauce over the top and then repeat layers of ladyfingers, jam, rind, sherry, brandy, fruit and remaining macaroons. Repeat custard layer. Chill.

Just before serving, top with whipped cream and slivered almonds.

HEAVENLY

FROZEN STRAWBERRY SQUARES

Serves 12 to 16

CRUMBLE:

1 cup flour
¼ cup brown sugar
½ cup chopped pecans
½ cup butter, melted

Melt butter and stir into other ingredients. Place in shallow pan. Bake at 325 degrees until brown. Stir occasionally. Sprinkle ⅔ of this mix into a 9 x 13 inch pyrex dish.

FILLING:

2 egg whites
1 cup sugar
2 tablespoons lemon juice
2 cups sliced fresh strawberries or 1 box frozen

Put all filling mix in bowl and beat with electric mixer rapidly for 10 minutes. Then fold in ½ pint of whipped cream. Place filling mix on top of crumbs in pyrex dish. Sprinkle remaining crumbs on top and freeze.

TO SERVE: Cut in squares.

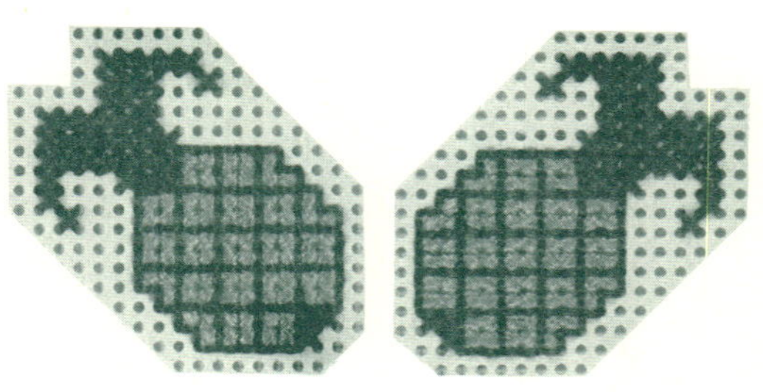

CHOCOLATE FONDUE

Serve at a morning coffee, or a cocktail party.

Yield: 1½ cups sauce

2 tablespoons honey or light corn syrup
½ cup half and half cream
1 (9 ounce) bar of chocolate
¼ cup finely chopped toasted almonds (optional)
1 teaspoon vanilla
2 tablespoons cointreau liqueur

Heat honey or corn syrup with cream over hot water in a double boiler. Add chocolate broken in pieces. Heat, stirring until chocolate is melted and mixture is smooth. Blend in vanilla and cointreau. You may add almonds, if desired.

Serve in a small chafing dish over hot water or in a fondue pot over very low heat.

HAVE READY ON A TRAY: Bite size pieces of cantaloupe, whole strawberries, pieces of banana, bites of cake, marshmallows or anything else you might like.

The sauce recipe may be doubled or tripled.

HELPFUL HINTS ABOUT BAKING

1. READ RECIPE ALL THE WAY THROUGH BEFORE BEGINNING.
2. Always preheat the oven unless recipe specifies doing it otherwise.
3. Use the kind of baking pan specified.
4. To grease pans, be sure to use solid shortening such as Crisco, not oil, butter, or margarine, unless specified in recipe.
5. To flour pans, grease first, dust lightly with flour, and then turn pan over and tap off the excess.
6. Assemble all the ingredients called for, making no substitutions. Let refrigerated ingredients come to room temperature before beginning.
7. Always sift cake flour before measuring.
8. Most recipes tell one to cream the shortening. This means to stir, rub against side of bowl with back of spoon, or beat with spoon or electric mixer until the mixture is soft, light, and creamy.
9. Use standard measuring tools.

GENERAL RULES FOR PUTTING CAKE TOGETHER

After all ingredients are assembled and are at room temperature...

Cream shortening thoroughly, until light and creamy. Add the sugar gradually. Beat until light and fluffy looking. This process might take from 6 to 10 minutes, depending on your type of mixer.

Add eggs one at a time, and beat after each addition only until blended well. If you beat the eggs too much, your cake will be heavy.

Add dry ingredients and liquid ingredients alternately to creamed mixture, beginning and ending with dry ingredients. Beat well after each addition but only until the batter is very smooth. Be sure to scrape sides and bottom of bowl with a rubber spatula several times during the blending process.

Be sure cake pans do not touch each other or the sides of the oven.

Do not open oven door to peek while cakes are baking. Be sure to let minimum baking time be completed before you open oven door. Test the cake for doneness. Use a cake tester or a toothpick or even a broom straw. Insert in center of cake. If it is clean when you take it out, cake is done.

Let cakes cool on wire racks before frosting. Remove from pans after 5 minutes out of the oven.

ALMOND CAKE WITH RASPBERRY SAUCE

Serves 12

ALMOND CAKE:

¾ cup sugar
½ cup unsalted butter, room temperature
8 ounces almond paste
3 eggs
1 tablespoon Kirsch or Triple Sec
¼ teaspoon almond extract
¼ cup all purpose flour
⅓ teaspoon baking powder
Powdered sugar

Preheat oven to 350 degrees. Generously butter and flour an 8 inch round cake pan. Combine sugar, butter, and almond paste in medium mixing bowl and blend well. Beat in eggs, liqueur and almond extract. Add flour and baking powder, beating until just mixed through; do not overbeat. Bake until tester inserted in center of cake comes out clean, about 40 to 50 minutes. Let cool. Invert onto serving platter and dust lightly with powdered sugar.

FOR SAUCE:

1 pint fresh raspberries or 1 (12 ounce) package frozen, and thawed
2 tablespoons sugar if using fresh

Combine raspberries with sugar in processor or blender and puree. Gently press sauce through fine sieve to remove seeds. Serve sauce as an accompaniment to almond cake.

Cut cake in triangular wedges, like slices of pie.

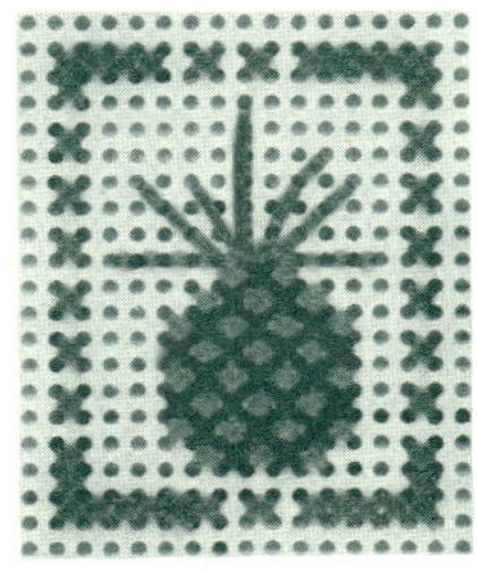

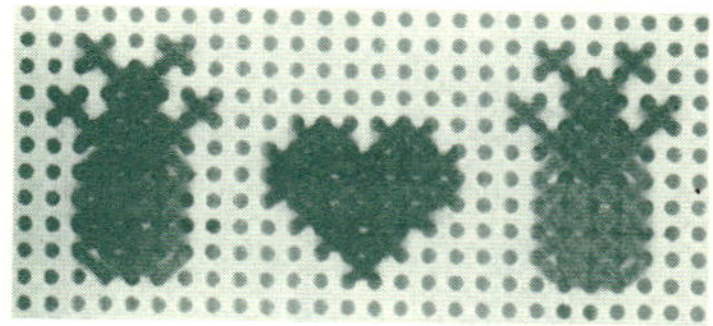

MARCIA'S PORTUGUESE ALMOND CAKE

Serves 8 to 10

1 cup all purpose flour, sifted
¾ cup sugar
½ teaspoon baking powder
½ teaspoon baking soda
¼ teaspoon salt
1 egg
½ cup buttermilk
½ teaspoon vanilla
⅓ cup melted butter, cooled to room temperature
⅔ cup sliced almonds
Hot almond syrup

Preheat oven to 350 degrees.

Sift dry ingredients.

In another bowl, beat egg and buttermilk together until smooth. Stir in melted butter. Add vanilla. Add flour mixture and mix with a spoon until nearly smooth. Turn into a buttered 9 inch springform pan OR a 9 inch square pan. Bake until center of cake springs back when lightly touched, about 35 minutes. Remove from oven.

While cake is hot, cover top with almonds. Slowly pour the hot almond syrup evenly over nuts letting syrup soak into cake. Then broil about 6 inches from heat until amonds are lightly toasted. Cool on rack.

HOT ALMOND SYRUP:

¾ cup sugar
6 tablespoons water
½ teaspoon almond extract

In a 1 quart saucepan, combine the sugar and water. Boil until it reaches 220 degrees on a candy thermometer. Remove from heat. Stir in almond extract. Pour over cake.

NOTE: Recipe may be doubled. You may then use a 13 x 9 inch oblong glass baking dish.

TO SERVE: Cut in squares. This is grand served while warm.

Marcia Via

BANANA SPLIT CAKE

A Fabulous Dish for a Crowd of Young Folks, and others.

2 cups graham cracker crumbs
1 large can crushed pineapple, AND/OR 1 package frozen strawberries, thawed and drained
1 cup nuts and cherries
½ pound margarine
3 cups powdered sugar
2 egg whites
3 or 4 bananas
1 large tub non dairy cream topping

Mix 2 cups crumbs, ¼ pound margarine, one cup powdered sugar and make crust for an 8 x 13 inch pan or glass baking dish.

Pour 1 large can drained crushed pineapple AND/OR drained strawberries over crust. (I use both).

Beat 2 egg whites until stiff, add 2 cups powdered sugar and ¼ pound melted margarine and pour over fruit. Slice 3 or 4 bananas on top.

Mix the topping with the nuts and cherries and pour over the bananas.

Chill for at least 2 hours before serving.

This is a good Pot Luck Supper Dish.

BUNDT CAKE

½ cup plus 2 tablespoons butter
2 cups sugar
5 eggs, separated
2 cups flour
2 teaspoons baking powder
¼ teaspoon salt
1 cup milk
2 teaspoons vanilla extract
2 teaspoons lemon extract

Cream together butter and sugar until fluffy. Beat in 5 egg yolks, one at a time, beating hard after each addition. Sift 2 cups flour with baking powder and salt. Stir flour into butter mixture alternately with milk. Mix in extracts.

Whip 5 egg whites until they hold a definite point and fold them gently into batter.

Pour into a BUTTERED and lightly floured Bundt cake pan and bake cake in a moderate oven at 350 degrees for 45 minutes. Increase heat to 375 degrees for 15 more minutes.

Cool on cake rack.

Sprinkle cake with confectioners sugar before serving.

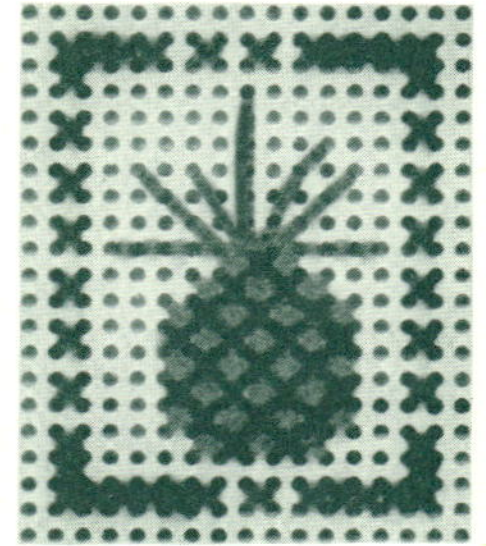

LETA'S CHARLOTTE CAKE

Serves 12 to 16

8 eggs separated (putting 4 yolks in each of 2 bowls)
½ teaspoon cream of tartar
1¼ cups sugar, sifted
1 cup flour, sifted 6 times

Beat egg whites until frothy. Add cream of tartar. Beat until stiff. Add slowly the 1¼ cups sifted sugar. Then add all 4 egg yolks which have been beaten together. Fold in the 1 cup of flour that has been *sifted 6 times.* Bake in an ungreased tube pan in a moderate oven (325 degrees) from 50 to 60 minutes. Turn upside down on rack to cool in pan.

CUSTARD FILLING:
2½ cups milk, scalded
4 egg yolks
1 cup sugar
½ cup flour, sifted
1 tablespoon unflavored gelatin
2 pints cream, whipped

Scald milk. Beat other 4 egg yolks. Add 1 cup sugar and sifted flour. Beat well. Pour scalded milk over egg mixture, stirring until smooth. Cook in a double boiler until thick.

Soak 1 tablespoon gelatin in 2 tablespoons milk. Mix with hot custard and cool. Just before the custard sets, fold in 1 pint of the whipped cream.

Slice the cake into 3 layers with a bread knife. Cover layers with custard. Top layer, too. Refrigerate until firm.

Frost entire cake with whipped cream sweetened a little to taste and flavored with vanilla or almond extract. Can also flavor it with sherry or brandy.

Serves 12 to 16 people.

A fabulous dessert.

Mrs. Alex W. Hulett

MARASCHINO CHERRY CAKE

Preheat oven to 350 degrees. Bake layers 30 to 35 minutes.
Grease and flour 2 nine inch cake pans.

⅔ cup shortening, softened
1½ cups sugar
3 cups sifted cake flour
2½ teaspoons baking powder
1 teaspoon salt
¼ cup cherry juice
¾ cup milk
½ cup chopped pecans
16 maraschino cherries cut in eighths
5 egg whites (⅔ cup) stiffly beaten

Cream shortening and sugar. Stir together the flour, baking powder, and salt. Add to shortening-sugar mix. Blend and mix alternately with cherry juice and milk. Stir in nuts and cherries. Fold in stiffly beaten egg whites.

Pour into prepared pans, bake, and cool.

Frost with cooked white frosting. Add a little cherry juice for color.

Decorate with well drained (and dried off with a paper towel) long stemmed cherries.

EASY TWO EGG CAKE

2 cups flour
2 teaspoons baking powder
¾ teaspoon salt
1¼ cups sugar
1 stick butter (½ cup)
1 tablespoon vanilla
2 eggs, unbeaten
⅔ cups milk

Cream butter, add sugar, then eggs. Alternate dry ingredients with milk. Add vanilla.

Bake in 2 layer cake pans for 25 minutes at 375 degrees.

Frost cake with your favorite frosting.

COCONUT LAYER CAKE

This cake is fantastically light and moist.

Serves 16 to 20

¾ cup shortening
1½ cups sugar
1½ teaspoons vanilla extract
1 teaspoon almond extract
2¼ cups sifted cake flour
2½ teaspoons baking powder
½ teaspoon salt
1 cup milk
6 egg whites

Cream softened shortening and gradually add sugar. This take about 8 minutes. It should be very light in color. Add extracts. Sift flour, baking powder and salt together. Add alternately to butter-sugar mixture with the milk. Be sure to end with flour. Beat after each addition.

ADD EGG WHITES ONE AT A TIME AND BEAT WELL. Place in 3 paper lined and greased 9 inch cake pans. Bake at 300 degrees for 15 to 20 minutes. Cool. You will think the cake is not done, however it is, it is just delicate. Turn out on wire racks.

TO FROST: Spread plenty of coconut icing between the layers, then frost entire cake. Sprinkle freshly grated coconut over top and sides of cake.

Frost with any white icing or use the following:

COCONUT ICING:

2 cups sugar
Freshly grated coconut (you will need 2). Be sure to save the coconut milk
2 egg whites, stiffly beaten
6 large marshmallows, melted
1 teaspoon almond extract

Bring sugar and 1 cup coconut milk to a rolling boil. To the beaten egg whites add ½ the milk mixture, slowly, while beating constantly. Add the marshmallows and keep on beating. Cook remaining milk mixture until it threads (about 238 on candy thermometer). While beating egg white mixture with mixer, add the syrup in a slow thin stream. Fold in ½ the grated coconut. Use the other half to cover top and sides of cake.

NOTE: A coconut cake should be refrigerated the second day.

CHOCOLATE ANGEL FOOD CAKE

My Children's favorite Birthday Cake.

NOTE: If you follow these directions exactly, this cake will never fail.

PREPARATION: Assemble ingredients and utensils needed before you begin.

Use a 10 inch deep tube cake pan and DO NOT GREASE.

Remove eggs from refrigerator and separate. Let stand until at room temperature.

Sift flour once before measuring. Then sift together 5 times, the following:

¾ cup plus 2 tablespoons sifted cake flour
¼ cup cocoa
¾ cup sugar

You must sift the above ingredients 5 times.

Then put into the large bowl of mixmaster:

1½ cups egg whites (11 to 13 whites)
½ teaspoon salt

Beat on No. 10 speed until foamy, about ½ minute.

Add 1½ teaspoons cream of tartar and continue beating on No. 10 speed until whites are stiff and stand in points, about 2½ to 3 minutes. Do not overbeat until dry.

SPRINKLE IN RAPIDLY: 1 cup sifted sugar while beating on No. 8 speed. Beat only until sugar is blended, about 1 minute. Scrape bowl gently toward beaters and up and over with a folding motion. Turn mixer to No. 2 speed. Add 1 teaspoon vanilla extract and 1 teaspoon almond extract.

Sprinkle in sifted flour mixture evenly and quickly. Beat only enough to blend, about 1½ minutes, scraping bowl gently toward beaters with folding motion to blend quickly.

Gently put into tube pan. Carefully cut through the batter with a knife or spatula, going around in a circular motion 6 times. This is to release large air bubbles.

Continued on next page

Bake in a pre-heated oven (375 degrees) for 30 to 35 minutes until done. Remove from oven. Invert pan on rack until cool. Then loosen cake with spatula and remove from pan.

Can be served plain or frosted with chocolate frosting. Use the Butter Icing with both variations a and b. (See Index).

NORMA'S CHOCOLATE ALMOND CAKE

3 squares (3 ounces) unsweetened chocolate
½ cup water
1 cup sour cream
2 cups sifted cake flour
1 teaspoon baking soda
1 teaspoon salt
1½ teaspoons baking powder
⅔ cup butter
⅔ cup firmly packed light brown sugar
1 cup granulated sugar
3 eggs
2 teaspoons vanilla

Melt chocolate with water on low heat. Cool. Add sour cream.

Sift dry ingredients. Cream butter and sugar, and add eggs. Add dry ingredients. Add chocolate-sour cream mixture.

Bake in layers at 350 degrees for 35 minutes. Frost with the following frosting.

NORMA'S CHOCOLATE FROSTING:

Yield: 2½ cups

6 tablespoons butter
1 teaspoon vanilla
2 egg whites
2 to 3 tablespoons milk
⅛ teaspoon salt
1 pound confectioners sugar
3 squares unsweetened chocolate, melted

Cream butter, add salt, vanilla, sugar, and whites. Add chocolate. Beat well. Add milk.

Toast almond slivers about 10 minutes in oven, watching carefully not to burn. Cool.

Frost cake and then stud all over with the almonds.

Very unusual and good.

Mrs. Richard Sessions

GERMAN CHOCOLATE CAKE

1 package (¼ pound) sweet cooking chocolate
½ cup boiling water
1 cup (2 sticks) butter
2 cups sugar
4 egg yolks, unbeaten
1 teaspoon vanilla
2½ cups sifted cake flour
½ teaspoon salt
1 teaspoon soda
1 cup buttermilk
4 egg whites, stiffly beaten

Melt chocolate in ½ cup boiling water. Let cool slightly while mixing other ingredients. Cream butter together with sugar until light and fluffy. Add egg yolks, one at a time, beating well after each addition. Add the melted chocolate with water in which it was melted and the vanilla. Mix well. Sift dry ingredients and add alternately with buttermilk. Beat until batter is smooth and well blended.

Beat the egg whites separately until stiff, then gently fold into the cake batter.

Turn into three 8 or 9 inch layer cake pans, greased and floured.

Bake at 350 degrees for 35 to 40 minutes. Cool for 10 minutes in pans, then turn out on racks to finish cooling.

Frost with Coconut Pecan Frosting.

COCONUT PECAN FROSTING:

1 cup evaporated milk or half and half cream
1 cup sugar
3 egg yolks
1 stick (½ cup) butter
1 teaspoon vanilla
1 to 1⅓ cup flaked coconut
1 cup chopped pecans

Combine milk or cream, sugar, egg yolks, butter, and vanilla in a sauce pan. Cook, stirring constantly, over medium heat until mixture thickens, about 12 minutes. Remove from heat, add coconut and pecans.

Beat until frosting cools and is of spreading consistency.

Makes enough to cover the tops of three layers. Leave sides unfrosted. Frosting will sort of drizzle down the sides automatically.

DIVINE CHOCOLATE LAYER CAKE

2 eggs
2 cups sugar
2 cups buttermilk
2 teaspoons soda
2 teaspoons vanilla
4 squares bitter chocolate
2½ cups flour
1 stick butter or margarine (½ cup)
½ teaspoon salt

Beat eggs with buttermilk and add vanilla. Sift dry ingredients and add to egg mixture, then add butter and chocolate which have been melted together in a small double boiler. Beat thoroughly.

Pour into 2 greased 9 inch cake pans and bake about 30 minutes in a 350 degree oven.

Frost with the following icing:

CHOCOLATE ICING:
1 pound confectioners sugar
½ cup evaporated milk
2 teaspoons vanilla
4 squares bitter chocolate
1 stick butter (½ cup)

Add milk and vanilla to sifted sugar. Melt chocolate and butter together and add to first mixture. If icing is not thick enough to spread nicely, add confectioners sugar.

CHOCOLATE POUND CAKE

1 cup butter
1 cup shortening
3 cups sugar
5 eggs
2½ cups cake flour
½ cup cocoa
½ teaspoon baking powder
1 teaspoon vanilla
1 cup milk

Cream butter and shortening. Add sugar and mix well. Add eggs one at a time and half of the dry ingredients. Add milk and the remainder of the dry ingredients. Add vanilla and beat well.

Pour into tube pan. Bake at 350 degrees for 1 hour and 15 minutes. Permit cake to cool at least an hour before removing from pan.

FROSTING:
1 box confectioners sugar
½ cup cocoa
2½ tablespoons margarine, softened
½ cup warm evaporated milk
1 teaspoon vanilla and ½ teaspoon almond extracts
1 tablespoon shortening, heaping

Cream margarine, shortening and vanilla together. Add confectioners sugar and cocoa. Add warm milk until creamy and smooth. Swirl onto cooled cake.

Recipe makes enough frosting to cover entire cake. Half a recipe is perfect to swirl over the top.

FUDGE CAKE

1 stick butter (½ cup)
2 eggs
2 tablespoons cocoa
1 cup sugar
¾ cup flour
1 cup nuts
Pinch salt

Melt butter and cocoa. Beat eggs and sugar together. Pour butter and cocoa into eggs and sugar. Add flour and chopped nuts. Bake for about 20 minutes.

Cover top of hot cake with marshmallows (the little ones).

Frost with Dot Chocolate Frosting. (See Index).

TO SERVE: Cut in small squares. This is very rich and a small piece will be plenty.

LANELL'S CHOCOLATE CAKE

Delicious and very easy

2 cups sugar
2 cups flour
4 tablespoons cocoa

Melt together 1 stick butter, 1 stick margarine and 1 cup water. Heat liquids to the boiling point and pour over dry mix.

Add the following:

½ cup buttermilk
2 beaten eggs
1 teaspoon soda
1 teaspoon vanilla

Mix all well. Batter looks unusually thin for a cake batter.

Bake for 25 minutes at 400 degrees in pan that measures 13 x 9 x 2 inches.

FROSTING:
1 stick melted butter (½ cup)
1 box powdered sugar
4 tablespoons cocoa
3 to 6 tablespoons milk
1 teaspoon vanilla

Mix and pour over hot cake that is still in pan. Cut in squares and serve.

Mrs. H. Wingfield Glover

TUNNEL O FUDGE CAKE

1 cup butter
6 eggs
2 cups self-rising flour
1½ cups sugar
1 package 2 layer double Dutch Fudge Frosting Mix
2 cups chopped pecans

Cream butter, add eggs, add flour, sugar, frosting and nuts. Pour into a greased Bundt cake pan.

Bake at 350 degrees for 65 to 70 minutes. Cool for 2 hours before removing from pan.

CHOCOLATE ROLL CAKE

6 eggs, separated
1 cup confectioners sugar
3 heaping tablespoons cocoa
2 tablespoons plain flour
Pinch of salt

Beat egg yolks about 3 minutes at high speed until lemon colored. Add sugar, cocoa, and flour. Beat about 5 minutes. Fold in beaten whites.

Grease and line with waxed paper a 11 x 15 inch jelly roll pan. Bake at 350 degrees about 12 minutes.

Take out on a barely damp cloth that has been sprinkled with powdered sugar. Remove waxed paper gently. Roll cake back up in the towel and set aside.

Whip 1 pint cream, 1½ tablespoons vanilla, 2 tablespoons sugar, until very stiff. Spread on cake evenly. Then roll up like a jelly roll. If it looks funny and messy, don't worry because you will cover it with frosting.

Frost with more whipped cream that has been flavored with cream de cocoa, or just plain sweetened whipped cream, or just sift powdered sugar over the top and sides. Let your imagination run wild. Can garnish with shaved semisweet chocolate, or fresh strawberries and mint leaves.

TO SERVE: Slice cake in about inch slices. Pass a pitcher of warm chocolate sauce.

CHOCOLATE SAUCE FOR CHOCOLATE ROLL CAKE:

2 squares chocolate
2 tablespoons butter
⅔ cup sugar
1 cup cream
½ teaspoon vanilla

Melt butter and chocolate in saucepan. Add sugar and stir until dissolved. Add cream and cook slowly, stirring until smooth and thick. Remove from heat and add vanilla. Yields approximately 2 cups of sauce.

Serve warm. Let each guest drizzle warm chocolate sauce over slice of cake.

THIS IS DIVINE.

VARIATION: Spread softened vanilla ice cream on cake. Roll up and freeze.

WHITE CHOCOLATE CAKE

This is a heavenly concoction.

1 cup butter, softened
2 cups sugar
4 eggs, separated
1 teaspoon vanilla
¼ pound white chocolate or almond bark, melted
2½ cups cake flour
1 teaspoon baking powder
1 cup buttermilk
1 cup chopped pecans
1 cup flaked coconut

Cream butter and sugar. Beat in egg yolks; add vanilla and melted chocolate. Sift together flour and baking powder; add to the chocolate mixture alternately with buttermilk. Fold in stiffly beaten egg whites. Stir in pecans and coconut.

Bake in three 9 inch round cake pans which have been greased and floured.

Bake at 350 degrees for 30 minutes. Cool on cake racks.

Frost with Caramel Frosting. (See Index).

LEMON CAKE

¾ cup butter or margarine
1¼ cups sugar
8 egg yolks
2½ cups cake flour
3 teaspoons baking powder
¼ teaspoon salt
¾ cup milk
1 teaspoon vanilla
1 teaspoon grated lemon rind
1 teaspoon lemon juice

Preheat oven to 325 degrees.

Cream butter and sugar until light and fluffy.

In separate bowl beat egg yolks until light and lemon colored. Blend into butter mixture.

Sift together dry ingredients. Then sift three more times. Add sifted ingredients in thirds, alternating with ¾ cup milk. Beat batter thoroughly after each addition. Add vanilla, lemon rind, and juice. Beat 2 minutes.

Bake in a greased Bundt pan for 1 hour or until a cake tester or straw inserted in center comes out clean.

FRUITCAKE DOBBINS STYLE

Recipe makes 2 large round cakes made in tube pans. We make these the first part of November each year. One cake is used for Thanksgiving; the other for Christmas.

The "cutting up" of the fruit is a Family Affair, using scissors. We usually cut the fruit one evening and I then bake the cakes within the next day or so.

To mix the fruit, I use the top of a large plastic cake cover. It works wonders although it certainly was not intended for this purpose.

FRUITCAKE INGREDIENTS:

2 pounds candied red cherries
2 pounds crystallized pineapple, using white and green
1 pound mixed, already cut candied fruit
4 ounces crystallized lemon peel
4 ounces crystallized orange peel
4 ounces crystallized citron
2 cups raisins (optional)
4 cups chopped pecans
8 ounces English walnuts, chopped
8 ounces or more sliced almonds
1 cup Damson plum jelly or jam
½ cup honey
1 dozen large eggs
1 pound butter
2 cups granulated sugar
4 cups flour
1 ounce lemon extract
1 ounce almond extract
2 cups bourbon whiskey
1 cup cocktail sherry or brandy
½ teaspoon ground cloves
½ teaspoon ground allspice
1 teaspoon ground cinnamon
1 teaspoon ground nutmeg

DIRECTIONS: Cut up fruit and set aside. Cut up nuts and set aside. Marinate the fruit in the bourbon and sherry overnight in a covered container in refrigerator.

Line pans with brown wrapping paper that has been greased on both sides with solid shortening. Do a thorough job on this.

MAKE BATTER: Separate eggs. Cream butter and sugar in large bowl of mixmaster. Add beaten yolks and flour alternately. Beat well. Add spices, extracts, jam and honey. Beat egg whites stiff but not dry. Fold into the flour mixture.

Pour fruit that has been marinating into the huge container. Add the chopped nuts and mix well with your hands. Pour in the batter. Again, with your hands, mix well, until all is blended together.

continued on next page

NOTE: Be sure to remove all jewelry on hands, and wash hands again thoroughly before mixing the fruitcake.

Pour mixture into prepared pans. I use a measuring cup to distribute evenly.

Bake for 3 or 4 hours at 250 degrees in greased, paper lined pans. Sometimes you can get 2 tube pans and 1 small loaf from this batter. When cakes are done, cool completely. Wrap each cooled cake in aluminum foil and store in air tight containers.

Keeps well. However, if at any time the cakes seem too dry, just saturate with a little more bourbon and re-wrap.

MILKY WAY CAKE

15 ounces Milky Way candy bars (8)
½ cup melted butter
1½ cups sugar
½ cup softened butter
4 eggs
1 teaspoon vanilla extract
1¼ cups buttermlk
½ teaspoon soda
3 cups flour
1 cup chopped pecans

Combine candy bars and ½ cup melted butter in saucepan. Place over low heat until candy melts. Cream sugar and butter. Add eggs one at a time and beat well. Add vanilla. Mix buttermilk and soda together and add to butter mixture alternately with the flour. Beat well. Add candy and nuts. Pour batter into a greased and floured 10 inch tube pan. Bake at 325 degrees for 1 hour and 20 minutes. Let cool in pan for 1 hour.

MILK CHOCOLATE FROSTING:
2 cups sugar
1 cup evaporated milk
½ cup melted butter
1 package (6 ounce) semisweet chocolate bits
1 cup marshmallow creme
Milk

Combine sugar, milk, and butter in heavy saucepan. Cook over medium heat until a soft ball forms when a small amount is dropped in cold water. Remove from heat. Add chocolate and marshmallow creme and stir until melted.

Frost cake.

(Cake has texture of a pound cake—It is very rich. Serve small, thin slices).

PLAIN POUND CAKE

½ pound butter
2 cups sugar
6 eggs
1 teaspoon vanilla
2 cups flour
1½ teaspoons mace
1 teaspoon salt

Cream butter and sugar well. Add eggs one at a time. Beat well each time. Add dry ingredients and vanilla. Bake for 1 hour at 300 degrees in a tube pan.

Test for doneness with straw or cake tester. Sometimes an additional 10 minutes cooking time is needed.

LORD BALTIMORE CAKE
(A gold cake)

2 cups sifted cake flour
2½ teaspoons baking powder
¾ teaspoon salt
1 cup sugar
⅓ cup soft shortening
4 egg yolks
1 teaspoon vanilla
1 cup milk
White Mountain Cream Frosting
Lord Baltimore Filling

Grease two 9 x 1½ inch layer cake pans, dust with flour, and tap out any excess.

Sift flour, baking powder, and salt. Set aside.

Beat sugar, shortening, egg yolks, and vanilla in large bowl of mixer at high speed 3 minutes. Remove bowl from mixer.

Stir in flour mixture alternately with milk, beating after each addition until batter is smooth. Pour batter into prepared pans.

Bake in moderate oven (350 degrees) for 30 minutes or until centers spring back when lightly pressed with fingertip. Cool layers in pans on wire racks 10 minutes. Loosen around edges with a knife and turn out onto wire racks and cool completely. Put layers together with Lord Baltimore Filling. Frost side and top with remaining White Mountain Cream Frosting. Decorate with pecan halves and cherry halves.

LORD BALTIMORE FILLING:
(Makes enough to fill two 9 inch layers)

½ cup flaked toasted coconut
½ cup finely chopped pecans
⅓ cup chopped candied red cherries
2 teaspoons grated orange rind
1 teaspoon almond extract
1½ cups White Mountain Cream Frosting

Combine coconut, pecans, cherries, orange rind, and almond extract in a medium sized bowl. Fold in the White Mountain Cream Frosting. Spread between layers of the Lord Baltimore Cake.

LADY BALTIMORE CAKE

(A silver cake)

2⅔ cups sifted cake flour
1½ cups sugar
4 teaspoons baking powder
1 teaspoon salt
⅔ cup soft shortening
1¼ cups milk
1 teaspoon vanilla
4 egg whites
White Mountain Cream Frosting tinted pink with red food coloring
Lady Baltimore Filling

Grease bottoms of two 9 x 1½ inch layer cake pans. Line pans with wax paper, grease and flour paper and tap out the excess flour. (Lining pans makes it easier to remove delicate cake).

Combine flour, sugar, baking powder, salt, shortening, ¾ cup milk, and vanilla in the large bowl of mixer. Beat at low speed until blended, then beat at high speed for 2 minutes. Add remaining ½ cup milk and egg whites; continue beating at high speed, scraping down side of bowl often, 2 minutes longer; pour batter into pans.

Bake in 350 degree oven for 30 minutes or until centers spring back when lightly pressed with fingertip. Cool layers in pans on wire racks 10 minutes. Loosen around edges with a knife and turn out onto wire racks. Remove waxed paper and cool completely.

Put layers together with Lady Baltimore Filling. Frost side and top with pink Mountain Cream Frosting. Decorate with maraschino cherry halves and pecan halves.

LADY BALTIMORE FILLING:

(Enough filling for two 9 inch layers)

½ cup finely chopped pecans
⅓ cup cut up dried figs
⅓ cup chopped raisins
3 tablespoons chopped maraschino cherries
2 teaspoons grated orange rind
1½ cups pink Mountain Cream Frosting

Combine pecans, figs, raisins, cherries, and orange rind in a medium size bowl and toss to mix well. Fold in the pink Mountain Cream Frosting until well blended.

continued on next page

WHITE MOUNTAIN CREAM FROSTING:
(For Lady Baltimore Cake)
(For Lord Baltimore Cake)
Makes enough to fill and frost two 9 inch layers.

1 cup sugar
⅓ cup light corn syrup
¼ cup water
¼ teaspoon salt
4 egg whites
⅛ teaspoon cream of tartar
½ teaspoon vanilla

Combine sugar, corn syrup, water, and salt in a small saucepan; cover. Heat to boiling; uncover; boil gently until mixture registers 242 degrees on a candy thermometer or until a small amount of the hot syrup falls threadlike from a spoon.

While syrup cooks, beat egg whites with cream of tartar in a large bowl until stiff peaks form when beaters are removed. Pour hot syrup onto egg whites in a very thin stream, beating all the time at high speed until frosting is stiff and glossy. Beat in vanilla.

POPPY SEED CAKE

½ cup poppy seeds
½ cup milk
2 cups sifted cake flour
3 teaspoons double-acting baking powder
1 teaspoon salt
3 egg whites
¼ cup margarine
1¼ cups sugar
½ cup heavy cream
1 teaspoon vanilla

Soak poppy seeds in ½ cup milk. Sift together the flour, baking powder and salt. Beat the egg whites until stiff but not dry.

Cream margarine and add sugar, gradually, creaming well. Combine cream with vanilla and add alternately with dry ingredients to the sugar-margarine mixture, beginning and ending with dry ingredients. Blend thoroughly after each addition, using low speed of mixer. Add poppy seed-milk mixture. Fold in beaten whites gently but thoroughly. Pour into 2 well-greased and lightly floured 8 inch round layer cake pans.

Bake in moderate oven at 375 degrees for 25 to 30 minutes. Cool, spread filling between layers and frost. Use a half recipe of the Charlotte Cake Custard Filling (see Index). Frost with whipped cream. Sprinkle poppy seeds lightly on top. Refrigerate.

LETA'S SOUR CREAM POUND CAKE

One of our favorites.

½ pound butter
3 cups sugar, sifted
1 teaspoon vanilla
6 large eggs or 7 to 8 small ones
¼ teaspoon soda
3 cups all-purpose flour, sifted
1 teaspoon mace (optional)
½ pint sour cream

Blend together well the butter, sugar, and vanilla until nice and creamy. Add the eggs one at a time, blending well after each addition. Add, sifted together, the soda, sifted flour and mace. Alternate dry ingredients with ½ pint sour cream.

Bake in a 325 degree oven for 1 hour in a Bundt pan or a tube pan. Don't forget to grease and flour pan.

Fabulous, served hot, right out of the oven.

SPICE CAKE

¾ cup dark brown sugar
1 cup white sugar
¾ cup shortening
3 eggs
1 cup buttermilk
2¼ cups plain flour
1 teaspoon baking powder
1 teaspoon vanilla
¾ teaspoon soda
¼ teaspoon salt
¾ teaspoon ground cloves
¾ teaspoon ground cinnamon
¾ teaspoon ground allspice
Dash black pepper

Bake in layer pans in a 350 degree oven, for about 25 minutes.

Frost with the following:

BROWN SUGAR FROSTING:

2 egg whites
⅓ cup cold water
1½ cups brown sugar
1 teaspoon vanilla

Cook 7 minutes or until stiff in a double boiler, beating constantly. Cover each layer with chopped walnuts.

Especially good in the Fall of the year.

STRAWBERRY CAKE

One of a very few "BOX" cakes I use. This one is unusually good and refreshing.

1 box white cake mix

ADD:
1 tablespoon sifted flour
1 package strawberry gelatin
¾ cup vegetable oil

Mix dry ingredients. Add oil, then add ½ cup water. Add ½ cup frozen strawberries into the above mix, saving remainder for filling. Mix well. Then add 4 whole eggs, one at a time. Beat and put into three 8 inch layer cake pans. Bake at 350 degrees for 25 to 30 minutes.

FILLING:
1 stick margarine
1 box powdered sugar
Pinch salt

Mix well. Add strawberries slowly until mix is of consistency to spread. Spread between layers and on top.

FROSTING: Frost cake with whipped cream sweetened with sugar to taste. Garnish with fresh whole strawberries and mint sprigs.

JOY'S VIRGINIA TIPSY CAKE

5 egg yolks
2 cups sugar
2 cups flour
5 teaspoons baking powder
½ cup cold water
1 teaspoon vanilla
5 egg whites
½ pound blanched almonds
1 pint sherry (use a good dry sherry)

Beat egg yolks. Add sugar, gradually. Sift flour and baking powder together. Add to egg yolk mixture. Stir in cold water and vanilla. Lastly fold in stiffly beaten egg whites. Pour batter into ungreased tube pan. Bake at 350 degrees for 50 to 60 minutes. Invert pan on wire rack and cool. Stick almonds all over top of cake. Pour sherry over cake and let stand overnight.

DIVINE.

Mrs. Gerald Mitchell

TREASURE COFFEE CAKE

Great for morning coffee at a ladies meeting.

1 cup butter
1 cup white granulated sugar
2 whole eggs
2 teaspoons vanilla
1 cup sour cream
Dash salt
2 cups cake flour
1 teaspoon baking powder
1 teaspoon soda

Cream butter, sugar, vanilla, eggs, and salt. Stir together flour, baking powder, and soda. Add half the flour mixture and half of the sour cream to butter mixture. Beat one minute. Then add rest of both and beat one minute more.

Grease and flour a Bundt cake pan. Spread half of the batter in pan. Mix icing mixture and sprinkle half on batter. Then carefully pour and spread remaining cake batter on top of this. Sprinkle remaining icing mixture on top. Bake in 350 degree oven for 35 to 40 minutes.

CRUMB ICING MIX:

½ cup firmly packed dark brown sugar
¼ cup white sugar
1 teaspoon ground cinnamon
1 cup chopped pecans

BUTTER ICING

This is very versatile...

½ cup butter
¼ teaspoon salt
2½ cups sifted confectioners sugar
3 or 4 tablespoons milk
1 teaspoon vanilla

Cream butter, add salt and sugar. Add milk as needed and flavoring. Beat until light and fluffy. Spread on cake.

VARIATIONS:

a. 2 tablespoons instant coffee (liquid)
b. 2 squares bitter chocolate, melted
c. Almond extract
d. Orange juice instead of milk and 2 teaspoons grated orange peel
e. Lemon juice instead of milk and 2 teaspoons grated lemon peel.

AUNT ALINE'S FABULOUS CARAMEL ICING

Place in a large sauce pan:

2½ cups sugar
¾ cups milk

Put ½ cup additional sugar in a small heavy skillet to caramelize.

START COOKING BOTH OF THESE AT THE SAME TIME. They need to remain at the same temperature for proper blending.

When sugar is melted and a light brown color (caramel), add it very very slowly to the hot milk mixture. This takes about 10 minutes to get the right color. The mixture will probably look lumpy but this condition will correct itself. Cook over medium heat. Insert candy thermometer at this point. When mixture bubbles up and reaches the soft ball stage on the thermometer, remove from heat. Add ½ stick butter and 1 teaspoon vanilla. Let cool just a little. Then beat with electric mixer until right consistency to spread.

Contrary to popular opinion, this is not difficult, it's just tedious. Pay close attention to what you are doing and you are bound to be successful.

Mrs. Marvin Koen

SEVEN MINUTE WHITE ICING

(Sufficient for the tops and sides of two 9 inch layers)

Place in the top of a double boiler and beat until thoroughly blended:

2 unbeaten egg whites
1½ cups sugar
5 tablespoons cold water
¼ teaspoon cream of tartar
1½ teaspoons light corn syrup

Place these ingredients over rapidly boiling water. Beat them constantly with a rotary beater or with a wire whisk for 7 minutes. You may also use your electric mixer. After the 7 minutes, remove the icing from the heat. Add 1 teaspoon vanilla. Continue beating until the icing is the right consistency to spread. Then you must work very quickly. Put the layers together with frosting. Secure with toothpicks. Then frost the sides first, then the top. Be sure to give the top a swirly look, not just plain and smooth.

This is a fluffy delicious icing that has never failed for me.

WHITE BIRTHDAY CAKE ICING

Crusty outside and soft inside.

4½ cups sugar
1 cup water
6 tablespoons light corn syrup
6 egg whites, beaten stiff
⅓ cup confectioners sugar

Mix sugar, water, and corn syrup and cook to the soft boil stage on candy thermometer (238 degrees). Add syrup slowly to egg whites which have been beaten stiff. Beat until mixture looks like cream. Add confectioners sugar and your favorite flavoring. Spread on cake. Always frost sides of cake first, then top.

I sometimes sprinkle colored sugar crystals on the finished cake for a more festive look.

DOT CHOCOLATE FROSTING

Yield: 1½ Cups

1 (15 ounce) can sweetened condensed milk
1 tablespoon water
⅛ teaspoon salt
2 squares (2 ounces) unsweetened chocolate
½ teaspoon vanilla extract

Put sweetened condensed milk, water, and salt in top of double boiler. Mix well. Add chocolate.

Cook over rapidly boiling water, stirring often, until thick (about 10 minutes).

Remove from heat. Cool. Stir in vanilla. Spread on cooled cake.

NOTE: For fudgecake, spread hot icing over the marshmallows.

FLAKY PASTRY

(Enough for 5 pie crusts to be frozen).

4½ cups sifted plain flour
1½ teaspoons salt
1½ cups shortening
8 tablespoons ICE water (cold)

Sift flour and salt. Heat cup with hot water before putting in shortening so that it will come out of cup better. Cut in shortening with 2 knives used in a crisscross motion or with a pastry blender until particles are the size of small peas. Then add water, a little at a time, working in lightly with a fork. Add only enough water to make pastry form a ball on end of fork. The less water, the more tender the pastry.

This recipe will fill 5 pie shells. Place aluminum foil between each plate and cover all 5 and put in freezer for later use.

PLAIN PASTRY

For one single crust pie or 4 to 6 tart shells:

1½ cups sifted all purpose flour
½ teaspoon salt
½ cup shortening
4 to 5 tablespoons cold water

For a double crust pie, or 6 to 8 pie shells:

2 cups sifted all purpose flour
1 teaspoon salt
⅔ cup shortening
5 to 7 tablespoons cold water

Sift flour and salt together. Cut in shortening with pastry blender or knife until pieces are the size of small peas. Sprinkle 1 tablespoon water over part of mixture and gently toss with fork. Push to side of bowl. Repeat until all is moistened. Form into a ball (or two balls).

Flatten on lightly floured surface by pressing with edge of hand 3 times across in both directions. Roll with rolling pin from center to edge until ⅛ inch thick. Fit into pie plate. Bake at 450 degrees for 10 to 12 minutes until golden. (Don't forget to flute the edge by pinching).

MAUD'S DUTCH APPLE PIE

1 stick margarine
1 cup firmly packed brown sugar (dark)
6 delicious apples, large
½ cup white sugar
2 tablespoons flour
1 egg

Mix sugar with flour and add to melted butter. Add beaten egg. Put layer of thinly sliced apples in uncooked pie crust. Pour over this, half of the sugar mixture. Add another layer of apples and the rest of the mixture. Sprinkle lots of cinnamon over the top and put the top crust on. (I use a lattice type top). Bake at 250 degrees for 1 hour.

This method is excellent using green apples.

FRIED APPLE PIES

Yield: about 15

3 cups sliced, pared, tart apples
½ cup water
1 teaspoon lemon juice
¼ cup sugar
½ teaspoon ground cinnamon
⅛ teaspoon ground nutmeg
Pastry for 2-crust pie
Vegetable oil for frying
Butter or margarine
Powdered sugar

Put apples into a saucepan, add water and lemon juice. Cover and cook over low heat for 15 minutes or until apples are tender. Remove apples and drain. Blend in sugar, cinnamon, and nutmeg.

Shape pastry into 2 balls. Using 1 ball at a time, roll on lightly floured board to about ⅛ inch thickness. Cut out rounds, using a 3½ inch cutter.

Heat shortening to 375 degrees.

Place 2 tablespoons apple mixture on each pastry round. Dot with butter. Moisten one half of the edge of each round with water. Fold the other half of round over filling. Press edges together with a fork.

Put pies into deep hot shortening. Cook about 3 minutes or until golden brown. Turn pies as they rise to surface, and several times during the cooking. Do not pierce. Remove from shortening and drain on paper towels. Serve warm with a sprinkling of powdered sugar. Delicious.

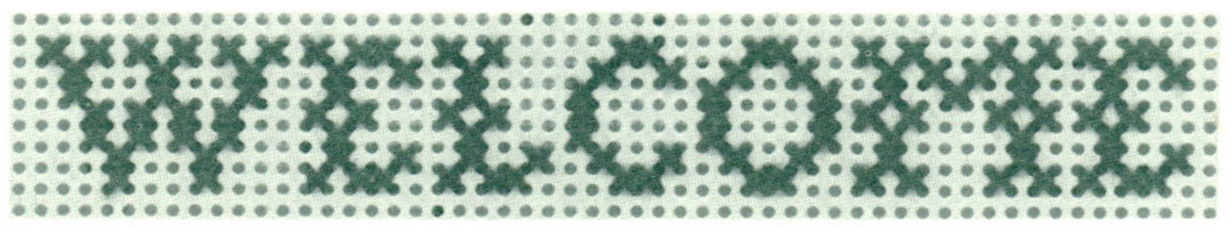

BLACKBERRY PIE

¾ cup sugar
¼ cup flour
½ teaspoon cinnamon
½ teaspoon grated lemon peel
¼ teaspoon nutmeg
⅛ teaspoon salt
5 cups blackberries, picked over, washed and drained well

In a large bowl combine sugar, flour, cinnamon, lemon peel, nutmeg, and salt. Add berries and toss well with your hands and set aside.

Pour berry mix into unbaked pie crust. Dot with butter. Either cover with a lattice top or a whole crust, pierced in several places.

Bake for 50 minutes in a 425 degree oven.

Serve hot with a scoop of vanilla ice cream on each slice.

WEIDMANN'S BLACK BOTTOM PIE

Serves 6 to 8

CRUST:
14 ginger snaps
5 tablespoons melted butter

Crush ginger snaps, roll out fine, add melted butter, pat into 9 inch pie pan. Bake in a hot oven 10 minutes and allow to cool.

FILLING:
2 cups scalded milk
4 egg yolks, well beaten
½ cup sugar
1½ tablespoons cornstarch

Add eggs slowly to hot milk. Combine and stir into above. Cook in double boiler for 20 minutes, stirring occasionally, until it coats spoon. Remove, and take out 1 cup. Add 1½ squares bitter chocolate to the cup you have removed, and beat well as it cools. Add one teaspoon vanilla extract, then pour this mixture into pie crust. Chill.

SECOND MIXTURE:
1 tablespoon gelatin
2 tablespoons cold water

Dissolve gelatin in cold water, and add remaining custard and cool. Beat up 4 egg whites, stiff, with ½ cup sugar and add ¼ teaspoon cream of tartar, and 2 tablespoons whiskey. Then fold into plain custard mixture on top of chocolate mixture. Chill.

Cover top of pie with whipped cream and shavings of bitter chocolate.

Weidmann's Restaurant
Meridian, Mississippi

CARAMEL PIE

Superb, but extremely rich. Serve small portions.

2 cups light brown sugar
1 cup milk
2 egg yolks
Lump of butter the size of a walnut

Cook sugar, milk, butter, until mixture thickens. (225 degrees on a candy thermometer). Add egg yolks, beaten well, and thinned with ¼ cup milk. Cook again until thick. Cool. Serve in individual baked pastry shells with a scoop of whipped cream on top.

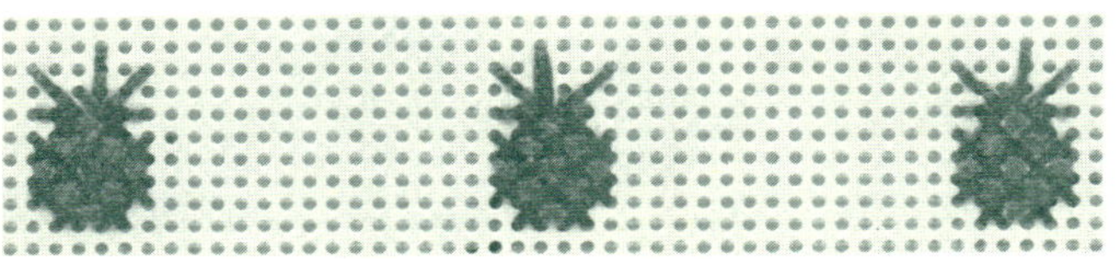

IRMA'S CHEESE CAKE

Exceptionally good and different

1 box Zwieback, made into crumbs
2 tablespoons butter
2 tablespoons sugar
¼ cup ground pecans
Dash of cinnamon

Line springform pan with above mix. (Be sure to reserve some crumbs for sprinkling over top of cheesecake).

3 packages (8 ounce each) cream cheese
¾ cup sugar
3 tablespoons flour
½ pint whipping cream
5 eggs, separated
Grated rind of 2 lemons
⅛ teaspoon salt

Cream cheese, sugar, flour. Add egg yolks one at a time. Beat well. Add cream, rind and juice. Fold in stiffly beaten whites to which the salt has been added. Beat until the whites form soft peaks. Gradually add 2 tablespoons sugar. Fold whites into lemon mix. Pour into shell and sprinkle Zwieback crumbs lightly over top.

Bake for 1 hour in a 325 degree oven. Cut off heat and leave in oven for another hour. DO NOT OPEN OVEN DOOR FOR ANY REASON UNTIL THE END OF THE SECOND HOUR.

Mrs. Lawrence Paine

EASY CHERRY CREAM CHEESE PIE

1 crumb crust (9 inch) or 1 baked pastry shell, cooled
1 package (8 ounce) cream cheese
1⅓ cups (15 ounce can) sweetened condensed milk
⅓ cup fresh lemon juice
1 teaspoon vanilla extract
1 can (1 pound, 6 ounce) prepared cherry pie filling

Soften cream cheese to room temperature; whip until fluffy. Gradually add condensed milk. Stir until well blended. Add lemon juice and vanilla. Blend well. Pour into crust. Chill two or three hours before garnishing top of pie with cherry pie filling.

CHOCOLATE CHIP-PECAN PIE

This pie is divine, and very rich.

Serves 12 to 16

½ cup butter
1 cup sugar
1 cup white corn syrup
4 eggs
1 teaspoon vanilla
6 ounces chocolate chips
1 cup chopped pecans
2 (9 inch) pie shells

Melt butter. Mix sugar, syrup, eggs in bowl. Add melted butter, vanilla, chocolate chips and pecans. Mix well. Pour mix into the two pie shells. Bake at 350 degrees for 40 minutes.

Delicious served with a scoop of vanilla ice cream.

CHOCOLATE MERINGUE PIE

1 cup sugar
3 tablespoons cocoa
½ cup flour
3 eggs, separated
1 teaspoon vanilla extract
1½ cups milk
¼ stick butter (2 tablespoons)

Mix well sugar, flour, cocoa. Add milk gradually, then well beaten egg yolks. Add butter. Cook in double boiler until very thick. Remove from heat and add vanilla. Beat with electric mixer until light in consistency. Pour into baked pie crust. Cool.

MERINGUE: Beat egg whites until slightly stiff. Add 3 tablespoons sugar gradually and beat until peaks stand (stiff but not dry). Cover pie with meringue and bake at 300 degrees for 30 minutes. Watch carefully and do not burn meringue.

VIOLA'S COCONUT PIE

All the way from South Carolina

1½ cups sugar
2 eggs
1 cup evaporated milk
1 tablespoon flour
1 package frozen coconut
1 stick butter (¼ pound)
1 teaspoon vanilla

Mix flour and sugar. Add eggs, butter, and milk, vanilla and coconut. Cook in unbaked pie shell at 350 degrees until firm.

FROSTED DAIQUIRI PIE

Serves 8

1 package (8 ounce) cream cheese, softened
1 can (14 ounce) sweetened condensed milk
1 tablespoon grated lime peel
½ cup fresh lime juice
⅓ cup light rum
9 inch graham cracker crust
1 cup heavy cream
1 tablespoon light rum
1 teaspoon grated lime peel

In medium bowl, with mixer, beat cream cheese until soft and fluffy. Beat in condensed milk gradually. Add 1 tablespoon lime peel, the lime juice and ⅓ cup rum, stirring until well combined. Pour into pie shell. Refrigerate 3 hours or overnight, or until stiff.

TO SERVE: Beat cream until stiff. Gradually add 1 tablespoon rum. Spread over top of pie. Sprinkle surface with lime peel.

Do not double recipe. Just make as many pies as needed.

GIRL SCOUT AND BROWNIE MINT PIE

14 Girl Scout Chocolate Mint Cookies
3 egg whites
Dash of salt
¾ cup sugar
½ teaspoon vanilla
½ cup chopped nuts
Sweetened whipped cream

Chill cookies and make into crumbs in your blender or food processor.

Beat egg whites with salt to form soft peaks. Gradually beat in sugar until stiff. Add vanilla. Fold in crumbs and chopped nuts. Spread evenly in buttered pie plate. Bake in a slow oven (325 degrees) for 35 minutes.

Cool thoroughly. Spread sweetened whipped cream over top and chill 3 to 4 hours.

Garnish with shaved chocolate or maraschino cherries.

LEMON MERINGUE PIE

Always good and T.K.D.'s favorite.

1½ cups sugar
⅓ cup cornstarch
1½ cups water
3 egg yolks, slightly beaten
3 tablespoons butter
¼ cup fresh lemon juice
1 tablespoon grated lemon rind
¼ teaspoon lemon extract
Meringue made with 3 egg whites
Baked 8 or 9 inch pie shell (Homemade is best)

Preheat oven to 400 degrees. Mix sugar and cornstarch in saucepan. Gradually stir in water. Stir over medium heat until mixture thickens and boils. Boil 1 minute. Slowly stir half of the hot mixture into slightly beaten egg yolks. Beat into remaining hot mixture. Boil 1 minute, stirring constantly. Remove from heat. Continue stirring until smooth. Blend in butter, lemon juice and lemon rind, and lemon extract. Pour hot filling into baked pie shell. Cover with meringue. Bake 8 to 10 minutes until a delicate brown.

MERINGUE:

3 egg whites, at room temperature
¼ teaspoon cream of tartar
6 tablespoons sugar

Beat egg whites with cream of tartar until very frothy. Gradually beat in sugar. Beat until stiff and glossy. Put on top of pie filling, being sure to seal edges well.

ORANGE MERINGUE PIE

¾ cup sugar
¼ cup cornstarch
¼ teaspoon salt
1½ cups orange juice
2 slightly beaten egg yolks
1 tablespoon butter
1 teaspoon grated orange peel
1 (8-inch) baked pastry shell
2 egg whites
¼ cup sugar

In saucepan, combine the ¾ cup sugar, cornstarch and salt. Gradually stir in orange juice. Cook and stir over high heat until thickened and bubbly. Reduce heat. Cook 1 minute more; remove from heat. Stir small amount of hot mixture into egg yolks and return to hot mixture. Cook and stir over medium heat 2 more minutes. Stir in butter and orange peel. Pour into pastry shell.

Beat egg whites to soft peaks. Gradually beat in the ¼ cup sugar until stiff peaks form. Spread meringue over hot filling, sealing to edge of crust.

Bake in 400 degree oven for 7 to 9 minutes or until meringue is golden. Let cool on rack before serving.

TINY PECAN PIES

Great for a Party.

1 (3 ounce) package cream cheese
½ cup margarine
1 cup flour

Cream above ingredients and chill for 2 hours. Then press small amount into small muffin tins. Do not grease.

Beat together:

1 egg, lightly
1 cup dark brown sugar
1 tablespoon butter
1 tablespoon vanilla
Dash salt
⅔ cup chopped pecans

Spoon into prepared muffin tins. Do not over fill. Bake at 325 degrees for 25 minutes. Let cool for 10 minutes in tins. Remove while warm to baking rack. You may have to prod with a knife.

These keep well in a tightly covered tin or they may be made way ahead of when you need them and frozen.

PECAN PIE

¾ cup sugar
1¼ cups white corn syrup
1 teaspoon vanilla
4 eggs
½ stick butter (¼ cup)
1 or more cups pecans

Mix above ingredients and pour into unbaked pie shell. Bake for 10 minutes at 450 degrees and then turn oven down to 350 degrees and bake for 40 minutes.

NORMA'S HEAVENLY STRAWBERRY PIE

1 baked pie shell
1 cup sugar
3 tablespoons cornstarch
1 quart strawberries
1 cup whipping cream

Wash and drain strawberries. Save half of berries and stand point end up in bottom of baked pie shell. Mash remaining berries until juice is well extracted. Bring to a boil, add sugar, mixed with cornstarch. Cook slowly for about 10 minutes, stirring constantly. Mixture will get a glazed look and very thick. Cool and pour over berries in pie shell. Chill. Top with whipped cream.

If tart shells are used, makes approximately 8 to 10 tarts.

Mrs. Richard Sessions

WEIDMANN'S RESTAURANT LEMON ALMOND ICE BOX PIE

CRUST:

2 cups finely crushed vanilla wafers or graham crackers
½ cup finely chopped toasted and buttered almonds
⅓ cup melted margarine

Mix well and fit nicely into a 9 or 10 inch pie pan. Bake until brown in a slow oven.

FILLING:

Mix 1 can sweetened condensed milk with 2 egg yolks, 1 teaspoon grated lemon peel, and ½ cup fresh lemon juice.

Pour into cooled crust. Use whipped cream generously over top; then sprinkle some toasted, buttered, and very well chopped almonds over top. Chill at least 1 hour before serving.

PATSY'S CHEESECAKE

Serves 8

CRUST:

20 graham crackers, sugar and butter

Follow recipe on graham cracker box. Press crust into a 9 x 12 inch glass baking dish. Bake 5 minutes at 350 degrees and chill.

FILLING:

3 egg yolks
1 cup sugar
Juice of 1½ lemons
3 egg whites
½ pint whipping cream, whipped
2 teaspoons vanilla extract
½ pound softened cream cheese

Beat egg yolks well. Add sugar and the juice of 1½ lemons. Beat well and set aside. Beat the 3 egg whites until stiff but not dry and set aside. Whip the cream and set aside.

Mix together the vanilla extract with the softened cream cheese. Beat until smooth. Add the egg yolk mixture, blending well. Fold in the egg whites and then fold in the whipped cream. Pour mixture into pie shell. Sprinkle top with graham cracker crumbs. Freeze over night.

Let dessert set out about 15 minutes before you cut and serve. Garnish with fresh or frozen strawberries.

Mrs. Brock O'Leary

Cookies and Candy

EASY ALMOND ROLL COOKIES

Yield: 3 dozen

⅔ cup canned slivered blanched almonds
½ cup butter
½ cup granulated sugar
1 tablespoon flour
2 tablespoons milk

In blender or food processor, grind almonds. Turn into a medium sized skillet.

Butter 2 cookie sheets well and sprinkle each with flour. Preheat oven to 350 degrees.

To the nuts in skillet, add butter, sugar, flour and milk. Cook over medium heat while stirring with a rubber spatula, until completely blended.

Then, on one of cookie sheets, drop, by full measuring teaspoonfuls, 4 widely separated mounds of cookie mixture. Bake 4 to 6 minutes or until edges are golden. While these are baking, get the second cookie sheet of cookies ready to bake.

Remove 1st cookie sheet from oven. Let stand a second or 2. Then, with a broad spatula tenderly loosen cookie. With left hand, quickly pick up farther end of one of the cookies, place the round handle of a wooden spoon under it, then roll cookie snugly around handle. Gently slip cookie from handle to wire rack to cool. Repeat the rolling with the other 3 cookies.

Repeat above steps until all are baked. Don't forget to rebutter and flour the cookie sheets.

APRICOT STICKS

3 egg whites
½ cup sugar
1 cup pecans
1 stick butter (½ cup)
1 cup sugar
4 egg yolks
Grated rind of 2 lemons
2 cups flour
1 teaspoon salt
½ teaspoon baking powder
1 cup apricot jam or preserves

Beat egg whites with ½ cup sugar and fold in cut up pecans. Set aside. Cream butter and sugar and add egg yolks and lemon rind. Blend in dry ingredients. Spread thin into a 11 x 17 inch pan which has been well greased. Then cover this mixture with the apricot jam. Spread the egg white mixture over the jam layer. Bake 30 to 35 minutes at 350 degrees. When cookies are slightly cooled, sift powdered sugar over tops lightly. Cut into any shape desired.

BEST OF ALL BROWNIES A LA PHYLLIS

1 stick margarine (½ cup)
1 cup sugar
2 eggs
1 cup sifted cake flour
1 pinch salt
2 squares semi-sweet chocolate, melted
1 teaspoon vanilla
1 cup chopped nuts (optional)

Soften butter and cream with sugar. Add eggs one at a time and mix well. Add flour, mix, then add melted chocolate and mix. Add nuts and vanilla. Put in greased 11 x 7 x 1½" pan and bake at 250 degrees for 1 hour.

NOTE: After brownies have baked a while, about halfway, take a cake tester and poke holes in cake. This helps keep top from cracking.

When done, cool in pan. Then cut in squares. Sprinkle with powdered sugar or frost some with chocolate icing.

These are so good, you might as well double the recipe.

FROSTING:
Bring to a boil the following:

1 stick margarine
6 tablespoons milk

ADD:
3 tablespoons cocoa
1 box powdered sugar
1 teaspoon vanilla

Beat until of spreading consistency.

Mrs. W. G. Campbell, Jr.

LEMON BROWNIES

¾ cup butter
½ cup powdered sugar
1½ cups flour

Cut butter into sugar and flour until mix looks like coarse crumbs. Then pat into a 9 x 13 inch pan. Bake for 15 minutes in a 350 degree oven.

THEN MIX:
3 eggs, beaten
1½ cups sugar
3 tablespoons flour
Juice and zest of one lemon

Pour this mix over top of hot cake. Then place back in oven at 350 degrees for 20 minutes. Cool. Cut in bars. Sprinkle powdered sugar on top.

So good that they almost taste like lemon pie.

MINIATURE CHEESE CAKES

Yield: about 48

Butter and graham cracker crumbs for muffin tins
2 packages (8 ounces each) cream cheese
¾ cup sugar
3 egg yolks
3 egg whites beaten stiff
¾ cup sour cream
2½ tablespoons sugar
1 teaspoon vanilla
Red preserves

Butter 4 miniature muffin pans and sprinkle with graham cracker crumbs until well coated. Preheat oven to 350 degrees.

Mix cream cheese with ¾ cup sugar and the egg yolks. Mix well in electric mixer. Beat egg whites until stiff and fold into the cheese mixture. Fill muffin pans almost full and bake for 15 minutes. Remove from oven and cool. They will fall or lose volume and even look funny. Don't worry.

Mix sour cream, 2½ tablespoons sugar and vanilla well. Drop about 1 teaspoon of this mixture into the center of each cake. Top each one with a tiny dab of preserves (preferably red) and bake again at 400 degrees for 5 minutes.

These may be frozen. You may also make in an oblong pan and cut in squares.

CHERRY MUFFINS

Yield: 36

1 stick margarine (½ cup)
½ cup dark brown sugar, scant
¼ cup white granulated sugar
2 egg yolks, beaten
1 small jar maraschino cherries
1 cup flour sifted with ¼ teaspoon baking powder
2 tablespoons brandy
2 egg whites, beaten stiff
½ cup pecans

Cream margarine and gradually add sugars. Beat well. Add beaten yolks, flour, baking powder, and brandy. Fold in egg whites. Grease and flour small muffin pans. Sprinkle bottom of pan with chopped nuts (about a teaspoon) and one cherry. Then spoon in batter.

Bake 10 to 15 minutes at 350 degrees. Sprinkle with powdered sugar when cool.

These will keep a long time in a covered tin.

GIANT CHOCOLATE CHIP COOKIES

Yield: 36 cookies

1½ cups brown sugar
½ cup granulated sugar
1 cup unsalted butter
2 eggs
1 teaspoon vanilla
1¾ cups flour
1 teaspoon salt
1 teaspoon baking soda
¾ cup chopped nuts
¾ cup semi-sweet real chocolate chips

Cream the butter and sugar together and beat in the eggs and vanilla until thoroughly blended.

Sift flour, salt and baking soda. Add to sugar-egg mixture and blend well. Stir in nuts and chocolate chips.

Drop in 2 tablespoon mounds onto a buttered cookie sheet. Spread mounds well apart. Bake in preheated 350 degree oven for 8 to 10 minutes until light brown and a knife inserted comes out clean. Cool on racks.

Children love these great big cookies.

CHOCOLATE CHIP CUPCAKES

Yield: 18 cupcakes

½ cup butter, softened
6 tablespoons sugar
6 tablespoons dark brown sugar
½ teaspoon vanilla
1 egg
1 cup plus 2 tablespoons sifted flour
½ teaspoon baking soda
½ teaspoon salt

Combine first four ingredients and beat until creamy. Add the egg. Sift together the dry ingredients and stir into butter mixture. Spoon into paper lined muffin tins (about 1 tablespoon per cupcake). Bake at 375 degrees for 10 to 12 minutes. Remove from oven and spoon 1 tablespoon topping over each cupcake. Return cupcakes to oven and bake for an additional 15 minutes.

TOPPING:
1 cup brown sugar
1 egg
Pinch salt
½ cup chopped pecans
1 cup semi-sweet chocolate chips
½ teaspoon vanilla

Mix together brown sugar, egg, and salt. Stir in nuts, chips, and vanilla.

CONNIE'S SWEETS

1 egg white
¾ cup light brown sugar
1 teaspoon vanilla
2 cups chopped pecans

Beat egg white until stiff. Add sugar, then vanilla. Blend and add nuts.

Drop by teaspoon on to a piece of parchment lined or an ungreased cookie sheet.

Bake at 250 degrees for 30 minutes. Turn off oven and leave cookies in oven for another 30 minutes.

Store in a covered tin.

CINNAMON NUT SQUARES

1 cup sugar
1 cup butter
1 egg
2 cups flour
3 teaspoons cinnamon
1 cup chopped pecans

Cream sugar, butter and egg yolk. Add sifted flour and cinnamon. Press out in ungreased jelly roll pan (15 x 10½ x 1″). Beat egg white until frothy and spread over dough. Press in chopped nuts. Bake at 300 degrees for about 30 minutes. Let cool slightly and cut in squares. Can also cut very small and therefore perfect for a tea.

DATE FILLED CHEESE PASTRIES

Yield: 4½ dozen

½ cup butter, softened
¼ pound Cheddar cheese, grated
1 cup sifted flour
1 box (7¼ ounces) dates, cut fine
½ cup light brown sugar
¼ cup water

Cream butter and cheese together. Gradually add flour, mixing to make a soft dough. Shape into a smooth round. Chill for 1 hour.

Meanwhile, combine dates, sugar and water in saucepan. On low heat, stir until soft (about 5 minutes). Cool.

Roll chilled dough 1/8 inch thick on lightly floured surface. Cut into two inch rounds. Place a rounded teaspoon or less of date mixture on half the round. Then fold over. Seal edges by pricking with fork. Bake at 350 degrees for 15 to 18 minutes, or until a light golden brown.

GERMAN CHOCOLATE COOKIES

Yield: 50 to 60 cookies

3 egg whites
½ teaspoon salt
½ cup sugar
¾ cup grated unblanched almonds
1 bar sweet chocolate, grated
1 drop almond extract

Beat salt and egg whites. Add sugar slowly. Beat 2 minutes. Fold in almonds and chocolate. Drop by teaspoon on to GREASED cookie sheet or use cookie press.

Bake at 275 degrees for 30 to 35 minutes.

GLORIA'S COOKIES

Like a brownie, only sort of butterscotch

2 cups light brown sugar
½ cup real butter
2 teaspoons baking powder
1 cup nuts, chopped
1½ cups flour
2 eggs, beaten
1 teaspoon vanilla
1 can flaked coconut

Melt butter and sugar in boiler on medium heat. Stir in all other ingredients, eggs last.

Bake at 350 degrees for 25 minutes. Leave in pan to cool. Then cut in squares, as brownies.

Children adore these.

Mrs. Mack Emmons

HAYSTACKS

1 small box dates, chopped
1 can flaked coconut
1 cup chopped nuts (pecans or English walnuts)
½ pound crystalized pineapple, chopped
½ pound candied cherries, chopped
Enough sweetened condensed milk to hold mixture together

Drop by teaspoons onto a buttered cookie sheet. Bake at 350 degrees for about 15 minutes, watching closely so as not to burn. Lift cookies onto a wire rack while hot. When cooled, store in a tightly covered tin.

ICE BOX COOKIES

The Old Fashioned Kind

¾ cup butter
1 cup firmly packed dark brown sugar
1 egg
1 teaspoon almond extract
½ teaspoon soda
½ teaspoon cream of tartar
2½ cups unsifted flour
½ cup ground or very finely chopped pecans

Cream together butter and brown sugar. Add egg and almond extract. Sift together the dry ingredients and add to the butter mixture. Mix well. Make into logs. Roll each log in waxed paper and refrigerate.

Slice and bake on ungreased cookie sheet at 400 degrees until delicately brown, about 8 to 10 minutes.

CHOCOLATE LEAVES

Beat 4½ tablespoons soft butter with a wire whisk until it is light and creamy. Gradually add 4½ tablespoons sugar and continue beating until it is white and fluffy. Stir in 6 tablespoons very finely ground blanched almonds and 1 beaten egg. Blend in ¾ cup sifted flour and flavor the dough with ¼ teaspoon rum.

TO FORM LEAVES: Lay aluminum stencil form flat on well buttered baking sheet. Spread about 2 tablespoons dough over stencil with a spatula. Press dough down smoothly and evenly, scraping off excess dough. Lift stencil straight up, leaving cookie on sheet. Be very patient.

Bake in a slow oven (300 degrees) for 10 to 15 minutes until edges are delicately golden. Remove from baking sheet while still warm and cool on a wire rack. (Stencils may be obtained from very large gourmet shops).

FROSTING:

CHOCOLATE: In top of double boiler, over hot water, melt 4 ounces dark sweet chocolate (2 squares) and work briefly with a small spatula or spreader. To ice leaves, turn them over and spread the undersides with a thin coating of chocolate, covering entire surface of leaves. With tip of spatula, mark the chocolate coating with lines resembling veins of leaf. Let stand on rack in cool place until icing is set. Store in tightly covered jars or tins. Will keep several weeks.

You can use a butter icing. Flavor with almond and tint green for Christmas.

BUTTER ICING:
Halve the recipe below for leaves.

¼ cup butter
2 cups confectioners sugar
1 teaspoon almond or vanilla
2 tablespoons cream

Soften butter and mix with sugar. Add flavoring and cream. Blend until of proper consistency.

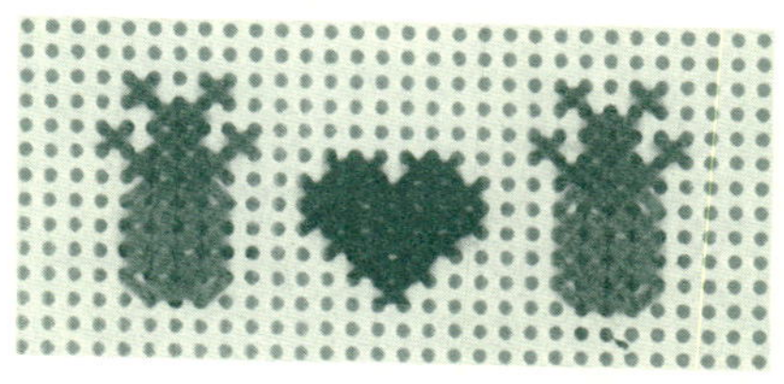

RAISIN NUT MUFFINS

½ pound butter
1½ squares unsweetened chocolate
1 cup flour
2 cups nuts
4 eggs, separated
1 cup sugar
2 cups raisins
2 teaspoons vanilla

Melt chocolate and butter. Add sugar, egg yolks, and flour. Then fold in egg whites that have been stiffly beaten. Add nuts and raisins.

Bake for 25 minutes at 350 degrees. Use small muffin tins.

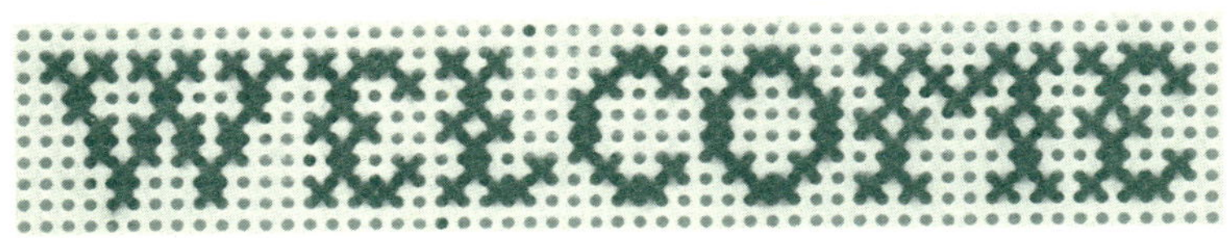

MADELEINES

Yield: 3 dozen cookies

These are lemon flavored, shell shaped traditional French tea cakes. To make them you will need special Madeleine pans that can be bought in most gourmet shops. Each pan makes 12 cookies.

1¼ cups sifted cake flour
½ teaspoon baking powder
¼ teaspoon salt
3 eggs
1 teaspoon vanilla extract
⅔ cup sugar
2 teaspoons finely grated lemon rind
¾ cup butter, melted
Confectioners (powdered) sugar

Sift cake flour with baking powder and salt. Set aside. Beat eggs until light. Add vanilla and gradually beat in the sugar. Continue beating until volume has increased to about four times the original. Fold in the finely grated lemon rind. Gradually fold in the flour mixture. Stir in the butter that has been melted and cooled.

Brush pans with additional melted butter and spoon about 1 tablespoon batter into each shell, filling them about ¾ full. Bake in a preheated 350 degree oven for 12 to 15 minutes, or until golden brown. Remove cookies to a wire rack. Cool and sift confectioners sugar over the tops.

THEY LITERALLY MELT IN YOUR MOUTH.

CHOCOLATE MADELEINES

Yield: about 2 dozen

These are delicious but not quite as light as the traditional Madeleines.

¾ cup unsalted sweet butter
3 ounces semisweet chocolate
1 cup all purpose flour
2 tablespoons unsweetened cocoa
Pinch salt
4 large eggs
⅔ cup granulated sugar
Powdered sugar

Preheat oven to 350 degrees.

Melt butter and chocolate in small saucepan over hot water. Cool.

Sift flour, cocoa and salt together twice.

Place eggs in stainless steel mixer bowl; place bowl over simmering water; bowl should not touch water. Gradually whisk granulated sugar into eggs; whisk until eggs feel warm. Remove bowl from water. Beat egg mixture on highest speed until mixture is pale and the consistency of whipped cream, 6 to 8 minutes.

Add chocolate and flour mixtures a third at a time to egg mixture; beat after each addition until no streaks remain.

Oil two madeleine pans; spoon 1 generous tablespoon of the batter into each cup. Bake.

TINY RUM CAKES
A Divine French Teacake

Yield: 2½ dozen

CAKE:
4 tablespoons sugar
2 eggs
6 tablespoons flour
1 teaspoon baking powder
Grated zest of 1 lemon

Beat sugar and eggs. Add remaining ingredients. Mix well. Fill tiny muffin tins ½ full or less. Bake at 350 degrees for 10 to 15 minutes.

SAUCE:
2 cups water
11 tablespoons sugar
Juice of 1 lemon
1⅓ cups light rum

Boil the first three ingredients at least 7 minutes, until syrupy. Add rum. Pour rum sauce over cakes while hot. Let set overnight in syrup.

These cakes must be small and only a bite, because they "leak."

BASIC DOUGH FOR TART SHELLS

Yield: 30 shells

1 cup all purpose flour not sifted
¼ cup granulated sugar
Pinch of salt
¼ pound butter
1 egg yolk
½ teaspoon almond extract

Let butter stand in room temperature until medium soft. Sift flour, sugar and salt into medium size mixing bowl, and add rest of ingredients.

With your hands, work all ingredients together, mixing well. Then turn dough on to lightly floured baking board and gently work a few seconds until dough is formed.

Chill dough for easier handling.

Pinch off pieces of dough to size of a big hazelnut and place in form and with your thumb even out and press dough on bottom and sides of form or mold.

Be careful not to let dough extend above edge of form, as edges might break when shell is removed from form. An easy way to eliminate that is to press finished form against palm of hand.

This recipe will make 30 tart shells. They may also be frozen.

CREAMY LEMON FILLING FOR TART SHELLS:

½ cup butter
1 cup sugar
2 whole eggs
2 egg yolks
Juice and rind from two lemons

Put whole eggs and other yolks into top of double boiler. Beat gently until whites and yolks are mixed. Add other ingredients. Stir with a wooden spoon and cook over gently boiling water until consistency of mayonnaise. Store in covered glass jar in refrigerator. Will keep for weeks.

TO SERVE: Spoon into shells just before serving. Top with a dab of whipped cream, if desired. Also a little sliver of lemon rind looks pretty.

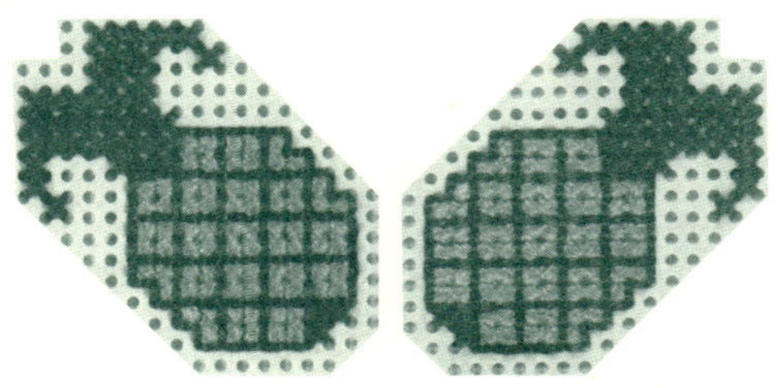

THUMBPRINT COOKIES

½ cup shortening
¼ cup brown sugar, packed
1 egg, separated
½ teaspoon vanilla
1 cup plain flour
¼ teaspoon salt
¾ cup finely chopped nuts

Heat oven to 350 degrees. Mix shortening, sugar, egg yolk, and vanilla. Measure flour. Mix flour with salt. Stir into dough mix.

Roll dough into small balls. Beat egg white slightly with a fork. Dip balls into egg white, roll in nuts. Place 1 inch apart on an ungreased cookie sheet. Press thumb gently in center to make a hollow place. Bake for 10 to 12 minutes.

When done and cool, fill thumb indentation with jelly or preserves, or chocolate.

CHOCOLATE TOFFEE SQUARES

Delicious and easy

Yield: about 80 squares

Whole graham crackers
1 cup dark brown sugar, packed
1 cup real butter
1 (11¾ ounce) package semi-sweet chocolate chips
1 cup ground pecans

Line a pan (at least 10 x 15 inches) with foil on bottom and sides. Cover this with separated graham crackers placed side by side. Set aside.

Simmer together for 3 minutes the butter and sugar. Pour mixture quickly over crackers and bake in preheated 400 degree oven for 5 minutes. Remove from oven.

Sprinkle chocolate chips over all, spreading to cover as they melt. Sprinkle pecans over top. Cool and cut into small squares. Makes about 80 squares.

RUSSIAN ROCKS

½ cup butter
1½ cups firmly packed brown sugar
3 eggs
½ teaspoon soda
1 tablespoon hot water
1 teaspoon cinnamon
3 cups raisins
1 cup nuts, chopped
3 cups flour

Mix well, then drop spoons of cookie dough on to cookie sheet and bake at 375 degrees for about 10 minutes.

MRS. KRATZER'S CREAM WAFERS

1 cup soft butter
⅓ cup whipping cream
2 cups flour, sifted

Mix all ingredients together. Chill. Roll out dough 1/8 inch thick on floured board. Cut with a round cutter. Roll only part of dough at a time, keeping rest refrigerated.

Transfer rounds to waxed paper, covered with sugar. Turn each round so that both sides are coated with sugar.

Place on ungreased baking sheet. Prick with fork about 4 times.

Bake 7 to 10 minutes at 375 degrees. Cool and put two cookies together with filling.

FILLING: Blend ¼ cup soft butter, ¼ cup sifted confectioners sugar, 1 teaspoon vanilla, and 1 egg yolk. Tint pink or green. Put between cookies.

ROSETTES OR TIMBALE CASES

1 teaspoon sugar
¼ teaspoon salt
1½ cups flour, sifted
2 eggs, beaten
1 cup milk

Mix and sift dry ingredients. Add beaten egg to milk. Combine mixtures and beat until smooth. Batter will look like thick cream.

TIMBALES: Use a timbale iron, available at most gourmet shops. Heat shortening to 365 degrees. (A deep fat fryer is perfect for this). Use enough shortening to cover the top of your timbale form. Heat iron in shortening about 30 seconds. Remove, drain, and dip in batter to the top of form. Then hold batter covered form in hot fat and fry until golden brown. Drain, and slip timbale off form and proceed again.

Timbales may be used like pastry shells for all sorts of dishes. Makes about 18 large timbales. Timbale irons also come in miniature shapes. These are wonderful for a tea or cocktail party filled with chicken salad or shrimp salad.

ROSETTES: Use Rosette iron. Follow above procedures for frying. Sprinkle powdered sugar over finished rosettes. These are great served on a tray for a tea or a morning coffee. Makes about 45 rosettes.

NOTE: Makes a hugh mess in your kitchen but they are well worth the trouble.

CHOCOLATE FUDGE

Yield: about 25 pieces or about 2 pounds

3 cups sugar
1 cup milk
3 squares unsweetened chocolate
2 tablespoons light corn syrup
½ teaspoon salt
3 tablespoons butter
1½ teaspoons vanilla extract
1 cup pecans, coarsely chopped

In a 4 quart saucepan over medium heat, heat the sugar, milk, chocolate, corn syrup, and salt to boiling, stirring frequently. Carefully set candy thermometer in place and cook without stirring until temperature on thermometer reaches 238 degrees or the soft-boil stage (when a small amount of chocolate mixture dropped into a cup of very cold water forms a ball that flattens on removal from water) about 10 minutes. Remove saucepan from heat.

Cool chocolate mixture without stirring, to 110 degrees or until outside of saucepan is lukewarm. Meanwhile, lightly butter an 8 x 8 inch baking pan.

When chocolate mixture is ready, add butter or margarine and vanilla extract. With wooden spoon, beat until mixture is thick and begins to lose its gloss, about 3 minutes. Quickly stir in chopped pecans; pour mixture into prepared pan. Cool fudge in pan on wire rack; cut into about 1½ inch squares. Store fudge in tightly covered container.

This recipe is the old fashioned kind of fudge and just melts in your mouth.

PRALINES

Yield: 32 pieces

1 pound light brown sugar
7 or 8 tablespoons water
1 cup or more pecans
¼ cup butter
4 tablespoons cream
1 teaspoon vanilla

Let sugar and water boil hard, then add pecans. Cook until mixture reaches the soft boil stage. Add butter, and remove from heat. Add cream and vanilla. Beat until creamy, but of the consistency that will spread. Drop by spoonfuls onto buttered cookie sheet or waxed paper and let harden. Be sure each spoonful has sufficient pecans.

Wrap each piece individually in squares of waxed paper and store in a covered tin.

MINTS I

50 to 60 mints

1 box confectioners sugar
5 tablespoons butter, softened or melted
7 drops food coloring
7 drops oil of peppermint (or more) (or lemon)

Mix with a fork until all is moist. Add 2 tablespoons evaporated milk. Mix with hands until workable. Might need a little more milk, but do not get too moist. Roll into little balls and place into mold. Unmold at once.

MINTS II

¼ of an 8 ounce package cream cheese
⅛ teaspoon oil of peppermint
1⅔ cups confectioners sugar
Food coloring to desired color

Mash cheese, add flavoring and coloring. Mix in sugar. Knead with hands until like pie dough. Roll in balls the size of marbles. Place on side in small amount of granulated sugar. Press sugar side in mold, unmold at once.

NOTE: Both recipes are quick and easy. Both recipes freeze well. A wonderful touch for a tea, they are both good and pretty. You can find the rubber candy molds at most gourmet shops in many shapes.

JUNIE'S KENTUCKY COLONELS

Yield: 4 dozen

1 pound confectioners sugar
1 stick butter (½ cup)
4 tablespoons bourbon (measure exactly, more is not better here)
¾ cup very finely chopped pecans
1 box unsweetened chocolate (8 ounce)
1 teaspoon paraffin (added to chocolate)

Cream sugar and butter and combine with bourbon and pecans. Roll into very small balls and let set in refrigerator at least 30 minutes. Melt chocolate and paraffin over hot water in double boiler.

Dip each little ball separately with a fork, using a teaspoon for balance and draining. Place on waxed paper and chill in refrigerator for several hours. Wrap separately in waxed paper and store in a cool place.

These are delicious.

Mrs. John T. DeMarines

PULL CANDY
(Some people call this Taffy)

3 cups sugar
¾ cup water
2 tablespoons vinegar
1 teaspoon butter

Cook mixture until it forms a hard ball in a glass of cold water. Take off stove and pour into a pan with 1 teaspoon butter spread in it. As soon as you can handle it, grease hands slightly with butter and pull until it turns white and hard. Stretch it out into long ropes. When hard, chop into short pieces with a knife. The pulling action is done with your fingers.

This is really fun for a group of older children. And it tastes good, too.

HELEN'S DIVINITY

Needs 2 people for preparation of finished candy.

Yield: about 50 pieces

3 cups sugar
½ cup light corn syrup
⅔ cup water
2 egg whites
⅛ teaspoon salt
½ teaspoon vanilla
1 cup nuts (optional)

Boil sugar, corn syrup and water together until mixture forms a HARD ball when dropped in water. (You may use a candy thermometer). Beat egg whites and salt until stiff on high speed of electric mixer. Pour syrup SLOWLY into beaten whites, keeping mixer on high speed. Continue beating until mixture is no longer glossy. Add vanilla and continue beating until mixture forms a definite peak when beaters are raised. If using nuts, stir in at this point.

NOW you need second person. Drop by teaspoonfuls onto waxed paper. You must work very quickly. Can garnish tops of candy with ¼ of a maraschino cherry or a pecan half.

NOTE: DO NOT MAKE IN DAMP, RAINY WEATHER.

Preserves, Pickles and Sandwiches

BLACKBERRY JAM

Yield: 3 pints

2 quarts fresh blackberries (Be sure to have a few that are not ripe, for tartness).

6 cups sugar

Pick over berries and wash well, gently. Cook in saucepan until juice begins to flow and the berries are soft. Mash or put some in food processor to obtain more juice and pulp. You need 4 cups of juice/pulp in boiler brought to a boil. Add the sugar and cook over medium heat until candy thermometer reaches about 221 degrees. This takes about 30 minutes.

Pour into sterile jars and seal. Makes 3 pints.

You may freeze the juice/pulp mix for later use.

BLACKBERRY JELLY

Yield: about 6 small jars

Use 2½ to 3 quarts blackberries, washed and drained in colander. Put berries in large saucepan and bring to the boiling point. Remove from heat. Mash berries with back of spoon or fork. Then strain into jelly bag or cheese cloth secured over larger container to drip. The object being, of course, to extract the juice. This takes a long time. You can get juice one day, refrigerate it or even freeze it for later use, then make jelly the next day.

3½ cups prepared berry juice (if juice is a little short, add water)

5 cups sugar

1 package Sure-Jell fruit pectin (DO NOT SUBSTITUTE)

Measure sugar and set aside. Put Sure-Jell in juice in a very large saucepan or Dutch oven. Pot should not be more than one-third full to allow room for rolling boil.

Bring juice and pectin to a full boil over high heat, stirring constantly. Add sugar all at once and stir. Bring to a full rolling boil (one that cannot be stirred down) and boil hard exactly one minute, stirring constantly. Remove from heat.

Skim off foam and immediately ladle into hot jars, leaving about ½ inch of space at top. Wipe off spills from jars with a damp cloth. Seal jars by spooning 1/8 inch hot paraffin onto hot jelly surface. Quickly cover with hot lids and screw bands on tightly.

BLUEBERRY CONSERVE

Yield: 5 half pints

4 cups sugar
2 cups water
½ orange, thinly sliced
½ lemon, thinly sliced
1 quart blueberries

Combine sugar and water in a large saucepan or Dutch oven and bring to a boil. Stir in orange and lemon slices and simmer, uncovered for 5 minutes. Add blueberries. Cook over medium high heat for 40 minutes or until thick, stirring frequently.

Quickly ladle conserve into hot sterilized jars, leaving ¼ inch headspace. Cover at once with lids and screw the bands tight. Process in a boiling-water bath for 15 minutes.

FIG PRESERVES

Wash figs by putting in sink, sprinkle baking soda over them and then pour boiling water over them. Rinse them about twice with very hot water, until the rinse water is fairly clear. This removes all of the fuzz on the figs. Drain well in colander.

TO MAKE PRESERVES: For each cup of figs, use one cup of granulated sugar. Do not use more than 10 cups of figs to a batch of preserves. Slice 2 lemons very thin, removing seeds. Put in pot with the figs. Simmer on low heat until the sugar melts. Be sure to stir from the bottom 2 or 3 times to make sure it has melted. Then simmer on a little higher heat until the figs are transparent while boiling. This takes several hours.

When done, spoon figs into sterile jars, being sure to have about 2 slices of lemon to each jar. Seal.

They are divine and our family almost fights over who is lucky enough to get the lemon slices.

LEMON MARMALADE

Yield: 5 or 6 half pints

2 pounds lemons
1½ cups cold water
2¼ cups sugar

Juice enough of the lemons to make ½ cup juice. Reserve juice and discard rinds. Rinse remaining lemons and pat dry. Cut off and discard ends; cut lemons lengthwise in half. Cut a V-shaped notch lengthwise in the center of each half; remove and discard piths and seeds. Slice lemon halves crosswise into paper thin slices.

Place lemon slices, reserved lemon juice, the water and ½ cup of the sugar in a large glass bowl. Let stand covered for 8 hours or overnight.

Place lemon mixture and remaining sugar in large enamel or stainless steel saucepan. Heat over medium high heat, stirring frequently, until thermometer registers 210 degrees, for 20 to 30 minutes.

Pack marmalade into hot sterilized half pint jars with tight fitting lids. Wipe jars clean and seal. Cool jars on wire rack to room temperature. Store in refrigerator up to 4 weeks.

SPICED PEACH PRESERVES

Yield: 7 or 8 half pints

1 (1¾ ounce) package Sure-Jel
3 pounds ripe peaches, peeled and chopped fine in food processor (about 4 cups are needed)
Juice of 1 lemon
5½ cups sugar
¼ teaspoon each of ground cinnamon, ground cloves, and ground nutmeg

Mix Sure-Jel, fruit and lemon juice and place in a large sauce pan over high heat. Bring to a boil, stirring constantly. Add the sugar all at once and bring mixture back to a rolling boil. Boil hard for 1 minute, continuing to stir constantly. Remove from heat and skim off the foam with a metal spoon. Add the spices. Pour into sterile jars and seal.

Fabulous served with hot biscuits.

(This is good to give as gifts, well liked by most people and a little bit different).

PEACH PRESERVES

1 cup peaches
1 cup sugar

Use this proportion of sugar to peaches. Four cups of each is easy to work with.

Peel peaches and slice thin. Remove seeds but do not throw away. Add sugar to peaches and seeds and let set overnight in the refrigerator or for several hours. Bring to a boil in a large pan. Then simmer for an hour. Remove seeds and skim off orange colored foam. Let cool completely.

Put into sterilized jars and seal. Four cups of peaches usually make 5 half pints of preserves.

MUSCADINE PRESERVES

Yield: 4 half pints

4 quarts muscadine grapes
2⅔ cups sugar

Wash muscadines and remove seeds from each grape. This takes a long time but it is better to seed them before cooking. Cut each grape in half after removing the seeds. Place in a Dutch oven or large saucepan with enough water to cover and simmer for 20 minutes. Add sugar to fruit and stir well. Cook over medium heat until it reaches about 220 degrees on a candy thermometer. This takes about 30 minutes. Skim off the foam. Ladle into jars and seal.

PEAR AMBER JAM

4 pounds Bartlett pears
2 oranges
1 (No. 2) can crushed drained pineapple
1 (8 ounce) bottle maraschino cherries
Sugar

Wash, peel, and remove core of pears. Cut in small pieces. Grind oranges, including the peel. Combine fruits, and measure. Add ¾ as much sugar as combined fruits. Mix. Spread in a roasting pan. Place in middle of oven and cook at 350 degrees for about 1½ hours. Stir occasionally. Add thinly sliced cherries and cook for another 20 minutes. If it doesn't look quite syrupy enough, cook a little longer.

Pour in hot sterile jars and seal.

NOTE: Oven cooking saves tiresome stirring to prevent scorching if cooked on top of stove.

STRAWBERRY PRESERVES

Yields: 2 glasses preserves

Very good and easy. This is a dark, rich, preserve.

4 cups strawberries
1½ tablespoons lemon juice
3 cups sugar

Hull and wash berries. Boil berries with the lemon juice for exactly 3 minutes. Add the sugar, mix well, and boil hard for exactly 6 minutes. Pour into shallow pyrex dish. Let stand for 24 hours, turning thoroughly several times to allow air to get into preserves.

Spoon into sterile jars. Cover with paraffin and seal.

SQUASH PICKLE

Yield: 5 pints

8 cups yellow crookneck squash
3 cups onion
3 large bell peppers
1 small jar pimento

Slice squash in rounds. Slice onions thin. Chop bell peppers fine. Alternate layers of squash, onion, and pepper. Sprinkle each layer with salt. Let stand for 1 hour. Then place in colander and drain.

SYRUP:
3 cups vinegar
2½ cups sugar
2 teaspoons celery seed
2 teaspoons mustard seed
¼ teaspoon turmeric and pimento
1½ tablespoons pickling spice tied in a cheese cloth bag

Bring syrup to a rolling boil. Add squash, onion, and pepper. Bring back to a full boil. Turn off heat. Discard spice bag.

Spoon into hot sterile jars and seal. Serve chilled.

ICE WATER CUCUMBER PICKLE

Pick cucumbers and add to brine made by dissolving table salt in warm water until it will float an egg. Allow cucumbers to remain in brine for 7 days. Remove from brine. Wash, and soak in alum water solution for 24 hours. This solution is made by dissolving 2 tablespoons powdered alum in 1 quart of water.

After standing overnight, heat cucumbers in alum solution until they are hot, but not boiling. Remove from heat and let stand 8 or 10 hours and heat again in the same way. Remove from alum water, wash in clear water, and place in ice water until cold.

Make a syrup of 2 cups of sugar to 1 cup of white vinegar and drop in a bag of mixed spices. Use pickling spices tied in cheese cloth or a child's new sock.

Heat cucumbers in syrup until it almost boils and cucumbers are hot.

The next day, take cucumbers out of syrup. Heat syrup and put cucumbers back in syrup. Heat until cucumbers are hot but do not boil. The third day, heat cucumbers in syrup and then pack in hot sterilized jars. Add 1 teaspoon yellow mustard seed to each pint jar and seal (the mustard seed is optional).

SCHEDULE:

Day 1 through 7	Soak in brine for 7 days
Day 8	Remove from brine and put in Alum solution
Day 9	Heat in alum solution until hot
Day 10	Reheat. Remove from Alum. Wash in clear water, place in ice water til cold. Make syrup. Heat cucumbers in syrup.
Day 11	Take cucumbers out of syrup. Reheat syrup and put cucumbers back in syrup. Let them get hot, not boiling.
Day 12	Heat cucumbers in syrup and pack in jars.

MARCIA'S GREEN TOMATO PICKLES

3 quarts green tomatoes
3 or 4 onions
1 cup vinegar
1 green pepper and 1 red pepper, cut in strips or chopped
½ teaspoon ground cloves
½ teaspoon allspice
1 teaspoon cinnamon
1½ cups white sugar
1½ cups firmly packed brown sugar
Celery seed, if desired

Slice tomatoes and onions. Sprinkle generously with pickling salt over each layer. Let stand until the salt has drawn through them well (about 2 hours). Drain and rinse with cold water. Add other ingredients and simmer 45 minutes to 1 hour. If more liquid is needed, add more diluted vinegar. Seal in sterilized jars.

Mrs. Marcia Via

TOASTED CHEESE SANDWICH DREAMS

Delicious served hot with a salad for lunch.

Yield: 30

1 pound Old English Cheese, grated
Dash hot pepper seasoning
Dash Worcestershire sauce
Dash paprika
½ cup cream

Mix ingredients well. Using very thin slices of bread, remove crusts. Spread slices with spread, sprinkle with paprika, and roll into a "blanket roll". Brush with melted butter and sprinkle with more paprika.

Put in a 400 degree oven to brown. Be sure to brown on both sides.

KENTUCKY HOT BROWNS

Toast bread and butter it. Using toasted bread as a base, top with a layer of sliced ham, turkey, and cover with crumbled crisp bacon. Spoon over this a rich white cream sauce (see Index) and cover with Parmesan cheese. Just before serving, run under broiler and heat until brown and bubbly.

SANDWICH LOAF

1 whole wheat sandwich loaf (2 pound, 14¼ ounce), unsliced
1 white sandwich loaf (2 pound, 14¼ ounce) unsliced
Chicken Filling
Egg Filling
Ham Filling
Frosting

With a sharp knife, remove all crusts from loaves. Cut four ½ inch slices lengthwise from each loaf. Cover slices with a damp towel until you assemble the loaf.

Make the following fillings separately, combining all ingredients of each.

CHICKEN FILLING:
4 cans (5 ounce size) boned chicken
¼ cup chopped celery
½ teaspoon salt
1 tablespoon lemon juice
⅓ cup mayonnaise

EGG FILLING:
12 hard cooked eggs, coarsely chopped
4 teaspoons capers, drained
1 teaspoon salt
1 tablespoon cider vinegar
⅔ cup mayonnaise

HAM FILLING:
3 cups ground cooked ham (about 1 pound)
⅓ cup sweet pickle relish
2 tablespoons prepared mustard
2 tablespoons light brown sugar
½ cup mayonnaise

FROSTING:
4 packages (8 ounce size) cream cheese
1 cup milk
Watercress sprigs

TO ASSEMBLE LOAF: Use whole wheat slice as a base. Spread with even layer of Chicken Filling. Cover with white slice; spread with even layer of Egg Filling. Cover with whole wheat slice; spread with even layer of Ham Filling. Top with white slice.

If desired, loaf may be covered with waxed paper and damp towel. Refrigerate overnight. Frost next day.

continued on next page

TO FROST: In large bowl of electric mixer, let cream cheese warm to room temperature. At medium speed, beat until light and fluffy. Gradually add milk, beating well after each addition. Reserve ½ cup frosting for decoration.

Arrange loaf on serving platter. Carefully frost entire surface. To decorate edges, press reserved frosting through desired decorating tip of pastry bag. Refrigerate overnight. Garnish top with watercress. Makes about 32 servings.

NOTE: Bread is sufficient for 2 sandwich loaves. If only one is desired, use only white or whole wheat loaf. Fillings and frosting are enough for one sandwich loaf.

BUTTERCUPS

Yield: about 30 sandwiches

4 hardcooked eggs
2 tablespoons radish, chopped
1 tablespoon green onion, chopped
2 tablespoons mayonnaise
1 tablespoon Italian salad dressing
¼ teaspoon salt
¼ teaspoon Worcestershire sauce
1 loaf whole wheat bread, unsliced

Shell eggs. Chop and combine with chopped radish, green onion, dressing, salt, and Worcestershire. Chill. Cut the loaf of whole wheat bread into slices 1 inch thick; cut into rounds with a small cookie or biscuit cutter. Hollow out rounds with kitchen shears, leaving about ¼ inch sides and bottoms.

To serve, brush inside of bread cups with mayonnaise and fill with about 2 tablespoons of the egg salad. Garnish with thin radish slices that have been quartered.

TEA SANDWICHES

TO MAKE TEA SANDWICHES: Be sure to prepare all the fillings first. They can stand while you prepare the breads. Do not let the bread dry out.

Line a shallow pan with several thicknesses of damp paper towels. Cover with a sheet of waxed paper. Cut the bread into the specified shape and put it into the pan. Cover with waxed paper and a layer of damp paper towels.

Work with one kind of filling at a time. Spread the bread first with a thin coating of soft butter to prevent the fillings from soaking through. Spread the bread with filling and roll or stack as called for in the recipe. Place again in same lined pan. Cover with waxed paper and more damp towels and refrigerate. Rolled and stacked sandwiches must be chilled before you slice them.

Sandwiches having a top decor should be handled slightly differently. After putting them in the lined pan, cover the pan tautly with plastic wrap, so nothing rests on the tops of the sandwiches. Chill them.

CHECKERBOARD SANDWICHES

Stack 2 slices whole wheat bread and 2 slices white bread alternately, filling with 1 or more spreads. Press each stack together, and trim crusts. Cut into ½ inch slices.

Stack 3 slices together so that whole wheat and white strips alternate, filling with 1 or more spreads.

Wrap in plastic wrap and chill several hours. Remove from refrigerator, and cut into ½ inch checkerboard slices. Cover with waxed paper and damp towel until serving time. Store in refrigerator.

RIBBON SANDWICHES

Stack 3 slices whole wheat bread and 2 slices white bread alternately, filling with 1 or more spreads. Press each stack together firmly, and trim crusts. Wrap each stack in plastic wrap and chill for at least 2 hours. Cut into ½ inch slices.

Then cut each slice into thirds or halves and place on serving tray.

If not serving immediately, cover with waxed paper and a damp towel. Store in refrigerator.

PINWHEEL SANDWICHES

Trim crust off a long loaf of unsliced bread. Slice loaf lengthwise into ¼ inch thick slices, and roll each slice with a rolling pin to flatten. Spread with softened butter and a filling. If desired, place olives, pickles, Vienna sausage, or a frankfurter across the short end of slice; roll up tightly. Wrap in plastic wrap and chill several hours or overnight.

Cut chilled rolls into ½ inch slices and place on serving trays. Cover with waxed paper and a damp towel until ready to serve; store in refrigerator.

NOTE: You might need to place an order for a loaf of unsliced bread with a bakery. Sometimes the bakery will slice the bread for you.

CUCUMBER SANDWICHES I

1 (3 ounce) package cream cheese softened
1 teaspoon grated onion and juice
1 teaspoon minced fresh parsley
2 tablespoons grated cucumber, well drained
2 teaspoons lemon juice
Salt and paprika

Combine ingredients. Spread on bread for sandwiches. Garnish rounds of bread with thin slices of cucumber. Shake a little paprika on top for color.

NOTE: This spread can be made into a dip by thinning with whipping cream or commercial sour cream.

CUCUMBER SANDWICHES II

1 (3 ounce) package cream cheese, softened
1 medium cucumber, peeled, grated, and drained
1 tablespoon grated onion
1 tablespoon sour cream
Salt and pepper to taste
Can tint pale green with green food coloring (optional)

Combine all ingredients for filling and stir until smooth. Spread on thin slices of bread.

Garnish with a very thin tiny slice of radish twisted.

GINGER CREAM CHEESE FILLING

Yield: filling for 25 finger sandwiches.

Thoroughly mix the following:

1 (8 ounce) package softened cream cheese
2 tablespoons light rum
¼ cup finely minced candied ginger

CHICKEN ALMOND FILLING

Yield: filling for 25 sandwiches

Grind together 2 cups chopped chicken and ½ cup blanched almonds. Stir in 2 tablespoons drained crushed pineapple and enough mayonnaise to make a spreadable mixture.

HAM FINGERS

Yield: about 30

3 tablespoons mayonnaise
½ teaspoon prepared mustard
1 cup ground cooked ham
½ cup shredded natural Swiss cheese
1 loaf thin sliced raisin bread
Softened butter for spreading bread

Combine mayonnaise, mustard, ham and cheese. Mix well. Spread about 20 slices raisin bread with softened butter. Spread half the slices with the ham mixture; top with the remaining bread. Trim crusts. Cut sandwiches into 3 inch fingers. Cover with clear plastic wrap or foil. Chill.

HAM SALAD SANDWICHES

Yield: 1½ cups

1 cup ground cooked ham
4 tablespoons finely minced green pepper
2 teaspoons prepared mustard
4 tablespoons mayonnaise
2 tablespoons finely minced onion
1 or 2 tablespoons Worcestershire sauce
MSG
Salt and pepper to taste

Mix together all ingredients for filling and chill. Bring to room temperature before spreading on buttered bread.

PIMENTO CHEESE SPREAD

8 ounce bar medium sharp Cheddar cheese, grated
¼ teaspoon grated onion
1 tablespoon Worcestershire sauce
1 (4 ounce) jar pimento, chopped fine
4 tablespoons mayonnaise (or more, if needed)
Pinch salt
Dash cayenne pepper

Blend well with electric mixer until light and fluffy. Refrigerate. Keeps well.

BEAUTIFUL LITTLE STRAWBERRY SANDWICHES
(OPEN-FACED)

Yield: 4 dozen

FOR SERVING 100, triple the recipe.

Soften 1 package (3 or 4 ounce) cream cheese in medium bowl. Blend in ½ cup sliced strawberries, 2 tablespoons confectioners (powdered) sugar, and a dash of salt.

Trim crusts off 12 slices thin white bread. Spread with softened butter. Then spread with cheese mixture. Cut slices into quarters or make rounds with biscuit cutter. Top each with a halved strawberry and a tiny mint leaf. Place on a tray lined with a damp clean towel; cover and chill. These may be made 1 day before using.

SWEET SANDWICH SPREAD

1 lemon, all grated
1 cup sugar
1 egg
1 tablespoon butter
1 cup mayonnaise
1 cup chopped pecans
1 cup raisins, chopped in food processor

Cook the first four ingredients until thick. Add mayonnaise, nuts and raisins. Cool and spread on sandwich bread.

Mix can be refrigerated for later use.

A delicious tea sandwich filling.

SWEET VIDALIA SANDWICHES

Serves 6 to 8

12 slices baked ham
12 slices Vidalia sweet onion
12 slices unpeeled cucumber
12 slices bread (thinly sliced salt-rising bread is divine)
Lettuce leaves

Place 1 slice ham, onion, and cucumber on each slice of bread in the order given. You may spread bread with a little mayonnaise, if desired. Serve on a lettuce lined tray. Yummy.

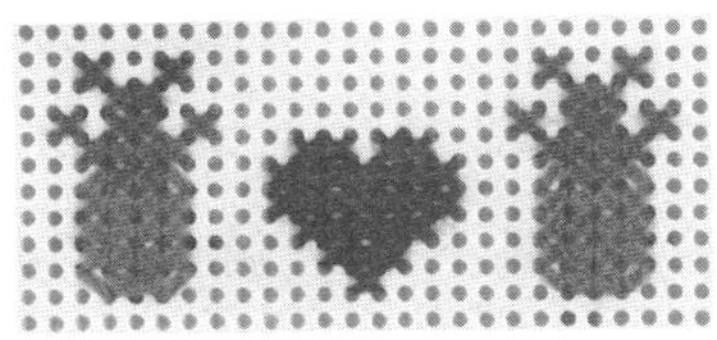

Holiday Treats

HOLIDAY MENU

Cocktail of Humor

Puree of Kindness

Generous portion of Friendship

Seasoned with Memories

Layers of Contentment

garnished with Good Health

Compote of Good Cheer

in a Happy New Year

CHRISTMAS BREW

Recipe given to me by Mrs. H. Wingfield Glover (Lanelle). She sends us a big jar every Christmas and everyone loves it.

1 gallon apple cider
1½ quarts cranberry juice
6 sticks cinnamon
2 tablespoons whole cloves
Brandy or rum flavoring to taste

Simmer for about 2 hours. The more it is heated, the better it gets.

EGGNOG

Yield: 2½ gallons

2 quarts heavy cream
2 dozen eggs
1½ cups sugar
1 quart bourbon (the best)
Vanilla ice cream (about a half gallon)

Separate eggs and beat yolks until creamy. Whip sugar into yolks. Set aside. Beat whites until they stand in peaks, adding ½ cup of sugar. Beat yolks and sugar together with the bourbon. Fold in the egg whites. Then fold in the whipped cream. Refrigerate until ready to serve.

At serving time, pour into punch bowl, adding as many scoops of vanilla ice cream as desired. Spoon into punch cups. Be sure to have grated nutmeg on hand to shake on eggnog.

Recipe halves easily and does fine.

A must for Christmas Day.

SPICED TEA MIX

2 cups sugar
2 cups orange-flavored instant breakfast drink
1 small jar lemon-flavored instant tea (1 ounce)
1 heaping teaspoon cinnamon
1 level teaspoon ground cloves
½ teaspoon each dried lemon rind and orange rind

Put all ingredients in a large bowl and mix well. Store in a jar. For 1 cup of hot spiced tea, put 2 teaspoons of mixture in a cup, fill with boiling water, stir, and sip.

HOW TO STOCK THE BAR FOR A PARTY

GENERAL INFORMATION: Host should count on serving each guest 2 to 3 drinks before a dinner and 3 to 4 drinks per person for a cocktail party. This is based on serving 1½ ounces of liquor per drink.

BEFORE DINNER:

8 guests	16 to 24 drinks	2 fifths
12 guests	24 to 36 drinks	3 fifths
20 guests	40 to 60 drinks	4 fifths
40 guests	80 to 100 drinks	6 quarts

FOR A PARTY:

8 guests	24 to 32 drinks	3 fifths
12 guests	36 to 48 drinks	4 fifths
20 guests	60 to 80 drinks	6 fifths
40 guests	120 to 160 drinks	1 case

The above is a solid base to start. To determine what kind of liquor to buy, you must rely on your familiarity with the tastes and habits of your guests. Also consider the general preferences that prevail in your community.

We usually have the following:

Scotch Bourbon Gin Vodka Rum
Good fairly dry white wine, as Chablis
Some beer.

MIXERS:
Club soda Coke 7-up or Sprite or Ginger ale
Diet cola Pitcher of water
Sliced lemons, limes and cherries.

COCOA MIX

1 box (1 pound) confectioners sugar
1 box (2 pounds) instant cocoa mix
1 box (8 ounce) non-fat dry milk powder
1 jar (6 or 8 ounce) non-dairy coffee creamer

Mix ingredients together well and put in airtight containers. Jars of this mix make a great gift for neighbors and friends.

TO SERVE: Use 3 or 4 tablespoons of mix per serving. Pour boiling hot water over dry mix in cup.

HOT MOCHA MIX

Yield: 8 cups

1 cup unsweetened cocoa
2½ cups sugar
2 cups dry non-dairy coffee creamer
2 cups non-fat dry milk powder
½ cup instant coffee
1 vanilla bean, cut into quarters

Combine ingredients in a large dry bowl. Stir until blended well. Pack into jars, making sure a piece of vanilla bean is in each jar. Seal and label. Store in the refrigerator at least a week before using so that vanilla flavor will be absorbed into the mix. Recipe makes 8 cups of dry mocha mix.

TO SERVE: Use 3 tablespoons mocha mix for every ¾ cup of boiling water. Top with a marshmallow or a little whipped cream.

RUTH'S CHEESE STRAWS

1 pound sharp Cheddar cheese
2 cups all purpose flour
1 teaspoon salt
¾ teaspoon cayenne pepper (more or less, depending on your taste)
1½ sticks margarine

Mix well together with your hands. Then use a cookie press, follow the directions for your press.

Bake in a hot oven at 350 degrees. Bake until barely brown.

Ruth Hulett

RUTH'S CHEESE DELIGHTS

Yield: about 75

2 sticks margarine
2 cups grated cheese (Use all of a 10 ounce bar sharp cheese)
2 cups flour
3½ cups oven-toasted rice cereal
1 teaspoon salt
½ teaspoon cayenne pepper
Optional: you may use 1 cup chopped pecans instead of the rice cereal

Mix together well. Roll in small balls, then press each one down flat with a fork. Bake for 8 to 10 minutes at 350 degrees. Watch closely.

At our house it just wouldn't be Christmas without Aunt Ruth's big tin of cheese delights and cheese straws. So good in the afternoon with a glass of sherry.

Ruth Hulett

STUFFED EDAM CHEESE

Yield: about 3 cups

1 whole edam cheese (about 1¾ to 2 pounds). Must place order at your grocery for this.
1 cup beer, any kind
¼ cup butter or margarine, softened
1 teaspoon caraway seed
1 teaspoon dry mustard
½ teaspoon celery salt

Let cheese stand at room temperature for 1 hour. Remove a slice from the top. With a spoon, scoop out cheese from the slice and from the big round red cheese, keeping the red shell intact. Discard top and refrigerate shell.

Grate scooped out cheese on fine grater into medium bowl (or use food processor). Let stand until very soft. Add beer, butter, seed, mustard, celery salt. Mix until well blended.

Fill cheese shell with mixture, mounding high.

TO STORE: Wrap cheese in plastic film, then in foil. Store in refrigerator for several weeks.

TO SERVE: Let stand at room temperature until soft enough to spread.

This is great to make around December 1 and serve all during the holidays.

OYSTERS ROCKEFELLER

A FABULOUS FIRST COURSE AND A CHRISTMAS TRADITION AT OUR HOUSE.

The mixture below will be enough for about 36 oysters on the half shell. It is best to use freshly shucked oysters, however you may use fresh oysters in the jar. Drain them well in a colander. Then place either 1 oyster to an oyster shell or use the shells available for au gratin dishes, placing 4 to 6 oysters to a shell.

NOTE: Once you acquire oyster shells, they may be used over and over again. Just wash them well in the dishwasher.

TO BAKE: Pack ice cream salt in flat baking pans and arrange the shells on top. Spread spinach mixture gently over each oyster. Bake at 450 degrees for 10 minutes. Serve shells on small plates with lemon wedges and a glass of chilled dry white wine.

SPINACH MIX:

Mix in food processor or in blender:

1 package frozen, thawed, uncooked spinach or a bunch of fresh spinach, washed and picked over well
½ cup fresh parsley, chopped
1 tablespoon finely chopped onion
1 clove garlic, minced
½ cup butter
½ cup white bread crumbs ground as fine as you can get them
A few drops hot pepper sauce
½ teaspoon salt

COFFEE CAKE RING

A CHRISTMAS MORNING TRADITION IN OUR FAMILY
ESPECIALLY FOR TOMMY

2 cups milk
½ cup sugar
½ cup shortening (margarine or butter)
1 teaspoon salt
6 cups sifted flour
2 packages yeast
1 cup melted butter (might take more)
2 cups sugar
1½ tablespoons cinnamon
1 cup or more chopped pecans

Place milk, sugar, and shortening in saucepan. Scald milk. Remove from heat, add salt, and cool to lukewarm. Dissolve yeast in two tablespoons warm water and add to mixture. Beat in flour and knead. Let rise until double in bulk, and knead again.

Break dough into balls the size of a large marble. Dip each in melted butter; then roll in the sugar, cinnamon mixture, and then in the chopped pecans. Place loosely in a buttered cake pan (tube or Bundt).

Bake in 350 degree oven for 45 minutes. Turn pan upside down on cake plate and cool. This lets any syrup in bottom of pan pour over ring and help hold it together.

Delicious. This recipe makes two coffee cakes. Serve hot. Each person breaks off a bite-size ball from the ring. Also good with after dinner coffee.

KIM'S APPLE CASSEROLE

Serves 8

Fill a buttered casserole dish ½ full of diced apples. Use Rome Beauty or Winesap apples. (Use 4 to 6 apples).

ADD:

½ cup sugar
½ cup cold water

Mix together until crumbly:

1 cup brown sugar
1 cup flour
½ cup butter

Put sugar, flour and butter mixture on top of apples. Sprinkle cinnamon over all and bake at 350 degrees for 1 hour.

Delicious for Christmas dinner.

Mrs. W. G. Campbell, Jr.

HOLIDAY BREAKFAST CASSEROLE

Serves 8

6 slices white bread cut in cubes
1 pound sausage, cooked, crumbled, and drained
1 cup shredded sharp cheese

Put the above ingredients in a buttered casserole (oblong glass, approximately 11 x 7 or 2 quart size).

Pour over the above mixture the following ingredients that have been beaten together:

6 eggs
2 cups milk
1 teaspoon salt
1 teaspoon dry mustard

Cover with plastic wrap and let set in refrigerator for 24 hours.

Bake for 1 hour or longer, until puffy and golden brown at 350 degrees. Serve hot.

Mrs. W. G. Campbell, Jr.

McMULLEN'S CRANBERRIES AND APPLES

Serves 12 to 16

2 cups fresh cranberries, washed and picked
3 cups sliced apples
1 cup sugar
1 tablespoon lemon juice
¼ teaspoon salt

Mix and pour into a 9 x 12 inch glass casserole dish.

1 cup light brown sugar, packed
½ cup flour
⅓ cup soft margarine
1 cup quick oatmeal

Mix together and sprinkle on top of fruit. Bake for 1 hour at 300 degrees.

Mrs. A. M. McMullen

MOT'S CHRISTMAS SALAD

12 to 15 servings

1 (3 ounce) package lime gelatin
1 cup boiling water
½ cup cold water
1 (8¼ ounce) can crushed pineapple, drained
2 (3 ounce) packages cream cheese, softened
1 (3 ounce) package lemon gelatin
1 cup boiling water
1 cup cold water
1 (3 ounce) package strawberry gelatin
1 cup boiling water
1 (7 ounce) can apricots, drained and pureed

I. Dissolve lime gelatin in 1 cup boiling water. Stir in ½ cup cold water and pineapple. Pour into a 11¾ x 7½ x 1¾ inch glass baking dish. Chill until firm.

II. Combine cream cheese and lemon gelatin. Mix well. Add 1 cup boiling water and then 1 cup cold water. Pour over first layer. Chill until firm.

III. Dissolve strawberry gelatin in 1 cup boiling water; stir in apricots. Cool. Pour over lemon layer. Chill until firm.

Cut in squares and serve on lettuce.

Mrs. Fred Hulett

AMBROSIA

8 or 10 Navel oranges
1 can crushed pineapple
Freshly grated coconut (may use frozen)

Either peel and section oranges or halve oranges and use a grapefruit knife to remove sections. Save juice.

In a clear glass bowl, layer the oranges, crushed pineapple, and coconut. Pour some of the orange juice over all. Cover with plastic wrap and refrigerate until ready to serve.

Ambrosia may be made ahead of time and frozen. To serve, just thaw before using. Can garnish with fresh strawberries.

We always have ambrosia at Thanksgiving and at Christmas. It is delicious at any meal. It is called the fruit of the Gods.

FAYE'S CHOCO-LUSCIOUS PIE

CRUST:

1 cup graham cracker crumbs
1 cup finely chopped pecans
⅓ cup firmly packed brown sugar
⅓ cup melted butter

Combine ingredients and press in a 9 inch pie pan. Bake in a 350 degree oven for 10 minutes and let cool.

FILLING:

1 envelope unflavored gelatin
¼ cup cold milk
⅔ cup sugar
2 eggs, separated
1¼ cups milk, scalded
1 teaspoon vanilla
1 cup whipped cream
1 square chocolate, shaved

Soften gelatin in cold milk. Combine ⅓ cup sugar; slightly beaten egg yolks, scalded milk, and cook, stirring constantly over very low heat until mixture coats spoon. Remove from heat and blend in softened gelatin. Add vanilla and let chill until mixture congeals. Beat thoroughly until light. Then beat egg whites with remaining ⅓ cup sugar until stiff. Fold into gelatin mixture. Next fold in whipped cream and shaven chocolate. Pour into crust and chill until firm. Drizzle chocolate topping on pie.

TOPPING: 2 squares unsweetened chocolate melted with 2 tablespoons butter. Drizzle over finished pie.

Mrs. Brock O'Leary

MRS. DEAR'S ORANGE, DATE, NUT CAKE

My Mother almost always had one of these cakes for Thanksgiving. Really good.

1 cup butter
2 cups sugar
4 eggs, separated
4 cups flour
1 teaspoon baking powder
1 teaspoon soda
½ teaspoon salt
1 teaspoon vanilla extract
1⅓ cups buttermilk
2 teaspoons orange rind, grated
½ pound dates, chopped
1 cup pecans, chopped

Sprinkle ½ cup of the flour on the dates and nuts. Mix well.

Cream butter and gradually add sugar. Then add beaten egg yolks. Sift in ¼ of the flour while beating. Dissolve soda in buttermilk and alternately add with remaining flour in thirds. Fold in dates, nuts, and orange rind. Beat egg whites until stiff and fold in.

Grease a large stem pan and bake at 325 degrees for 1½ hours. Test and cook longer, if necessary. If cake appears to be cooking too fast, turn oven down to 300 degrees about halfway through cooking.

TOPPING: Before starting cake, mix together and let stand, so as to be completely dissolved:

2 cups sugar
1 cup orange juice
2 tablespoons orange rind, grated

Stir occasionally, but DO NOT COOK. Set aside until cake is done.

After cake comes out of oven, while still in pan, punch lots of holes in cake, using an ice pick. Pour orange juice mixture on top. This will take a while and it has to be done gradually, letting each soaking seep into the cake. Cool cake in pan.

Delicious served plain. You may also serve with a little extra sauce and whipped cream.

(The recipe was given to me by Mrs. Everette Crudup, who obtained it directly from Mrs. Dear. Mrs. Dear made cakes for many Meridianites on special occasions. Her cakes were so popular that orders had to be placed weeks ahead of time).

SUSAN'S DAIQUIRI SOUFFLÉ

Serves 20

½ cup light rum
2 envelopes unflavored gelatin
10 eggs, separated
2 cups sugar, divided
½ cup lime juice
½ cup lemon juice
Grated rind of 2 limes
Grated rind of 2 lemons
Dash of salt
3 cups whipping cream, divided

Cut a piece of waxed paper long enough to fit around a 1½ quart soufflé dish, allowing a 1 inch overlap. Fold paper in half; wrap around dish, allowing paper to extend 5 inches above rim of dish to form a collar. Secure with tape. Lightly grease and set aside.

Combine light rum and gelatin; let stand 5 minutes. Beat egg yolks until light and fluffy, gradually add 1 cup sugar, beating constantly until thick.

Combine yolk mixture, fruit juices, grated rind and salt in a 2½ quart saucepan; stir well. Cook over low heat, stirring constantly, until thickened (about 12 minutes). Remove from heat. Add gelatin mixture and stir until dissolved. Cool.

Beat egg whites (at room temperature) until soft peaks form, gradually adding ½ cup sugar and continue to beat until stiff peaks form.

Combine remaining ½ cup sugar and 2 cups whipping cream in a large chilled mixing bowl, beat until stiff peaks form.

Pour cooled yolk mixture into a very large bowl (about 6 quarts); fold in beaten egg whites, then whipped cream. Pour into soufflé dish. Chill until firm.

Whip remaining 1 cup cream and spoon in mounds on top of soufflé to garnish.

Before serving, carefully remove collar from around soufflé dish.

This is a beautiful dessert and so good, especially during the holiday season. Recipe was given to me by my good friend, Nell McMullen.

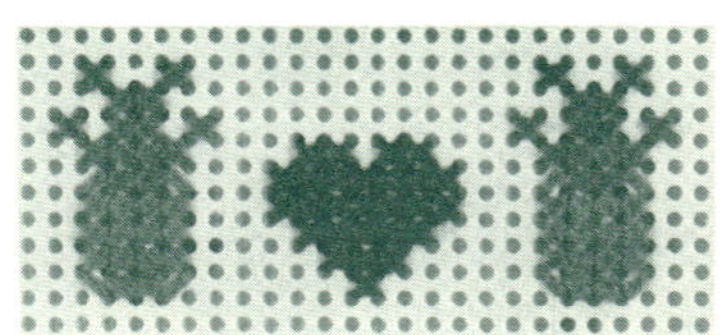

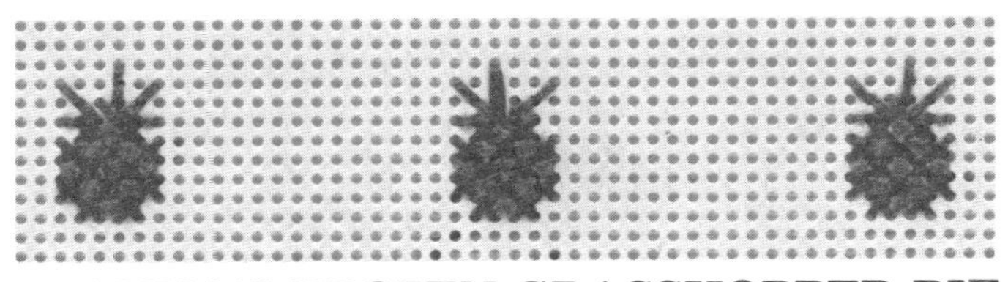

DEANNA'S FROZEN GRASSHOPPER PIE

Serves 8 to 10

24 chocolate sandwich cookies, crushed
¼ cup margarine, melted
Green food coloring
¼ cup green Creme de Menthe
1 jar marshmallow creme
2 cups heavy cream, whipped

Combine cookie crumbs and margarine. Press lightly into a 9 inch springform pan, reserving ⅓ cup of mixture for topping.

Blend Creme de Menthe with marshmallow creme, mixing until well blended. Add a few drops green food coloring to color desired. Fold in whipped cream; pour into pan. Sprinkle with remaining crumbs; freeze overnight.

Mrs. Richard Wilbourn

LETA'S FRUITCAKE COOKIE SQUARES OR CHRISTMAS COOKIES

These little squares are delicious and not as much trouble as fruitcake. Great just to have in a tin to pass to guests for a nibble of something sweet.

1 cup flour
1 teaspoon baking powder
1 cup powdered sugar
4 eggs
½ pound crystallized cherries
½ pound crystallized pineapple
1 pound dates
2 cups chopped pecans
2 tablespoons whiskey

Sift dry ingredients over pecans and the fruit that has been finely cut. Add beaten eggs and whiskey. Spread mix into a pan 1 x 11 x 15 inches or similar. Bake at 275 degrees for 1 hour. Cut in squares while hot. Lift squares to a wire rack to cool. When completely cooled, store in a tightly covered tin.

If you wish to be a little bit fancy, they may be frosted with a buttercream frosting.

COCOONS

Nice to have in a tin around Christmas

2 sticks butter, creamed
2 cups flour
4 tablespoons confectioners sugar
1 teaspoon vanilla
1 heaping cup pecans, ground or finely chopped (can use more)
Pinch of salt

Sift dry ingredients. Mix with butter. Add nuts. Shape and bake in 350 degree oven for 15 to 20 minutes. When cooled, sprinkle with powdered sugar. These are better if made very small. Just shape them with your hands. The finished cookie will be exactly as you mold them, for they do not rise.

GINGERBREAD MEN

Yield: 3 dozen

1 cup butter
1½ cups sugar
1 egg
4 teaspoons grated orange peel
2 tablespoons corn syrup (dark)
3 cups flour (sift before measuring)
2 teaspoons soda
2 teaspoons cinnamon
1 teaspoon ginger
½ teaspoon ground cloves
½ teaspoon salt

Cream butter, add sugar and egg. Mix well. Add other ingredients. Mix well and chill. Roll out on lightly floured surface and cut in desired shapes. Brush flour from cookies. Even a trace of flour on gingerbread spoils the looks. (You may lightly brush each cookie with water, if need be). Bake on ungreased cookie sheet at 375 degrees for 8 to 10 minutes. Cool 1 minute before removing from pan. Cool thoroughly before decorating with icing.

NOTE: Add raisins for eyes, etc. before baking.

HOLIDAY SURPRISE COOKIES

Yield: 4½ dozen

1 cup butter
⅔ cup sugar
1 teaspoon vanilla
1⅔ cups flour
½ cup cocoa
1 cup pecans, finely chopped
1 package milk chocolate kisses (about 54 for recipe and extra for nibbling)

Cream butter, sugar, and vanilla. Add flour and cocoa gradually. Add the chopped nuts. Beat at low speed until evenly mixed. Chill for 30 minutes. Unwrap paper from candy kisses. Shape a teaspoon of dough around each kiss. Roll in your palms and pinch away the excess to make a small ball. Place a few inches apart on an ungreased baking sheet. Bake in a preheated oven at 375 degrees for 10 to 12 minutes. Cool on a baking rack. These are a chocolate lovers dream.

SUGAR COOKIES

We make and decorate at Christmas each year.
It's a great Mother and child project.

2½ cups cake flour
2 teaspoons baking powder
½ teaspoon nutmeg
1 cup sugar
Grated rind of 1 lemon
1 tablespoon cream
½ cup butter
2 eggs, well beaten

Sift flour, baking powder and nutmeg. Cream butter thoroughly. Add sugar gradually. Add eggs, lemon rind, and cream. Add flour. Beat well. Roll thin on lightly floured surface and cut in shapes with assorted cookie cutters. Bake in a moderate oven, about 350 degrees. Watch closely so they do not burn.

NOTE: We do all decorating except frosting before the cookies bake.

AUNT BERNICE'S DATE AND PECAN ROLL CANDY

A delicious Christmas Confection.

3 cups sugar
1 cup milk
6 candied cherries
1 small package pitted dates
1 cup chopped pecans
1 tablespoon butter

Heat sugar and milk to boiling point. Add chopped dates and cherries. Boil slowly until mixture forms a soft ball in cold water. Add butter. Set in pan of cold water to cool. When cool, beat until thickened. Add nuts. Place in a damp cloth and roll. Chill roll at least overnight before slicing. Keeps a long time.

Mrs. J. Lyman Mason

JANE'S FUDGE

3 cups sugar
¾ cup margarine
⅔ cup evaporated milk
1 package (12 ounces) chocolate chips
1 jar (7 ounces) marshmallow creme
1 cup chopped pecans
1 teaspoon vanilla

Combine sugar, margarine, and milk; bring to a boil, stirring constantly. Boil 5 minutes over medium heat or until candy thermometer reaches 235 degrees, stirring constantly. Remove from heat. Stir in chocolate chips until melted. Add marshmallow creme, nuts, and vanilla. Beat until well blended. Pour into well greased 13 x 9 inch pan. Cool and cut into squares.

Mrs. A. M. McMullen

ORANGE PECANS

Juice of 1 large orange
Rind of 1 large orange
1 cup sugar
1 quart pecan halves

Let orange juice, grated rind and sugar come to a good quick boil. Add nuts a few at a time. Stir thoroughly. Stir until all the syrup is absorbed, stirring constantly. Remove from heat and continue stirring until each pecan is alone. Turn onto waxed paper to harden.

Keeps indefinitely in a closed tin.

Good to have around the Christmas Holidays.

POPCORN BALLS

1 cup sugar
⅓ cup white corn syrup
⅓ cup water
¼ cup butter
½ teaspoon salt
1 teaspoon vinegar
1 teaspoon vanilla
3 quarts popped popcorn

Combine the first 5 ingredients and cook, stirring until sugar is dissolved. Continue cooking without stirring until syrup reaches 270 degrees or forms a brittle ball when dropped in cold water. Add vanilla.

Pour syrup over popped corn, stirring until all kernels are covered.

Grease hands well and shape into balls. Makes 12 nice size popcorn balls. Do not double recipe. It is easier to work with in small batches.

This is really fun for children to make, with appropriate supervision, of course.

AROMA OF CHRISTMAS PUNCH

Let your house smell like Christmas...

1 fresh ginger root, split
3 sticks of cinnamon
16 whole cloves
1 teaspoon ground allspice
1 to 2 tablespoons pickling spice

To mix: add dry ingredients to 1 quart water and simmer on your stove. This makes your kitchen and your entire house smell wonderful, just like Christmas.

NOTE: THIS PUNCH IS NOT FOR CONSUMPTION. DO NOT DRINK.

HOLIDAY PINECONES

Adds color to the fire.

Soak pinecones in the following solution for 24 hours.

SOLUTION:
1 pound borax
3 pounds copper sulfate
1 pound ice cream salt
3 ounces boric acid crystals
3 gallons water

Use a plastic garbage can to soak the pinecones. Lay them out on newspapers to dry. Be sure to wear gloves to protect hands. Also be sure to protect surfaces.

These make nice gifts for neighbors for the holidays. Put them in a basket and tie with a red bow.

Menus

AFTER THE BALL BREAKFAST

Pitchers of chilled tomato juice and chilled orange juice
Sliced baked honey glazed ham
Breakfast roll with shrimp
Ambrosia with fresh strawberries
Hot buttered biscuit
Blueberry muffins, apple muffins
Assorted homemade preserves
Lots of hot coffee

BRUNCH

Choice of chilled fruit juices
Sliced baked ham
Quiche Lorraine
Watermelon filled with fresh fruit served with a custard sauce
Miniature Danish pastries
Biscuit served with assorted preserves
Coffee

BRUNCH

Bloody Marys, Screwdrivers, or just plain fruit juices
Little pig sausages served hot in chafing dish
Mot's Brunch Casserole
Curried Fruit Casserole
Assorted muffins
Champagne
Coffee

LUNCH JUST FOR THE GIRLS

Chicken salad in a fruit gelatin ring
Stuffed celery (stuffed with seasoned cream cheese)
Salted nuts
Bran muffins
Iced mint tea
Parfait

LUNCHEON

Shrimp Newberg spooned over cheese soufflé
Fruit salad with poppy seed dressing
Rolls
A good rich fattening dessert with coffee

LUNCHEON

Deviled Shrimp
Asparagus with Hollandaise Sauce
Cantaloupe ring with pineapple chunks and Honeydew melon balls
Poppy seed dressing
Muffins
Iced tea
Frozen lemon pie

LUNCHEON

Shrimp and crabmeat casserole
Green bean casserole
Avocado and grapefruit salad, sprinkled with raspberries,
served with a sour cream dressing
Lemon Chiffon ring
Coffee

BUFFET SUPPER

Appetizers:
Crab claws and cocktail sauce
Cheese ball with crackers
Assorted cocktails

Turkey Tettrazini
Sensation salad or a congealed fruit salad
Rolls
White wine
Leta's Charlotte Cake
Coffee

INFORMAL BUFFET SUPPER

Beef Bourguignon
Steamed rice
Marinated vegetables or a tossed salad
Crisp French bread and butter
Red wine
Norma's Chocolate Almond Cake
Coffee

BUFFET

Seafood Thermidor over Rice
Apricot salad in lettuce cups
Cheese biscuit
Parfait and cookie
Coffee

SUMMER SUPPER

Barbecued chicken cooked on the grill
Green rice casserole
Layered gourmet salad
Rolls
Homemade ice cream and brownies

SPRING DINNER

Cocktails
Salmon or crab mousse
Stuffed snow peas

Leg of Lamb
Steamed new potatoes in their jackets
Ratatouille
Symphony carrots
Small green salad (optional)
A good wine, white or red (you could even serve champagne).
Norma's heavenly strawberry pie
Coffee

DINNER

Appetizers and cocktails
Cream of peanut soup
Eye of the round roast with Bearnaise sauce
Spinach Madeline
Small baked stuffed potatoes
Hot rolls
English trifle
Coffee

DINNER

Dubonnet Cocktail
Appetizer: Green olives and cheese straws

Oysters Rockefeller (serve with a White wine, Loire)
French onion soup with toasted French bread
Quail in wine
Wild rice
Glazed baby carrots
Curried fruit casserole
Rolls
Cheese cake or chocolate soufflé
Coffee

NOTE: Serve a more dry white wine with dinner, as Soave

DINNER

Cocktails
Hors d'oeuvres:
Pickled shrimp with crackers
Black olive spread with crackers

Quail in Sherry
Wild rice with broiled mushrooms
Apricot casserole
Marinated vegetables (Broccoli, carrots, cauliflower,whole green beans, artichoke hearts, cherry tomatoes)
Chocolate angel food cake and coffee

MENU FOR THANKSGIVING DAY

Pickled Shrimp
Cheese ball with crackers

Turkey, Dressing, and Giblet gravy
Baked Ham

Green bean casserole
Sweet potatoes in orange shells
Broccoli Casserole
Bing Cherry Congealed Salad

Relish tray: olives, pickles carrot sticks, celery, cherry tomatoes
Homemade Rolls
Cranberry Sauce and fig preserves

Dessert:
Caramel Cake
Fruit cake
Chocolate Roll Cake
Tray of: tiny pecan pies, cheese cakes, and lemon tarts

Coffee

CHRISTMAS OPEN HOUSE FOR 100

Assorted cocktails (set up a bar with a bartender)
Punch bowl of Eggnog (set up somewhere other than bar area or dining room)
Tray of Sweets and salted nuts (have these with the eggnog)
Tray of sliced baked ham and turkey
Bowl of half mayonnaise and half mustard mixed together for spread
Basket of assorted small bread (party rye, white, wheat)
Cheese mold with assorted crackers
Broccoli dip with big corn chips
Rich Crab dip in chafing dish with toast rounds OR pickled shrimp with crackers
Tray of assorted raw vegetables served with a good dip
Meatballs a la Marilyn
Pickled blackeyed peas with saltine crackers

MENU FOR CHRISTMAS DAY

At our House Dinner is served about 2:00 p.m.

Punch Bowl of Eggnog
Other Cocktails
Cheese Straws

1st Course: Served in Den or Living Room
Oysters Rockefeller
Oysters Bienville
Sesame toast fingers
White wine (such as a Moselle)

Roast Turkey, Dressing, and Giblet gravy
Mot's Christmas Salad
Carrot Sticks, Celery, Ripe Olives and Pickles

Sweet Potato balls rolled in nuts
Asparagus Supreme
Corn Pie
Fresh steamed Broccoli with lemon butter

Gloria's Ice Box Rolls
White Wine (Vouray)

DESSERTS:
Ambrosia
Charlotte or Charlotte Cake
The Christmas Fruit Cake
Something Chocolate

GRADUATION PARTY

Assorted finger sandwiches
(Strawberry, chicken salad, ham salad, cucumber)
Miniature lemon tarts
Rosettes
Cheese rings or cheese straws
Fudge cake cut in tiny squares
Toffee-chocolate squares
Strawberry punch

SUMMER BUFFET FOR 24

Smoked turkey
Shrimp and Crabmeat casserole
Green rice casserole
Watermelon filled with fresh fruit
Poppy seed dressing
Rolls
White wine (A Vouray is nice)
Dessert:
White chocolate cake with caramel icing
Chocolate roll cake frosted with Amaretto flavored whipped cream
Coffee

BIRTHDAY SUPPER FOR A 12 YEAR OLD

Fried chicken wishbones (allow 2 per person)
Ham sandwiches cut in triangles
Potato chips
Soft drinks
Birthday cake and ice cream

TAILGATE PICNIC

Fried chicken or Baked chicken breasts
Ham and Swiss cheese sandwiches on rye bread
Marinated vegetable salad
Brownies (both chocolate and butterscotch)
Chilled white wine and lemonade

DESSERT BUFFET

Charlotte Cake
Tray of tiny tarts, lemon and pecan
Fresh coconut cake
Chocolate mousse
Tray of fresh strawberries to dip in rich, warm chocolate sauce
Caramel cake
Chilled Champagne
Coffee
Assorted liqueurs

INDEX

INDEX

INDEX

INDEX

INDEX

INDEX

PINEAPPLE GOLD
419 Windover Circle
Meridian, Mississippi 39301

Please send me ______ copies of **PINEAPPLE GOLD** at $10.95 plus $1.50 postage and handling. Mississippi residents add $.55 sales tax.

Enclosed is my check or money order for $ ______.

Name ______

Address ______

City ______ State ______ Zip ______

PINEAPPLE GOLD
419 Windover Circle
Meridian, Mississippi 39301

Please send me ______ copies of **PINEAPPLE GOLD** at $10.95 plus $1.50 postage and handling. Mississippi residents add $.55 sales tax.

Enclosed is my check or money order for $ ______.

Name ______

Address ______

City ______ State ______ Zip ______

PINEAPPLE GOLD
419 Windover Circle
Meridian, Mississippi 39301

Please send me ______ copies of **PINEAPPLE GOLD** at $10.95 plus $1.50 postage and handling. Mississippi residents add $.55 sales tax.

Enclosed is my check or money order for $ ______.

Name ______

Address ______

City ______ State ______ Zip ______

Reorder Additional Copies